THE GENTLE ART OF FAKING FURNITURE

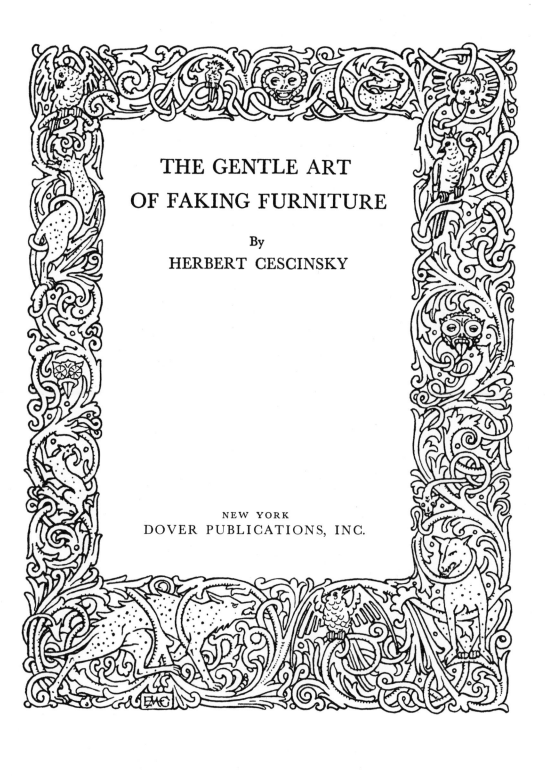

THE GENTLE ART
OF FAKING FURNITURE

By
HERBERT CESCINSKY

NEW YORK
DOVER PUBLICATIONS, INC.

This Dover edition, first published in 1967, is an unabridged and unaltered republication of the work originally published by Chapman & Hall, Ltd., in 1931.

NOTE ON THE PLATES

This edition conforms to the original in that no illustrations are used for plate numbers 93, 108, 124, 135, 136, 156, 192, 258 and 289.

Standard Book Number: 486-21862-7
Library of Congress Catalog Number: 67-28636
Manufactured in the United States of America
Dover Publications, Inc.
180 Varick Street
New York, N.Y. 10014

"The Buyer needs a thousand eyes;
The Seller but one."

TO

THE MEMORY OF THE LATE

A D O L P H   S H R A G E R

who acquired
A Second-hand but First-rate knowledge
of both

ENGLISH LAW AND ANTIQUE FURNITURE

by the simple process
of
PAYING FOR IT
in
1 9 2 3

—

THIS BOOK IS DEDICATED
by
THE AUTHOR
in
1 9 3 1

—

READER
DO THOU NOT LIKEWISE

PREFACE

THE preface to a book of this character should consist of a clear exposition of its scope and purpose; a brief statement as to what it does, and does not, contain. It is proposed to set this forth in as clear a way as possible.

This book has been written in the manner of a signpost, which points the way to a place but does not go there. If the reader have the idea that it is possible to acquire an accurate and comprehensive knowledge of faking and its detection from the following pages, without further reinforcement by way of technical experience and long and keen observation of many examples of English furniture and woodwork, then he, or she, will be disappointed. So much should be obvious, but the obvious is not always apparent. If it were possible to obtain such a knowledge at the cost of a week's study of this or any other book, then no expert would waste many years of time on the subject, and then have to make the confession that he learns anew day by day. The road to expertize must be a long one, necessarily; there are no short cuts—and there are no carrots.

It may be asked, if the differences between the genuine and the spurious be so slight, why not collect the fake? The answer is, why not, PROVIDING THAT ONE KNOWS THE DIFFERENCE BETWEEN THE TWO. Without entering into the question that inability to discern the difference between a real pearl and an imitation does not alter the fact that the one is real and the other imitation, it is of some importance that one should not pay pearl-price for the substitute, especially if one comes to sell again. The matter goes deeper even than this, in the case of antique furniture. Genuine old pieces are a part of the social history of bygone times, be that history ever so unknown or unwritten. To weave romances round a thing of only yesterday—and one the natural life of which has been seriously shortened in the attempt to give it the spurious appearance of age, and to do this through sheer ignorance—is neither satisfactory nor clever. To pay Queen Anne price for Mary Anne is still more stupid, and as all collecting is in the nature of an investment, either immediately or in the ultimate reality (one does not usually give a hundred pounds for an article which one knows will never realize five, even if the article be bought to keep for ever), to buy old English furniture without knowledge is akin to investing money in a mine which has never had an existence outside the lively imagination of a promoter of bogus companies.

This book, then, while it does not attempt to supply expert knowledge to the inexpert (not even an entire library could do this), yet does endeavour to point the ways in which such knowledge can be obtained. If it succeed only in this, then it has accomplished all that I set out to do.

CONTENTS

Preface   *page* vii

Chapter I   Introductory   1

II   About Fakes in General   6

III   The Genuine Antique and its Merits   13

IV   The Woodworker of the Olden Time   19

V   Detective Methods and the Problem of Restoration   25

VI   Early Oak Furniture and Woodwork   41

VII   Oak Panellings and Woodwork   53

VIII   Oak Furniture of the Seventeenth Century   61

IX   The Large Panel in English Woodwork   69

X   Walnut Furniture from 1660 to 1700   77

XI   Marqueterie Furniture   85

XII   Lacquer Work   93

XIII   Needlework and Stump-work   97

XIV   Queen Anne and Georgian Walnut   103

XV   Mahogany Furniture   111

XVI   The Work of the Chippendale School   119

XVII   Furniture of the Hepplewhite School   125

XVIII   Furniture of the Sheraton School   131

XIX   English Wall Mirrors   135

XX   Long-case and Bracket Clocks   141

XXI   Discursive and Conclusive   151

Index   157

CHAPTER I

INTRODUCTORY

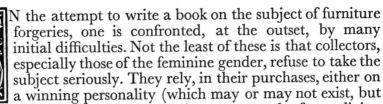N the attempt to write a book on the subject of furniture forgeries, one is confronted, at the outset, by many initial difficulties. Not the least of these is that collectors, especially those of the feminine gender, refuse to take the subject seriously. They rely, in their purchases, either on a winning personality (which may or may not exist, but is rarely effectual against a dealer who is out to get the fattest living possible from the wares which he sells, and who has, long since, ceased to be amenable to feminine charms) or on what they call "an eye" or "flair"—whatever the latter may mean, or imply. I know, by experience, that it has nothing to do with knowledge or training.

"Flair" may be all very well in judging a piece of furniture by its line, colour, or even its workmanship, but it is of no more avail in the detection of a clever fake than it would be in the diagnosis of Addison's disease. Of course, it may be pleaded that the latter is a serious matter, and may cause death if neglected, while the former is not of much account, after all. That may be true, but I fail to see why the collector of Chippendale or Queen Anne should not seek to acquire the necessary knowledge to protect himself, in his purchases. Personally, were I ever so rich, if I collected, and paid big prices for Queen Anne, I should like to get it, and not Mary Anne instead.

I know all about "dealers of repute," but I decline to admit this as any guarantee, and for two reasons. In the first place, one does not require an expert, but an actuary, to tell the collector of English Furniture that, in one year, more is shipped to America than could have been made in the whole of the eighteenth century. The population of Great Britain, in 1800, was rather less than twelve and a half millions. Taking an average of six to a family (it was the age of large families, remember), we get about two million families. In the eighteenth century these numbers would be considerably less. There was a sharp line of demarcation between families who could afford furniture of any note and others who had to put up with what they could get, and the numbers on the wealthy side were remarkably small. In these days, when wealth is far more evenly distributed, out of our great population, with an income-tax exemption limit, in practice, of about £250 per annum, the numbers who do pay this tax are surprisingly few. With a similar tax, in the eighteenth century, and making allowance for the greater purchasing value of money at that period, the proportion would have been much less. I have estimated that, in 1750, there were not 140,000 families in the whole of England who could have afforded to order furniture from a man such as Chippendale. Of these, the number who did refurnish at this period must have been small indeed, probably not more than 2,000 in all, and this may be a greatly exaggerated figure. Yet what these 2,000 families had made from 1730 to 1790 (and one can hardly imagine the same house being twice completely refurnished in this space of time) has equipped most of the millionaires' houses and apartments from New York to the Pacific Coast, to say nothing of the huge stocks in the hands of American dealers and department stores. What has been left has to be divided into what remains *in situ* and the residue left to reinforce English dealers' stocks. Little wonder, therefore, that the term "scarce" hardly describes the state of the market so far as genuine English furniture is concerned.

So much for reason number one, and our actuary. Remains the other, one equally as important. I have found that one lifetime has not been enough to learn what I should like to know about one subject: English Furniture and Woodwork from Gothic to Sheraton. I have not had to sell goods for a living, so have been able to keep my mind reasonably open and unprejudiced. I have had no geese which I have had to strive to promote to swans. I have gathered some little knowledge of clocks, old silver, Chinese porcelains and the like, but I have learned enough to know that I would not trust to my unaided judgment in the buying of the two latter for my own collection. I cannot afford to make blunders.

If I am not equipped to buy for myself, how can I be knowledgeable enough to buy for others or to sell from my stocks? I may be honest, but that is only half the battle. A collector can be taken in by a fool no less than by a knave, yet consider an average dealer's stock, and see what he offers for sale, and guarantees as genuine. Furniture of all periods and nationalities, tapestries, needlework, Oriental, European, and English porcelains and potteries, enamels, *bijouterie*, clocks, watches, jewellery, glassware, panellings, carvings, pictures, carpets, rugs, old silver, and a hundred other objects. Now remember that, in the world, there are thousands of really clever people engaged in forging any of these objects which are high-priced enough to make the game worth while, and who each specialize in one particular field. Yet we expect the dealer to know more than the whole army of these fakers put together. The collector who really imagines such a thing must put his thinking out with his washing.

2

A collector who specializes in one particular field, say Chippendale furniture, can and should know more than any of these general dealers. I am not impugning the honesty of any of the latter, any more than I doubt the good faith of the surgeon who trepans a patient in the endeavour to locate some trouble of the kidneys, but I do impugn his knowledge.

Another of the initial difficulties which I outlined at the commencement of this chapter is, that to ask an expert to write a book on fakes and their detection is to require him to publish his armoury of detective weapons. It is akin to demanding that the faker shall expose all his secrets to the gaze of the public. In the case of the former, it may well mean he has to begin all over again, to learn all the new tricks and deceptions which have grown up as the result of his book. In that of the latter, the result will be that he has either to retire from the business or to recast his methods.

The better a book on fakes is the more it warns the faker that he has been found out, and that he has to alter his plans. Yet, at the same time, it does not really educate the untechnical in anything like a corresponding degree, even if the knowledge, so imparted, did not become obsolete in the process. An expert in English Furniture and Woodwork MUST be technical. A bench or workshop education does not make an expert necessarily, although I have often seen a "common workman" point out something of the greatest importance to an "expert." The real expert in furniture MUST begin with a workshop training; what he learns in the handling of timber and the making of pieces he can acquire nowhere else. It is like "walking the hospitals" is to the medical student; he learns, by practical experience, what no books can teach. Taking an example from the medical profession; a specialist examines a patient, and by auscultation and percussion, diagnoses something is wrong with the heart or the lungs. To him, his stethoscope tells something which is unmistakable, yet, to the layman, tells nothing whatsoever. If the specialist were to explain, his words would have no meaning to the uninitiated. Similarly, a furniture expert may point out to a student that a piece under examination must be modern, as the mahogany used in the making is of a kind which has only been discovered during recent years, and was never imported or known in the eighteenth century. He may go on to show the signs of modern tools, the marks of the circular saw, or the power-driven band, or fret-saws, the presence of modern screws, modern brass-work, modern polish, and modern everything else, yet the untechnical student will know just as much—or as little—as when he began. I have found this so often in a piece where something has been added and something else taken away—which is the case with the generality of fakes which

3

have not been made outright. The signs which must be left in the process are—or should be—unmistakable to the expert, yet it is rare to have them apprehended, intelligently, when pointed out. It is not the faculty of seeing, but observing deductively, which is absent.

But the faker! He is technical, and he is out to learn—what the expert does and does not know. It is his livelihood. Faking is expensive; the better one fakes, the more money it costs and the greater time it takes—which is, perhaps, the same thing. The faker is out to spend the minimum of time and money on what will pass expert examination, and if there are only one or two who know more than the rest of the trade, he is willing to take a chance, if he can save money by doing so. It must not be forgotten that the faker is a commercial man. He may get a fair or even a good price for his work, but the mammoth profits round about the thousand per cent mark are not made by him. He cannot disguise the source, and he is at the mercy of the dealer. That is why the former runs a second-hand Ford, perhaps, but the latter has a Rolls Royce, and a new one at that, as a rule. The faker, like Gilbert's burglar, is really doing good by stealth, and merely catering for a popular demand (usually the desire to possess the antique which never existed, or would never have come into being had not the faker lent his aid), and his reward, in this world, is likely to be small. After all, is there much difference, in essence, between the chair which Chippendale might have made, had he thought of it, or the coat of arms which the Heralds' College has conjured up out of the *Ewigkeit* for William Boggs, who has made a fortune out of "iron rations" for our dear boys at the front?

The faker, therefore, is quite a worthy individual, and when I bowl him out—as I do, sometimes—he is quite nice about it, as a rule, just as he would be if I had knocked down his middle stump, actually. But —he is out to learn all the time, and I rarely catch him out twice running on the same detail. This is what one would expect, naturally. Can one imagine that if a spurious coin were exposed, in a reasoned manner, that the counterfeiter's next batch, from his illegal mint, would not be an improvement on the first?

Returning to our initial difficulty, from which I have wandered somewhat. I am asked to write what must be a technical book, and for the untechnical reader. Now, no other professional man does this, and for the best of reasons. A surgeon does not publish a book entitled "Every Man his own Operator," nor do medical instrument firms advertise handy kits of operating instruments for home use by paterfamilias on the family. The surgeon writes for his colleagues or for students, or, perhaps, to show the world what a really fine surgeon he is, and medical instrument firms sell their wares to the surgeon, not to the amateur. I did buy a scalpel once, but I used it for sharpening pencils until Mr. King Gillette came along with his safety-razor blades, which I found preferable, but this was only because the average pocket-knife, sold in tool shops, is usually made from anything but tempered steel.

Messrs. Chapman & Hall, who have the faith which moves mountains, appear to think that I can write a book setting forth all I know, or should know, about the detection of fakes in English Furniture and Woodwork, and I have promised to do my best. I have, therefore, written this introductory chapter before starting on the book itself, mainly as a species of self-heartening. They think the book will appeal to a large public; I fear that such public will be very restricted, simply because if the book is to be of real service it will be understood by very few, and if it is to be popular—that is, to have a large sale—it will not be true to its title. Perhaps, however, if this book does command a wide circulation, I may have the task, later on, of writing another to explain the first. Who knows?

CHAPTER II

ABOUT FAKES IN GENERAL

THERE are two kinds of slang. One is merely a collection of vulgarisms, the other is both economical and expressive. So cogent indeed are some slang terms that they can only be explained by a sentence; sometimes they require almost a chapter.

Every hobby begets its own vocabulary, as a rule, and the collecting of old furniture is no exception. Thus "antique" has been promoted from adjective to noun, and covers an infinitely wider field in its altered status. The expressive word "fake" is one which must be accepted almost as a First Principle, as not only is it a word unique in the language, but it requires more than a phrase to elucidate its full meaning and implications. It is, above all, pithy, and it is proposed, therefore, to use it here.

"Fake" and "reproduction" are often loosely used as if they were interchangeable terms, which is, emphatically, not the case. A reproduction, in its best sense, reproduces everything but the appearance of antiquity, and, as a rule, it falls far short even of this. Let us take an eighteenth-century chair as an example. Here we have the wood, the design, the constructional methods, the finish and the age with its surface wear. The reproduction will aim only at producing a modern copy. If the model be of mahogany, then the copy will be of mahogany only, although the one may have been made from the old Spanish timber from San Domingo, the other from Honduras, Guatemala or Nicaragua, even from Africa. The design may be literally copied, more or less, but with the earlier and more primitive methods, which produced certain definite results, replaced by those of the machine, the band- or the fret-saw driven by power, and even the gouges and chisels of the carver will be different. It is not impossible, with modern mass-production methods, that the carving machine may have been used for the general roughing-out of the ornament, or even for the fashioning of the cabriole legs. The finish will be vastly different, as so many of the eighteenth-century models were merely oiled and left for the friction and the rubbing of years to produce what collectors know as "original patine." Others were lightly varnished and waxed, and the years have filled up the grain of the wood, dusting, rubbing and wear have produced a gloss, and friction and use have softened down all sharp edges. The reproduction will, as a rule, be shellac- or "French"-polished, with the edges left sharp. No attempt will have been made to produce even the effect of age, other than, perhaps, by a vile so-called "antique shading" of the surface or by a glass-papering which leaves the bare wood exposed through its stain, known in the trade as an "antique finish" because it resembles no antique piece ever known. In this respect even the faker (who aims at deception for the sake of profit) is often guilty of the like practice, chiefly because so many "collectors" (whose knowledge of the genuine article has been acquired by diligent, but unwitting study of the spurious) refuse to accept a straightforward piece unless it has been so maltreated.

Although "fake" is a useful portmanteau word, it still demands some explanation here, at the outset, if confusion of ideas is to be avoided. "Faking" and deception may be intrinsic or extrinsic. Thus if a dealer were to sell an American roll-top desk as a genuine Hepplewhite tambour writing-table, there would be no intrinsic deception at all; the desk would not become a fake by being sold under this description. Proceeding by stages, we reach the honest reproduction (which may have had some years of wear, but was never made with any idea of posing as an antique), which is sold as "genuine." It never was a "fake" at the outset, and neither a few years of wear and usage, nor the false description under which it has been sold, can be strictly said to have made it one. From this to the piece specifically made to deceive is often an orderly unbroken progression, so it will be seen, therefore, that the term "fake" must be an elastic one and difficult to define. It would almost appear that the faking element belongs as much to the method of selling as to the making. Wherever used here, therefore, it must be subject to a reasonable interpretation, and this must be a necessary stipulation, before proceeding further.

Developing our economical slang vocabulary as we go, old furniture may be divided into two main classes, the "fakeable" and the "unfakeable." These will be elaborated in later chapters, but may be briefly treated here.

If the genuine article does not command a price on the market which will pay for its reproduction, then faking is out of the question. It must be remembered that the fake, if it is to be worthy of the name, is much more—and expensively much more—than a mere modern copy.

Into this category of the "unfakeable," on account of price consideration, we can place such pieces as plain tallboy chests-of-drawers, tray wardrobes, square pianos (usually erroneously known as "spinets"), four-post bedsteads, and the like. It must be borne in mind that there are fashions in antiques, as in everything else, and the "unfakeable" of to-day may be the "fakeable" of to-morrow, and sometimes was the "fakeable" of yesterday. This latter is important.

There is another class of antique which really commands a high price but which still does not pay to reproduce. Tapestries of the seventeenth century, or later, are examples. If the price of antiques bore any relation to their manufacturing costs (which is emphatically not the case), then tapestries should be the finest collecting investment at the present day. The same might be said of the eighteenth-century straw-work or the scrolled-paper pieces, of which more will be said at a later stage.

On the reverse side of the mirror we have such pieces as easy chairs, especially those of walnut, which command fabulous prices when it is considered that one buys, as a rule, two elaborate and two plain legs, some worthless beech framing, often more or less rotten, and a bundle of rags. Sometimes one may add two or four castors of doubtful authenticity. Here is a veritable gold mine for the faker which will be explored subsequently.

Proceeding with our classifications, we can again divide fakes into two classes, those made to deceive a real expert, and those made to satisfy others whose sole criterion of antiquity is dirt or the presence of worm. Dirt is cheap and the making of worm-holes, as a trade, is wholly apocryphal. An old worm-eaten piece of wood, if left in the dark with a pantechnicon full of modern furniture, from February to June, will "antique" the lot, so as a criterion of antiquity worm-holes are not to be trusted. Yet I know of certain treatises where elaborate directions are given of the methods of detecting genuine worm-holes from the spurious or "manufactured" variety. It is one of life's little ironies that one meets many who will believe a worm much more readily than a man. Perhaps they have had a lot to do with men, and very little with worms.

Faking is commercial, and for the multitude, the collectors of two hemispheres. Experts are rare, that is, those who have any real right to the title. It pays, therefore, to ignore them, in a general way, or to regard them as a justifiable business risk. Good faking, which commences only where the reproduction finishes, is expensive, and may be wholly wasted if the article will deceive the generality of collectors without it. Thus we get the rubbed edge and arris of the commercial faker, and the "antique finish" and the "made from old wood" of the quasi-antique dealer, as if any full-grown wood could ever be young. The so-called "lady decorator" (who is, as a rule, only a decorative lady, with a nice eye for the colour of chintzes) is the usual medium for the marketing of these pieces, and is often prepared to guarantee their authenticity with the same fearlessness with which she would endorse

Queen Elizabeth's motor-car, if pressed to do so, or if she had it in stock or on approval, at the moment.

It is not proposed here to waste any time with such pieces, antiques which would not deceive any ordinary furniture remover, even although, not so many years ago, there was a famous case in the Courts where nearly every piece was in this category. The faked furniture which really matters is that which might take in an expert, as if that can be described and exposed the poorer stuff can be left to take care of itself. The counterfeit half-crown which really rings true is worthy of attention; the one which falls like a disc of dull lead can be dismissed.

Furniture fakes of any note are rarely made outright, even from old wood. There is no virtue in old timber; it is the original surface which counts, and on this point one finds the greatest confusion of ideas, as a rule. So many have the idea that new wood will shrink, warp or crack —which is true—but they imagine that old wood is free from these defects—which is true also, but only if the original surfaces be undisturbed. What is known as "seasoning" is really, in part, a case-hardening. True, the sap dries up in the pores, but the wood is still alive, as dead wood is rotten, and totally unfit for furniture. Polishing or varnishing, even a coating of wax or dirt, will assist this case-hardening of the surface, but if the wood be scraped or planed, it is just as liable to warp or shrink as if it had only been cut twelve months before. Some original seasoning is implied in all cases, as freshly cut or "green" timber will not stand, as a rule. There are exceptions even to this, however, as oak beams, as employed in old roof-construction, were often used "green," but here shrinking, warping or "casting" was not of great importance. I can remember, however, some twenty years ago, buying a load of genuine fourteenth-century oak beams, of large scantling, at Frankfort-on-Main, when some of the old houses were being pulled down. The timber was of a rich brown shade right to the heart of the beams, yet when they were cut on the saw, to panel or framing thicknesses, the boards warped and shrank almost as much as if the wood had been newly bought from a timber yard. So much for the virtues of "old wood."

Not only has the original surface a value in the preservation of the timber, but it possesses a further merit, as it can never be really imitated. It is one of the proofs of authenticity for which the expert looks. It follows, therefore, that to construct a piece of furniture outright, and to leave each original surface and edge intact, is a manifest impossibility, and a cut edge is almost as patent as a freshly planed surface. The faker, therefore, as compared with the reproducer, rarely makes outright; he seeks for a plain piece which he can alter or embellish. Thus a simple

9

tripod table can be carved up, and if well done, and if the lines of the old table are good (which is rarely the case), may be very difficult to detect. One meets with so many of these finely carved but badly designed tripod tables in well-known collections, and I have always distrusted them on sight. I maintain that a shop capable of producing carving of this quality would be cultured enough to design the stem and the tripod with just proportions and graceful lines. Another point to be noted is that, twenty years ago, plain country-made tripod tables were plentiful enough; they are now very rare. The obvious inference is that they have all been carved up since, and now ornament so many collections as "original untouched Chippendale." I can account for their scarcity in no other way, as at no time during this period would any such piece, unquestionably genuine, decorative and useful, be wilfully destroyed. This might have happened, and undoubtedly did happen, fifty or sixty years ago, but not since 1910. Reasoning on the basis of probabilities is really one of the most powerful weapons in the armoury of the expert, if used with discretion, yet it is one which is often despised by the untechnical.

Carving added to a plain piece may be either cut into the wood, as in the case of a tripod table, or it may be glued on the surface. It must be borne in mind that one cannot glue a piece of wood on an old surface; the presence of wax, polish, varnish, grease or dirt will prevent the glue from adhering, and the piece will fall off. Glue will not stick everything, by any means, although many imagine that it will. To apply carved ornament to the front of a drawer, for example, it is necessary to trace the outline of the ornament on the face of the drawer-front and then to scrape away the surface with a sharp chisel, to make a key for the glue. It is almost impossible to do this without leaving signs which indicate what has been done. With a fret, with its open spaces, the operation is more difficult still, as the original smooth surface cannot be left in the fret-openings, for obvious reasons, yet this involves a re-surfacing of the fret-bed which should deceive no one with keen observation and an unprejudiced mind.

General descriptions of the methods of the faker are often misleading just because they are general and not specific. An actual example of a much-improved piece is shown here at the end of this chapter. It is rare that specimens offer which are definitely illustrative, as photography is practically valueless in the illustration of really good fakes. It is one of the inherent difficulties in a book of this character that fine fakes and authentic pieces look equally genuine—or the reverse—in a photograph. Even in this illustration one has to take the description of what has actually occurred largely on trust.

Here is a commode which has begun life as a chest-of-drawers, probably quite plain. The lower drawer has been taken away and the sides cut. The next drawer has then been reconstructed by being cut into two narrower ones, the outside sides being left intact, but inside ends added. Each section has thus been made up with two narrow drawers, leaving a knee-hole between. It is obvious what has been done, as the outer sides are veneered on oak, but the inner ends are of solid mahogany, which would have been highly improbable had the piece been made outright in its present state. The splayed corners are original, but the carving is all a later addition. The carved cabriole legs have also been added and the original top carved up on its moulding. To one acquainted with the work of the eighteenth century, the whole piece *looks* wrong. There are limits to what one can do, in the alteration of an old piece, and here they have been exceeded, and the imposture is evident.

Examples of demonstrable fakes which can be realistically illustrated must, obviously, be rare, but the next example is instructive in showing the way in which a suspected piece should be examined. It should be obvious that it is just the details which make a piece valuable which should be scrutinised first. If they are original, nothing else matters very much; if they are late additions, then the rest matters still less. Yet one so often sees a so-called expert begin his examination of a piece such as this by opening the drawers and examining the insides, while it should be evident that, with any fake possessing any pretensions to a genuine character, the drawers would be original, from an old piece. I have always held that one can detect an expert in furniture by the way in which he begins his examination. Here it is the carving of the top and of the splayed sides, and the elaborate plinth which make the piece valuable. Without these details, it would be merely a serpentine-fronted chest-of-drawers, worth very little; with them, it is a very valuable commode. An examination of this piece shows that it is just these details which are quite recent additions, and ignorant in their character, as one would never expect a cultured cabinet maker to design this coarsely splayed plinth, and, if original, it would have been broken or trodden to pieces long ago. It is true that not all the furniture of the eighteenth century is fine, much of it is positively bad, but this is nearly always true of the design and the execution alike; it is rare to find finely carved details on a badly designed piece. In the attempt to "tinker" with an old piece, also, one is conditioned by one's material. Thus, a plain cabriole leg of a chair cannot be carved up, successfully, with a device, such as the head of a lion, which demands great projection, as the wood does not exist, and that is why a flattened lion-mask on the knee of a cabriole leg should always be suspected. If it had been so carved at the outset, thicker timber, allowing for the necessary projection, would have been used, or the leg would have been built out; there is no reason why it should not have been, but with an old chair the carver is conditioned by his lack of material.

To illustrate fakes by photography is difficult, not only for the reasons previously outlined, but because no one appears to possess them, or, at any rate, will acknowledge their ownership.

The necessary permissions, therefore, are rarely forthcoming. By a fortunate—or unfortunate—chance, I happen to be in a somewhat favourable position. Twenty years ago, when I wrote my first book, I commenced with the idea that pieces acquired by millionaires, and paid for from a bottomless purse, must be, *ipso facto*, genuine. I have taken photographs of many of the pieces which were the ornaments of collections of that time, but which have been dispersed since. It is proposed, therefore, to use these in the illustration of succeeding chapters, and to indicate in what manner they fall from grace.

A mahogany Commode which has begun life as a ser-pentine-fronted chest of four drawers. The bottom half has been cut away (probably to make a second com-mode), and the bottom drawer has had its central part cut away to form a knee-hole, with pierced and carved brackets between. The legs and the applied carvings on the canted corners are modern; so are the handles. The top is new, so are the serpentine ends.

Plate number One

Genuine Commodes of the finest period of Thomas Chippendale
Examples illustrating the difference between the "fakeable" and the "unfakeable"

The Commode above could have been made up, by the addition of the trusses and the carved "apron," from a plain serpentine-fronted chest of drawers, and should be thoroughly examined at these points. The other details are unimportant.

Plate number Two

Genuine Commodes of the finest period of Thomas Chippendale
Examples illustrating the difference between the "fakeable" and the "unfakeable"

The Commode above, from its design, must have been
made in its present state either originally, or outright, at
a recent date. The drawer-ends being bowed to follow
the sweep of the corner trusses could not possibly occur
in any simple piece, therefore if any part is old we may
be certain the whole is genuine.

Plate number Three

An original plain mahogany serpentine-fronted Chest of Drawers which has been "improved" by a set-back top, carved base moulding and "bracket" feet, ornamented splay sides and elaborate handles and lock plates. It is safe to say that no one, in the eighteenth century, would have designed ugly sprawling feet of this kind on a piece of this presumed quality. Note how the splay sides have been widened, to contain the carved pendants, at the expense of the upright drawer rails, which have disappeared entirely.

Plate number Four

There is a suspicious similarity between these two mahogany Settees, and of a kind which one would not find in original work, made when furniture was merely a commercial product.

Plate number Five

An example of an "Improved" Chair. Note how the line of the front cabriole leg contains the whole of the lion mask instead of the head projecting beyond. This was probably quite a plain chair originally.

Mahogany Arm Chair of important and expensive character, which has been made up entirely from old fragments. Note the lack of projection of the satyr masks on the front legs. To an expert, the whole chair *looks* wrong, both from the point of detail and proportion.

Plate number Six

CHAPTER III

THE GENUINE ANTIQUE AND ITS MERITS

THE history of a nation's handicrafts is the history of a people, and its art works mark the measure of its culture and education. With the furniture of the various periods, we enter the homes of the people; each piece is, or was, a part of their everyday life. It will be seen, therefore, that the real antique plays a part, and fulfils a purpose, to which the fake cannot even pretend. We may never know, in the greater majority of instances, anything of the inner history of each piece, but we can weave our romances round particular things; imagine the letters of joy, hope, gladness, sorrow or bitter misery which may have been penned at our bureau, or the riotous or decorous feasts which may have been witnessed by our dining-table, and, in a hundred other ways, we can live the lives of the past, in the present day, but it needs the faith of the schoolboy to weave such romances round the fakes of yesterday.*

There are collectors and collectors—and yet again collectors. Some collect merely for profit, watching for the rise in the market; others desire to possess things to which the average man cannot aspire. Yet others seek for unwritten history, some are led away by the lure of the antique, and they are satisfied with anything, however crude and ugly, so long as it is old. Last of all—and rarest of all—is the collector who loves old things for their beauty of line, finish of workmanship, and that mellowness of tone which only age can give. To such, each piece must be fine first and old afterwards, as every antique worth collecting should be. It will be seen, however, that the fake fulfils none of the conditions demanded by any collector, no matter how useful it may be in reinforcing the stock of the dealer. To the cultured eye, it is a thing of sham and deceit. Sunlight and time can fade oak, walnut or mahogany to lovely mellow shades which are the despair of the faker, with his caustics and strippers. The gentle friction of rubbing and use is totally different to the violent methods of the steel, the wire-brush or the stone. If one would only train the eye by observing the genuine unrestored piece, instead of tolerating anything from the re-surfaced antique to the out-

* "Faith," said the schoolboy, "is the capacity of believing what we know to be untrue."

13

and-out fake, there would be fewer mistakes made, and the faker would cease to flourish. Unfortunately, very few pieces of furniture are in this untouched state at the present day, and their numbers are being reduced year by year.

Wear alone is a very unsafe criterion, of course, as extensive usage may not indicate any great lapse of time. There are some chairs in the smoking-room of a well-known Pall Mall club which were made less than twenty years ago, but, at the present day, have a really gorgeous patine, finer than the surface of many eighteenth-century pieces. I know of one house in Cheshire where there are many examples of Queen Anne walnut which were made for the house at the time, and have never been out of it, but which some collectors of my acquaintance would reject as utterly modern. It is evident, therefore, that the genuine character of the pieces must be judged by something more than mere surface conditions.

It was pointed out, in the first chapter, that to be an expert one must be technical. Perhaps it would be as well to elaborate this somewhat. To explain the tools of the various periods and the evidence of their use is impossible in a book. Such knowledge can only be acquired in the workshop. Yet it must be obvious that tools, which were utterly unknown in the eighteenth century or earlier, cannot have been used on the furniture of that period, and if one finds indications of the circular saw, for instance, it must be evidence of modern origin. Conversely, one would hardly look for signs of the adze—the tool of the primitive carpenter—in the furniture of Georgian days. Side by side with this acquaintance of tools goes the knowledge of woods. There are nearly thirty different kinds of mahogany at the present day, and more than half that number of walnut. There is English oak of at least two kinds,* oak from Riga, Holland, France, Germany, Italy, Austria, America and even Japan. Even with English oak, at the present day, the timber is not that from the age-old trees such as was used in the sixteenth and seventeenth centuries; these have been cut down long ago.

It would be utterly out of place, in a book of this kind, to enter upon a technical treatise on the subject of timbers, but the necessary knowledge is indispensable to the expert, nevertheless, if judgment is to take the place of mere guesswork. One prevalent error must be corrected here. It appears to be the custom to regard the cabinet-maker of the eighteenth century as one of a far higher class than his present-day fellow. The statement has been definitely made in many books on English furniture. It is a half-truth only, which is more misleading than an actual false statement. The trade had better traditions then, it

* *Quercus sessiliflora* and *Q. pedunculata*.

is true, and greater time could be spent on the production of fine furniture, but that is only to say, in other words, that the average patron was relatively richer, and the workman paid far less in proportion than the present-day rate. If mere perfection of workmanship be the criterion then the maker of the present-day is far better equipped, and can do, without effort, what his eighteenth-century fellow achieved only with great labour and skill. The modern "overhand" planing machine flattens a surface automatically; the "thicknesser" will plane up a board equal in thickness everywhere. The jointing of edges is child's play in a machine shop, but, with the long "trying" plane, to get an edge straight and in square at the same time (without which the jointing of two boards is an impossibility) is at once the hope and the despair of the beginner. What is then implied by this ignorant laudation of the old makers? Design and proportion? We select the best from a trade and ignore the second and the third rate. Also, it is in the nature of things, with English furniture passing through a long period of neglect, that only the finest should be preserved and the rest allowed to decay or to be relegated to the scrap-heap. What has aroused this interest in the fine models of the seventeenth and eighteenth centuries (and they are fine) is the revulsion from the work of the Dark Ages of the nineteenth century, when furniture was valued for its weight (like the Brides of the East), and when such atrocities as "Early English" and "Domestic Gothic" were regarded as the last word in taste. In an enquiry such as this, it is as well to begin by freeing our minds from cant. The subject is intricate enough without needless further complications.

The historical aspect of English furniture is of considerable importance in judging the genuine and the spurious, strange as this may appear at first sight. We can only estimate the age of pieces by changes in fashion (which are a part of the history of the people themselves), and if we can date accurately we know what to expect at the various periods, and what to reject. Thus fashion originated the sideboard with drawers and cupboards in the later years of the eighteenth century, probably as a survival of the oak "Welsh" or "Suffolk" dressers, but still a distinct innovation in itself. Knowing this, we can say, with certainty, that a walnut sideboard cannot belong to the walnut period, from Charles II to George I, but must be later.* We can narrow this enquiry down, and with profit. The fake is rarely a pure copy; more often it strives after the wonderful; the thing which never existed at all. Herein lies its rarity, and, in consequence, its value, if it can pass as genuine. If one could really know everything which had been made at various periods, we would go far towards condemning these wonderful

* Actually, a walnut sideboard belongs to no eighteenth-century date at all; it must be modern.

fakes out of hand. This is impossible, of course, but not nearly as much so as one would imagine. We are not really concerned with what was actually made, but with what has survived, as genuine pieces cannot arise from furniture graveyards. It is true that many pieces may still be hidden in obscure country houses, utterly unknown to the world at large, but the great show houses are open, more or less, and these demonstrate the fashions of the various periods, and illustrate, in a general way, what was made, as a cabinet maker would, as a rule, make his pieces in the prevailing styles. To depart from them to any serious extent would be to endanger his chances of a sale. In addition, furniture produced at all times was, as a rule, made for use first, and to ornament a room only in a secondary degree. It was the commercial product of its time, and, while it might be elaborated and even rich in character, it would stop far short of the miraculous. It is here where the elaborate fake fails, as a rule. It is far too wonderful. Dealers refer to these specimens as "Museum Pieces," which is another way of stating that they would be utterly out of place in a home.

From the foregoing, it follows that while we may not know, in detail, each piece which was made at various periods, we can surmise, in a general way, the kind of thing which was produced. It must also be recognized that the more wonderful a piece is the more widely known it is likely to be. It is not the mammoths but the microbes which are likely to remain hidden from the collecting world. The more elaborate a piece is, therefore, the more it should be scrutinized and suspected. Remember also that a notable thing must have a pedigree, of sorts; it is only the fake which grows, Topsy fashion, yet collectors are notoriously careless when enquiring into its origin, and will, generally, accept any old wives' tale as to the provenance of any purchase. In other words, they often ask to be swindled, and their prayer is frequently answered.

To treat of fakes in a general sense is misleading and useless, yet it has been done, to a great extent, in books which have dealt with this subject. To say, for instance, that pieces are usually altered in this or that way is positively false, as, in the faking world, pieces are not *usually* altered in any way whatsoever. A good fake, beginning with the substructure of a simple genuine example, is conditioned by the piece itself, necessarily, and it is rare to find two exactly alike. I know the old legend of the chair which is taken to pieces and a portion used in each of a set of six others, but I doubt if this was ever done, and it would be an idiotic proceeding in any case, if to deceive anyone with knowledge were the aim. Fakes are not produced in this way, and with all the single chairs which I have seen, with arms added at a later date, I have never found one where the addition has been made with any intention of deceiving, or where the attempt has been successful, which is much the same thing. What has happened is simple. Someone possessing a single chair, and desiring one with arms, has had the arms added by a local cabinet maker or carpenter, with no thought whatever of posterity or the collectors of the future. It is only the finders of mares'-nests who would hold up such a chair as an example of a fake, intended to deceive the unwary, and, at the same time, to show their superior knowledge. Similarly, to cut away the "apron" and upholster the seat of a Chippendale commode-chair is not necessarily intended to enhance the value of the chair, although the result may be an improvement. It simply means that with greater knowledge of sanitation and hygiene the commode becomes a useless piece of furniture, and is, accordingly, altered to one with a decided use. Had deception been the aim, the alteration would be done in quite another fashion, as a rule, and one which would certainly take in our mares'-nest-finding expert.

Good fakes—that is, those which commence on a genuine basis—being infinitely varied, it is necessary to avoid the general and to deal with the particular. I propose, therefore, to take each section of English furniture and woodwork, from the Gothic to Sheraton, and to show, if possible, how each piece may be forged, and in what manner, and to indicate the details to which particular attention should be paid in making an examination.

One pitfall must be pointed out here, in concluding this chapter, and that is the later copy. It is so usual to imagine that oak furniture belongs to the seventeenth century or earlier, walnut from the Restoration to the early Georgian period, and mahogany from about 1725 onwards, that we forget the possibility of later copying. It was the instance of the long-case or "grandfather" clocks which first gave grounds for these suspicions. Here we have dials signed with names that have been recorded, with the dates of their business careers, and we know, positively, that clocks of early character were often produced long after their fashion had departed. True, these late examples are generally depraved, and were never in the same class as those of the fine early makers such as Tompion, Knibb, Clement, Quare, East and others, but the point here is rather that they ignore the current fashions and revert to the styles of a bygone period. The same is true with furniture, but this, being unsigned, and rarely dated, is more difficult to verify. Thus I know of court cupboards in the Restoration manner, and walnut chairs of James II style, which have been established as of late eighteenth-century date, made actually in the satinwood period, when one would have imagined that the fashion for oak and walnut had utterly departed. We are so accustomed to date pieces from the periods of the inception of the various fashions that we rarely think how far out we may be as to the actual age of the pieces themselves.

17

There is another point to be considered, that of the literal copying of Chippendale and Hepplewhite models in the nineteenth century. I know of many such which have acquired a tone and a surface in less than half a century, and which would deceive anyone not thoroughly acquainted with woods and technical details. A good deal of nonsense has been talked and written about these late examples, and one would imagine that expertize was merely a game of guesswork, carried to anything but a fine point. Thus it is so easy to speak of a fine chair as "London made" and a clumsy one as "Provincial," yet I have traced some of the best specimens I have found, *in situ*, in large country houses (where inventory records have existed for centuries, affording evidence which is incontrovertible) to small makers in obscure towns and villages, while some of the documented pieces of the great Chippendale himself leave much to be desired. He, or she, who would qualify as an expert, and be capable of detecting forgeries, must have a wide knowledge of genuine pieces, technically, artistically, constructionally, and historically. In addition, it is necessary to train the eye to observe as well as to see; to reason inductively and instantaneously. To the practised eye, every little detail has a meaning. Above all, many of the great houses themselves are open to the public on occasion, and one cannot see too much. To acquire a really good knowledge of English furniture, and of fakes, is a long and arduous process, and there are no short cuts. The truth of this may be more apparent in the later chapters of this book.

Oak Cupboard or Aumbry. The cornice is embattled (probably an addition), the two doors are pierced with Gothic tracery of primitive type. An example of crude post-Dissolution work of the "huchier" or "arkwright."

Plate number Seven

One of three mahogany Stalls or Pews in West Wycombe Church, Bucks. Each is on a dais stand with drawers, with a reading-desk in front of the chair. A choice example of fine mahogany of the

Plate number Eight

eighteenth century in original condition. These chairs have never been re-polished or re-surfaced. They have every appearance of being actual work from Thomas Chippendale's London workshop in St. Martin's Lane.

Plate number Nine

An oak Standing Cupboard, probably French but of English oak in parts. Some allowance must be made for restorations on these early sixteenth-century pieces, and at this date there was a considerable intermingling of French and English influences, especially in the extreme south-west of England. There is also the probability that this piece may have been made up, long ago, from carved fragments of ecclesiastical origin.

Plate number Ten

A Standing Cupboard in oak, made up entirely from
German fragments of carving of fine quality. A piece
such as this is valueless as an antique.

A walnut double-chair-back Settee. This is English both in design and workmanship, and has all the restraint of the best period, *circa* 1705. The cabriole legs are almost straight, and the broad central splats are severe and dignified. The inside balusters of the backs are joined together and finish in a single back leg. The seat rail is cut out and dips down to the knees of the legs, which crest up at the corners, but not in the centre.

Plate number Twelve

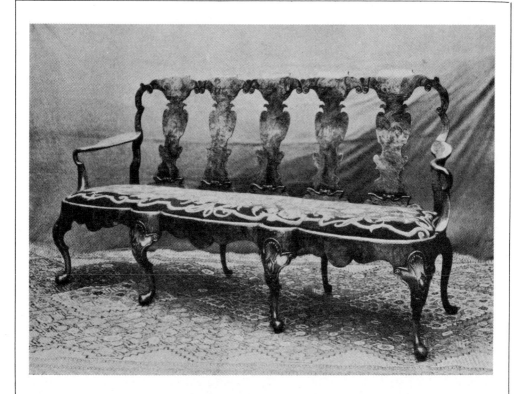

A walnut chair-back Settee with five splats. This is a piece the nationality of which is questionable. The design is Dutch, shown in the elaborate shaping outwards of the seat rail, the bandiness of the legs, and the joining together of the top rails without balusters. On the other hand, the arms, although bold in sweep, are of a type found in English arm-chairs, and the veneers are the burrs of English walnut (*juglans regia*). This settee was probably the work of a Dutch chairmaker domiciled in England, and constructed with English woods.

Plate number Thirteen

A Standing Cupboard of walnut. Highest quality of French work of the late sixteenth century. Apart from the cornice, cushion-moulded top and moulded base, it is instructive to note the great constructional differences as compared with English work of the

same date. The two double-caryatid supports with the central lion mask are hewn from solid baulks of timber without any construction. This is possible with seasoned walnut; it would be almost impossible, or at least dangerous, with English oak.

Plate number Fifteen

Two views of an interesting Coat of Arms on a mantel at
the Feathers Hotel, Ludlow, Salop. The mantel has been
re-adapted and altered (the shelf above, with its brackets,
are Victorian additions), but the central panel is original
work of *circa* 1625 date.

Plate number Sixteen

The Dining-room at the Feathers Hotel, Ludlow, Salop. The mantel is one of the finest examples in England, of fine mellow tone, with original surfaces everywhere. The stone lining is modern. This mantel is reputed to have come from Stokesay Castle, but this is doubtful. That it is not in its original room is shown by the fact that it has been reduced in height, and its former broad cushion-moulded shelf removed. The original oak cornice has also disappeared.

Plate number Seventeen

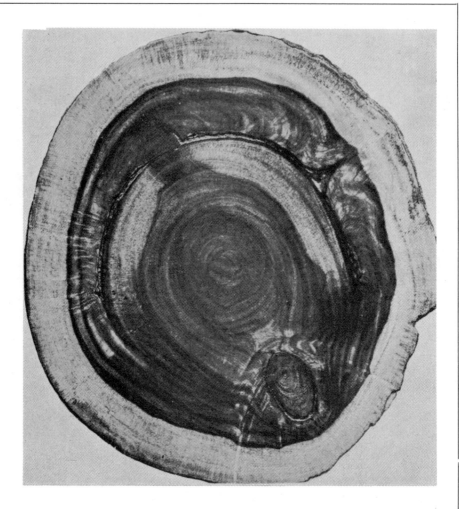

A transverse slice cut from a sapling of laburnum wood. These veneers are known as "oyster-pieces" and are used for surface veneering, jointed together with the plane (see next illustration). Walnut, laburnum and lignum vitæ are the usual timbers cut in this way. In this piece, note the heart wood and the outer sap ring.

Plate number Eighteen

An English walnut Cabinet of *circa* 1700. The inside faces of the doors and the fronts of the interior drawers are veneered with "oyster-pieces" banded with light cross-cut almond tree. On the outside the entire surface is veneered with thuja—an African wood of rich figure.

Plate number Nineteen

Two views (open and closed) of a rare, and very unpractical, Bureau on a cabriole stand. This was discovered not four years ago, since when two others, practically identical, turned up, illustrating the proverb that there is nothing new under the sun.

Plate number Twenty

CHAPTER IV

THE WOODWORKER OF THE OLDEN TIME

IT was Herbert Spencer who first stated the principle that all development was from the simple to the complex, from the homogeneous to the heterogeneous. This law applies to the evolution of furniture and woodwork. The terms were synonymous in Plantagenet times, when furniture was scanty in amount and limited in variety, and wainscotings of timber, in houses, had not yet evolved. This homogeneity applied, not only to the furniture which was made, but also to the craftsmen who made it. The carpenter was the sole artisan in woodwork for domestic or clerical purposes. After the Dissolution of the Monasteries, in the first half of the sixteenth century, there arose a race of inferior craftsmen, the "huchiers" or arkwrights. The "ark" was the familiar name of the chest or coffer, an important piece of furniture designed to hold articles of value, linen, silver and plate, fabrics, vestments and the like, at a period when wealth was tangible and real, not held by token. Towards the close of the sixteenth century the two trades, which had hitherto been quite distinct and on widely differing levels, appear to have partly coalesced, the result being the "joyner" or joiner, who concerned himself with such woodwork as was not constructional in the sense of bearing large strains, as in roofs, chancel screens, and the like.

Right up to the Restoration we find this arkwright-carpenter, or joiner, engaged on furniture of all kinds, including chairs. Then the trade of the woodworker splits up again, and we get the chair maker as a distinct trade, followed by the cabinet maker. Carvers and wood turners were always apart from very early times, but they were in the nature of accessories—embellishers, one might term them—to the woodworking trade as a whole. At a later stage we find lacquer workers, marqueterie cutters and other subsidiary trades, but gilders and sawyers persist from very early times, the former rarely employed for furniture. Perhaps the earliest craftsman was the pit-sawyer, and from very early records we find that the man on the ground, who guided the saw, was always more highly paid than the man in the pit, who merely pushed the saw up and pulled it down; hence the term "top-sawyer" descriptive of skill or command.

19

Oak was almost the universal timber up to Tudor times, although Memel red deal must have been sparingly imported, as we know of certain deal wainscotings which must have been highly prized, as they are specifically mentioned in inventories. Fruit wood, pear, apple, damson, plum and almond were used, in small pieces for spindles and appliqués, and chests of cypress wood date from very early periods, although their nationality is often questionable.

Of the tools of the Plantagenet carpenter we know very little beyond the fact that saws ("kytting-saws"), augers ("wymbils"), adzes and such primitive appliances are mentioned in records from very early times. One is apt to be led astray by the fact that oak logs were so often split into boards with the beetle and the wedge or by the riving iron, which appears to suggest that the saw was not used, and was, therefore, unknown. Actually, the early woodworkers, who were most particular about their timber, found out that split oak, riven on its natural cleavage lines, possessed a stability which sawn oak did not possess. Even to this day, with power-driven saws, oak exposed to the weather in thin planks, as in park palings, is nearly always riven instead of sawn. The quartering of oak shows also that the discovery was made, quite early, of the stable qualities of oak when cut parallel to the medullary rays. It may be accepted, almost without exception, as a definite fact that all oak, other than in beams or posts, was quarter-cut right up to the middle of the eighteenth century, even for carcase construction or drawer sides. This is an important point, especially in judging the authenticity of panellings, so it is necessary to add some explanation to the diagrams illustrated here.

Oak cut on the quarter invariably exhibits the medullary ray figure in a series of splashes on the surface. The first two or three boards cut right through the centre of the trunk show this "silver figure," as these boards are almost parallel to the medullary ray itself. Beyond, however, it is necessary to cut on an inclined plane, the angle of which must vary with each succeeding cut. Between each board there falls out a small wedge piece which is more or less wasted. What is important to remember is that the saw, in quartering, almost follows the natural cleavage lines of the timber, and that the river, when he uses the "thrower" or riving iron to split the wood into "panel stuff" for wainscotings, produces quartered oak as a matter of course. The wood will split in no other way. It will be found that oak panels in wainscotings up to the end of the reign of Charles II (1685) are almost invariably split, and vary greatly in thickness, even in the same panel, whereas the framings, the stiles and rails, are nearly always sawn.

One would like to establish a rule that all original oak pieces were made from quarter-sawn timber, but this would be misleading. First of all, there is no secret about this method of cutting, and quartered oak is used, to this day, in all good shops. Secondly, in Tudor and Stuart times, these matters were in the hands of the Trade Guilds, who had the power to seize all oak intended for furniture or interior woodwork, which was not cut "on the quarter." The records of the Carpenters' Company abound with entries as to the "restynge of stuffe," i.e. the impounding of defective timber. To these powerful Guilds, partly clerical in character, we owe many of the fine halls as at Cirencester, Lavenham and elsewhere, and also the fact that Tudor and Stuart oak has survived to our day. Had the oak used been cut "on the straight" the furniture and panellings would have shrunk, warped or otherwise have fallen to pieces. As the usual panel grooves in seventeenth-century wainscotings are very shallow, as a rule, we know that the panel timber cannot have shrunk to any appreciable extent.

Unfortunately for our present purpose of proper co-ordination, the arkwright does not appear to have been subject to Guilds as strict as those which regulated the carpenter, with the result that in the inferior post-Dissolution Gothic pieces from about 1550 to 1600 one finds straight cut and quartered oak used indiscriminately. Added to this, not only the workmanship but even the tradition is crude in the extreme. It must be obvious that the cruder a piece of furniture is the more difficult it is to separate the fake from the genuine. It is akin to attempting to date two rabbit hutches of uncertain age. There is nothing in the way of art-craftsmanship to act as a guide. Some examples of this primitive post-Dissolution Gothic are illustrated here. Unfortunately they command prices high enough to make faking well worth while, and it is exceedingly difficult to detect these forgeries if they are well done. It is like attempting to allocate dates to two stacks of firewood.

It is only within recent years that this crude post-Dissolution Gothic has been placed in its proper sequence in the chronology of English furniture. Even in our national museums the authorities have been led astray by its primitive constructional character and have dated it as far back as the fifteenth century, ignoring the fact that constructional knowledge had advanced far beyond this stage even at this period. Church woodwork shows us that framing and panelling were known and practised even in the fourteenth century, whereas, in these debased Gothic pieces, doors are often mere slabs of wood pierced in rough geometrical designs. It is notable, also, that while we find standing cupboards, chests and tables in this debased style, we never meet with chairs or stools in the same manner, and this absence alone should have aroused suspicion. Actually, two distinct schools of woodworkers arise after about 1540. The one, infinitely the more scholarly and skilled in the craft, follow in the new manner, the Renaissance, which was

21

introduced from Italy by Pietro Torrigiano in his design for the tomb of Henry VII in Westminster Abbey, or which permeated through France into Somerset and Devon, or arrived from the Low Countries and influenced the work of the East Anglian counties. There remained others, no longer under the tutelage of abbey or monastery (and all art-crafts had, hitherto, emanated from the clerical houses), who ventured on the old style, dimly remembered in vague ornamented forms, but with the former fine constructional traditions absolutely forgotten.

There is one striking phenomenon in the development of English woodwork which it may be instructive to notice here. The early carpenter followed the mason, and used timber in much the same way as the latter used stone. It was long before the greater possibilities of timber dawned on the woodworker. Stone can bear great crushing, but very little tensile strains. A tie-beam of stone would have to be far more massive than one of wood to remain stable on an equal span. The mason chisels a panel with its frame from the solid, and even when he builds up, his mitre is merely carved ornament, with the butt-joint below it. The early woodworker followed this lead, at first, and even in the late seventeenth century, when framing and panelling had been fully understood for more than a century, it is usual to find this mason's mitre in wainscotings and even in furniture.

These constructional possibilities of timber as compared with stone appear to have been almost unknown to the post-Dissolution woodworker, who avoided drawers (which involved dovetailing), and made his doors from mere slabs of oak. There is also the suspicion that his tools were similarly primitive, as, in many examples, the carver appears to have come to his aid, and to have carved flat surfaces to hide the unskilled use of the adze or the absence of the plane. Tools of precision could only have been possessed by the few. We know they were costly and greatly prized, as there are numerous records of where they are left to descendants in wills, and described in great detail in inventories.

There is no doubt that the custom of the shop providing the tools for the workman existed almost to the close of the eighteenth century. Going back no more than forty years ago, in Germany, Holland and parts of France, the only tools which were expected to be furnished by the "journeyman" were a metre rule and perhaps a few special planes and gouges. Very often the travelling workman possessed only an apron; the shop provided everything else. There were exceptions to this at all times, as examples of elaborate tool chests exist which date from the middle of the eighteenth century at least;* but whether these were the property of workmen or belonged to a master man, or his shop, it

* One, in the Geffrye Museum, in Shoreditch, London, has drawers inside with the fronts inlaid with marqueterie!

is difficult to say. It must be remembered that, at this date, transport of heavy chests of tools from place to place must have been a far more arduous undertaking than it would be at the present day.

There is every evidence to show that tools must have been rare in the earlier periods, as so few have survived, and those which have persisted are often of a very ornate character, which suggest that they were highly prized and would, therefore, not be lightly destroyed or allowed to perish. Thus I have seen planes and the frames of saws finely carved, and sometimes inlaid with ivory and bone. This rarity, therefore, indicates that tools belonged rather to the shop than to the workman, and in pre-Dissolution days, when all the fine woodwork was executed more or less under the protection of the Church, tools must have belonged to the local abbey or monastery. With the post-Dissolution Gothic, it is not only the design and the workmanship which is cruder and unskilled, it is the tools themselves which are scanty and primitive. A mortise, for example, can only be made with the mortise chisel; no other tool will serve. The dovetailing of drawers demands a fine saw and sharp chisels of various sizes. Undercut carving requires finely tempered gouges and V-tools, among others.

When we examine this post-Dissolution Gothic (of which several examples will be illustrated later on), we find that mortise-and-tenon framing is exceptional and dovetailed drawers still rarer. Carving is flat and crude, often a mere scratching with a sharpened divider (the so-called "chip carving"), and piercing shows that the saws must have been very coarse. The true Gothic built-up tracery is replaced by crude "plate tracery," where the design is sometimes sawn through the solid wood, more often hacked out with chisels. If one compares true fourteenth-century work, such as the chests in Dersingham Church or Pershore Abbey, with this mid-sixteenth-century crude furniture, it will be seen that the latter exhibits late and uncultured details, yet, judged by its primitive character, should be referred to a much earlier date than the former. At the same time it must be borne in mind that the woodworkers, even as early as the dawn of the fifteenth century, were in two distinct classes at least. At the top was the skilled and highly paid carpenter, usually in the fee of the Church, and generally engaged on elaborate works, such as screens, stalls with their canopies, and timber roofs. Occasionally he would make furniture, such as the chests in Pershore Abbey, St. Michael's Parish Church at Coventry or the triple Guild throne in St. Mary's Hall in the same city. His work is to be distinguished by its skill and constructive knowledge; he joints and frames accurately, and his oak is always quarter-sawn.

Side by side with the carpenter, although possibly not working in the same shop, and certainly not belonging to the same Guild, was the "huchier" or "arkwright," who uses oak very much in the stone mason's manner rather than in that of the carpenter or woodworker proper. It is only in minute details that the work of the early fifteenth-century arkwright differs from that of the post-Dissolution maker of furniture. If anything, the latter is the cruder of the two, and there is no doubt that, after the Dissolution, such skill as still remained after the fostering art of the Church had been scattered abroad turned its attention to the new manner, the Renaissance from Italy and France, leaving the Gothic with its former fine traditions lingering only as a remote memory, to the unskilled arkwright with his lack of knowledge and artistic education, and his imperfect and clumsy tools and methods.

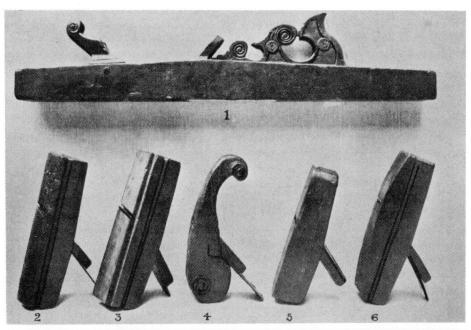

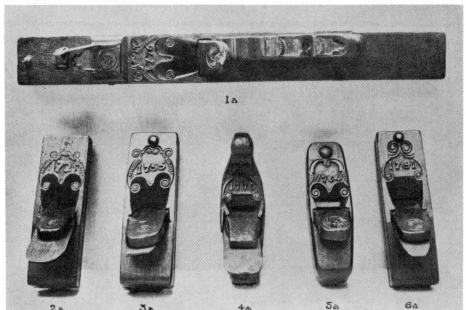

Early Planes, seen from the side and from above:
(1, 1a) Long trying plane.　　(4, 4a) Shaping plane.
(2, 2a) Smoothing plane.　　(5, 5a) Roughing plane.
(3, 3a) Smoothing plane.　　(6, 6a) Shaping plane.
Note. These planes are dated, but are all of the "single-iron" type,
and must have been difficult to use for fine work.

Plate number Twenty-one

Right

Using the Adze. This was the tool used for smoothing up large roof timbers. Note the timber "knee" on the right-hand side, of the type used for windbraces of timber houses.

Left

The Pit-saw at work. The modern power-driven circular saw has largely displaced the pit-saw, but the latter is still used in country districts for large timbers. Note the "top" and "bottom" sawyer.

Plate number Twenty-two

Using the Riving-iron, or "Thrower," in the splitting of oak. *Above*, using the "Beetle" to enter the log; *below*, levering the log open with the Riving-iron.

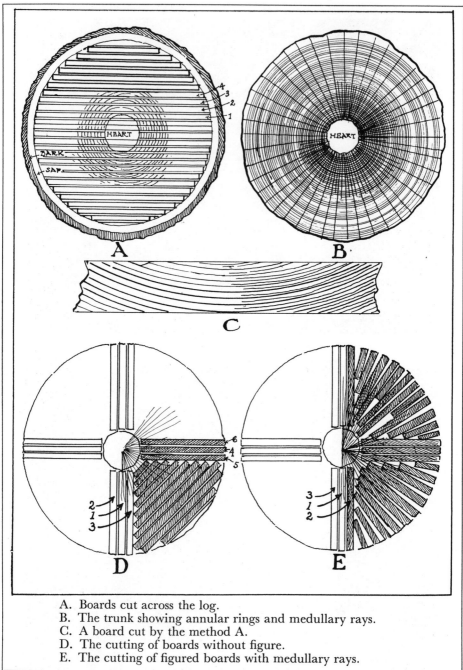

A. Boards cut across the log.
B. The trunk showing annular rings and medullary rays.
C. A board cut by the method A.
D. The cutting of boards without figure.
E. The cutting of figured boards with medullary rays.

Plate number Twenty-four

CHAPTER V

DETECTIVE METHODS AND THE PROBLEM OF RESTORATION

S the succeeding chapters of this book will be devoted to the consideration of English furniture and woodwork in chronological detail (there is no other method if the result is not to be a disorderly and disjointed effort), it may be as well to establish certain formulæ which will serve as a basis for the examination of pieces. After such formulæ have been stated, it is then possible to indicate the scope of the knowledge which is necessary before they can be employed with advantage. It must be remembered that, with constant practice, these points tend to become automatic. They can be briefly stated thus:—

(1) Is the piece English?
(2) Of what wood is it made?
(3) What is its probable date, or to what period does it purport to belong?
(4) If the example be earlier than 1650, to what county or district can it be referred?
(5) Is it a valuable example, and, if so, in what does the value consist? In rarity, detail or workmanship?
(6) Are the valuable details original to the piece?
(7) Can the piece have been something else originally?
(8) Has it been altered in any way, either by additions or repair?
(9) Is it the kind of thing which was made at the period to which it purports to belong?
(10) Are the tools which have been used those of the period or are they of modern character?
(11) Is the piece in its original state as regards finish, making reasonable allowance for wear, friction or polishing by rubbing? If not, to what degree has it been renovated?
(12) Are the wood thicknesses correct for the period?
(13) Is the construction of the period?
(14) Has the piece a history or a pedigree?

Having thus established a method of procedure, we can proceed to examine and elaborate each point. It is obvious that the necessary knowledge must be presumed, and this can be acquired only by actual experience in the handling and examination of genuine pieces. Books can afford some measure of instruction, but no photograph, however good, can convey an accurate idea of surface condition or of constructional details. With oak furniture and woodwork, at least, there is no finer school than the small parish churches which are scattered up and down England and Wales. Of all the churches which I know (and I have visited hundreds, and on many occasions), I have never found a deliberate fake in a single one. I have seen plenty of altered pieces, but the alteration has been frankly done with no intention, whatsoever, of deceiving. Even with the later furniture of the walnut and mahogany periods (much of which when in churches must have come into clerical possession soon after it was made) there is the same purity, and, in addition, one can often study the original condition of such furniture when it left the shops, without the adventitious aids of rubbing and waxing over a long period of use in the home.

To those who are interested in what the collector so often miscalls "original state," the reader can be safely recommended to examine, at some leisure, the three magnificent mahogany stalls or chairs in West Wycombe Church, in Buckinghamshire (only a short run from London), the mahogany table and chairs in the Monypenny Pew in Rolvenden Church, or the pair of fine walnut Restoration chairs flanking the altar table at Biddenden (both in Kent), and for original oak I know of no finer examples of detail and surface condition than the pew-ends in Ufford Church in Suffolk, and the miserere-seats and choir-stalls at Ludlow in Shropshire. At the latter, one can stay at the "Feathers," and, in the dining-room, inspect one of the finest oak mantels in England, even although it is not in its original home, and, in its adaptation to its new-old surroundings, has lost its cornice and its broad cushion-moulded shelf and stone lining. I know of no more valuable experience for the budding collector than an attentive examination of the examples cited above, allied to a good memory for detail and surface condition. It is a pity that so many vitiate their taste and spoil their eye by looking at nothing else than fakes, things of yesterday which are "planted" all over the country for the special benefit of the bargain-hunting "collector." It is akin to living with pictures of the Alma Tadema order—if not worse—as a preliminary to the study of Italian primitives.

Reverting now to our formulæ we can begin, in order, with:

(1) Is the piece English?

There is often considerable confusion regarding the nationality of both oak and walnut pieces. We must remember that Plantagenet England was still largely French in language and customs, and foreign artisans greatly influenced many of the oak pieces of the fifteenth century. Thus one finds examples such as the standing cupboard at the end of this chapter, where the timber is English oak but the whole manner is that of the French Gothic. With these early pieces, which are exceedingly rare, it matters very little if they be French or English, their value is much the same; but with the walnut furniture of the late seventeenth century the fact whether a piece is Dutch or English makes a considerable difference in price. Apart from the question of the timber and the veneer (to one well acquainted with woods there is a marked difference between English walnut and that from the Low Countries, but this implies special knowledge), it is not difficult to distinguish between English and Dutch examples when both are characteristic. Unfortunately, at this period, from 1670 to 1705, some furniture was made outright in Holland and imported; other pieces were produced by Dutch workmen domiciled in this country; still others originated from English workmen designing under Dutch influence, and, to confuse matters yet further, walnut was often imported both in the log and the plank. There is a measure of safety in this, that if a piece be designed and constructed in the English manner, it does not affect its value, in any great measure, even if it be, actually, an outright importation, whereas one made in England, from English walnut, but in the pronounced Dutch manner, is worth far less. This point can be well illustrated by a chair-back settee of English walnut, but in the full style of Holland of the 1700 period. If this be compared with the next, which is another settee in the English manner, the points of difference can be noted. The shapings of the former are over-flamboyant, and the cabriole legs are bandy. With the latter, these details are graceful and refined, and the fashion in England was always for the coupled chair-backs instead of the back with many splats. Had the first been in the English manner, with its fine veneered splats, it would have been worth three times as much as the other at least, as such a detail as five splats in the one settee is almost unknown in England. The Dutch style makes the value of the two about equal. The question of nationality is of great importance, therefore, apart from the fact that a collector of English furniture would hardly wish to add Dutch pieces unwittingly or under a mistaken idea as to their country of origin.

With furniture of the sixteenth century there should be no possibility of error, especially with French pieces, as, while oak is almost the invariable wood in England, walnut was nearly always used in France. A very notable French cabinet of the period, in walnut, is shown here and, apart from the general style and decoration, the marked difference in structural methods cannot fail to be apparent at once. In some ways it is more advanced than the English cabinets or wall-pieces of the same date, but English woodworkers of the sixteenth century would never have dared to hew the double caryatid supports, with the centred human mask, from a single baulk of timber. In any case, the restrictions of his Guild would have interdicted such a practice.

This question of nationality is a very wide one, and could be protracted if the scope of this book permitted, but I have dealt with this matter at great length, and in many volumes (to say nothing of the works of others), so it must be left for the student to reinforce his knowledge from these books.

(2) Of what wood is it made?

The second point, as to the wood from which an example is made, is also inexplicable here, for the same reason. The proper places to study timbers are in the workshop or in the yards of merchants. No book can teach the student anything. To differentiate between oak, walnut, mahogany, satinwood, cherry, chestnut, sycamore, rosewood, ebony and other furniture timbers is easy, but to place the nationality of each variety, or the locality of origin, is far more difficult, yet it may make all the difference, not only in the judgment of a genuine piece, but also in the detection of a fake, if the mahogany, for example, be Central American or African. It will be found, throughout this book, that a certain standard of knowledge has to be presumed. No work of this character can undertake to teach all that there is to learn about English furniture. The experience which may take an expert half a lifetime to acquire cannot be attained in a few hours or days by simply reading this or any other book. So much must be obvious, yet to be able to direct studies into the proper channel is already a marked step forward.

Years ago I found it a very good plan to make a friendly association with one or two timber merchants, and to take one wood at a time (mahogany, for example), and to study this in plank and veneer, directly the logs had been "opened" by the saw. I preferred timber yards to workshops, as, with the former, the country of origin could be definitely ascertained from the bills of lading, whereas many of the shop ideas, while thoroughly sincere, were often inaccurate. I found, in all, that there were nearly thirty defined species of mahogany imported from Central America and Africa, and certain bastard species from other parts of the globe. In the eighteenth century the wood originated almost entirely from San Domingo, or other parts of Cuba and Honduras.

An important point is to learn from a narrow piece of, say, eight inches, either in the plank or the finished article of furniture, if it has been cut from an old full-grown tree or not. In the years from 1725 to 1780 only the largest trees were felled, as the supply was plentiful, and young timber, therefore, is an almost infallible indication of later importation. To judge of the width of the full plank, one must be able to discern the heart-wood at once and without hesitation, as this is the centre of the tree.

There is much to be learned about the old and the modern methods of cutting veneers. Those of the eighteenth century were always cut with the saw; no other means was known. At the present day, in addition to the saw, the knife is used in two ways. Rotary cutting is done with a broad knife which cuts round the log, in exactly the same way as one unwraps a music-roll such as is used on a mechanical piano-player. This rotary-cut veneer is the width of the trunk, and, by its method of cutting, is practically endless. Cut in this way, the veneer is thin and absolutely without figure. It is, or should be, only used for the cheapest work, yet I can recollect the top of an old Sheraton semi-circular side-board which had been re-veneered in this way, and which featured in a certain notorious case in the Law Courts only a few years ago, yet when I pointed out this veneer as certain evidence of modern work, I could see it was wholly incomprehensible to the "experts" on the other side, none of whom had received a technical training in the workshop or the timber-yard.

The second method of veneer-cutting is by the pendulum knife, a broad blade which swings in a segment, cutting a broad leaf with each sweep. A man stands by to watch each cut and to see that the line of cleavage is such as will produce the maximum figure. If this shows any tendency to "fade out," the knife is stopped and the pitch of the log changed in its "dogs." The baulk of timber is kept saturated with water to prevent splitting of the leaves of veneer as they are cut. This pendulum-knife-cut veneer is generally stouter than the rotary-cut, and, cleaving the log straight through, the same figure of the wood is preserved as with the saw-cut method.

There are several other intricacies in veneer-cutting which should be studied, such as the cleaving of burr (or, as they say in America, "burl") veneers from the boles of old walnut trees. The merchant who deals in fancy veneers is always on the look-out for freak growths, and trees which have been polled offer many varieties. Thus the pollarded olive (often incorrectly styled as "maza-wood"), walnut, elm or ash yield rich veneers, although only in small pieces, and these excessively brittle. Another method is to cut saplings and branches transversely into what are known as "oyster-pieces," which are merely slices of "end-wood," or cross-grain. Laburnum, with its dark heart and yellow sap-ring, produces very decorative "oyster-pieces," and walnut, almond, kingwood and other timbers are used in the same manner. The greatest care has to be exercised in "laying" these pieces (which are carefully jointed together with the plane or the fine marqueterie saw), as not only

29

are they very fragile, but "end-wood," or cross-grain, does not adhere to its ground without elaborate precautions in the glueing.

It is a common idea that glue will stick anything, but this is the greatest fallacy. To joint two pieces of wood together, it is necessary that they shall fit with the greatest accuracy. The hand-screw or the cramp will help a bad joint only for a time, until the glue has thoroughly dried, and has contracted in consequence. To lay a veneer, it is necessary to roughen both its under surface and its bed to give a "key" to the glue, which is usually done with the "toothing-plane," a tool where the edge of the "iron" is serrated. Any grease, however slight, must be removed, or the veneer will not adhere. There are many pitfalls for the amateur in veneering, which will be pointed out in a later chapter on marqueterie furniture.

Sufficient has been said here, for the moment, to emphasize the necessity for the technical education of the expert. There is no royal road to knowledge in this field, nor in any other of a similar character. It is assumed that it is the desire of the expert to know, not to guess, or, as our American cousins say, expressively, to "opinionate." We can, therefore, leave the question of woods and return to the third point in our list after a somewhat lengthy digression.

(3) What is the probable date or to which period does the piece purport to belong?

The word "probable" is inserted here, as no one, with knowledge enough to recognize his limitations, can state an actual date for any antique piece of English furniture. When we name a date we really mean the period when a certain definite general fashion originated, and pieces possessing characteristics in common must have been produced in numbers before such fashion can be said to have become established at all. It must also not be forgotten that it is the detail which follows the latest fashion which indicates the period. One must ignore, to a large extent, the possibility of the later copy of sufficient age to have acquired the surface appearance of an original model, although here a good knowledge of timbers, methods, and tools will often enable the cultured expert to detect such a copy.

A knowledge of the various fashions in English furniture of the various periods, together with a minute acquaintance with the details of each, is an indispensable preliminary to expert knowledge in the detection of the fake. This, in itself, is a wide subject, and the reader must be referred to the bibliography at the end of this book for further information on this subject. It is obvious that a piece which exhibits details which do not conform to the era to which it purports to belong cannot be of that period, and it may be either a later bad copy or a modern fake.

(4) If the example be earlier than 1650, to what county or district can it be referred?

This is an important branch of our subject, as, in the early oak period, each section of England had its own characteristics, and the conditions of labour and transit, at the time, were such that the possibility of the interchange of ideas, models, or workmen was very remote. That pieces of, say, Somerset, Warwickshire, Shropshire, Wales, Devonshire or East Anglia have been scattered up and down the country since does not affect the point that they were segregated at the time when they were made, and for many years after, and any example which combines Warwickshire and East Anglian details is almost certainly a later copy, if not a modern forgery. Right up to the middle of the Stuart period the laws regulating labour were arbitrary and savage, and the workman who roamed from his native village without the consent of his Lord of the Manor, or (in the fifteenth and sixteenth centuries) that of the abbot or head of the neighbouring monastery, ran a serious risk of being summarily hanged from a tree, without trial, as a rogue and a masterless man, in any strange locality in which he sought employment.

I was the first to point out the importance of these localities of origin, so far as the history of English furniture was concerned, in *Early English Furniture and Woodwork* (1922), but I did not consider, at the time, the relation of this knowledge to the detection of fakes. We are far from possessing accurate knowledge of this branch of our subject, as it is a field which calls for patient and wholly unremunerative labour, and one with innumerable false side-tracks. I have elaborated the nature of the problem in the book referred to above, and do not propose to traverse the same ground again. It is sufficient here to point out the great archæological interest which attaches to this division of the subject. Not so long ago I found a very fine oak mantel in an old house in a remote part of Wales. It had been there for a couple of centuries, at least, but it had, obviously, been adapted to its position, as the cornice had been removed to get it into the height of the room. I made the claim that it was of East Anglian origin, but this was ridiculed by the owner, who admitted, by the way, that it might have come from a local thirteenth-century castle, now ruinous. I left the matter at that, but I received a letter recently from the same man, in which he informed me he had discovered, from his records, that his family had owned a house at Great Bealings in Suffolk, which was sold in 1622 and pulled down shortly after. He admitted the probability of his fine mantel having been removed from that house.

There is one guide which may assist the student in his investigations into localities of origin, and that is to be found in church woodwork and furniture. Even in the somewhat rare instances where pieces have been brought into the church at a later date there is every probability that these came from houses in the same neighbourhood, as it is hardly possible for a church in Wales, for instance, to receive a gift of a chair or a chest from a house in Norfolk. There is also the added advantage, with church possessions, that it is almost impossible to get furniture out again once it has been placed inside, as the Monypennys of Hole Park found to their cost when they claimed the return of the furniture in the family pew in Rolvenden Church many years ago. A faculty was necessary, and this was never obtained.

(5) Is it a valuable article, and, if so, in what does the value consist? In rarity, detail or workmanship?

Here, again, we have three distinct problems which must imply special knowledge and experience. No one who has not seen many things, and over long periods, can judge of the rarity of any particular example, and it is one of the uncanny facts in relation to English furniture that, after many years, one encounters a very exceptional piece and regards it as unique, yet, within a comparatively short space of time, a second and even a third turns up. I am alluding here to genuine pieces. I have illustrated rare models in my books and have seen the market literally flooded with others soon after, but this is duplication rather than discovery.

A bureau on a cabriole stand, of curious design and workmanship, is illustrated here. It is an interesting example of the "unfakeable," as the method by which the flap doors are disposed of, when the bureau is opened, is more ingenious than practical. No faker would dream of reproducing such a piece, yet I saw this ten years ago, and it was utterly novel to me. Within two years I found another, not identical but very nearly so, and in this year of 1930 I have found another, complete with the lunetted drawers in the stand which are missing in the illustration here. It serves to illustrate the point that, in English furniture, there is no such word as "unique." It is only by a prolonged experience that one can judge of the rarity of any example which turns up, but a judgment as to its artistic merits is quite another matter. Culture in the estimation of detail, however, can only be acquired by laborious study, and one is very prone to be influenced, in one's estimate of the fine, by considerations of value. To judge accurately of workmanship requires a definite technical training; there is no alternative method.

The appreciation of the points which make the value of a piece under examination should be practically intuitive, and it is these details to which close attention should be directed. If they are genuine, nothing else matters very much; if they are recent, then the faker has enhanced the value of a piece intrinsically worth very little. Take a commode with elaborate carved splay angles and plinth, and with costly ormulu handles. The proper way to commence an examination is to concentrate on these details, and if one sees an "expert" begin by opening the drawers and scrutinising the inside, one may be sure that between his "opinion" and mere guesswork there is about the same difference as between an attorney and a solicitor. The same is true of every trade and profession; the pretender is at once apparent to the technical expert, and this is equally true of boots (to the shoemaker) or obscure diseases of the body (to the surgeon or physician). I can say, however, with literal truth, that quacks in the medical profession are not nearly so numerous—or so assertive—as charlatans in the antique trade. The latter often rely on the fact that only the technical workman can, as a rule, expose them, and from the social position of such workmen, or commercial considerations, such exposure is very unlikely to be effective. These pseudo-experts are usually pachydermatous enough to care very little about what is said behind their backs.

(6) Are the valuable details original to the piece?

This problem is largely dealt with in the foregoing, but there is the one of "marriage," which has always to be considered. I have seen valuable old cabriole legs removed from an otherwise ugly chair and grafted on to another with a fine back but simple front legs, and this addition is very difficult to detect. I also knew an instance, not so long ago, where a dealer acquired two finely carved mahogany floral pendants, and who was searching the trade for a serpentine-fronted chest-of-drawers with splay corners of the necessary width. He found one, eventually, in a shop where I was almost a weekly visitor, and I saw the same chest, in its beautified state, in a West End dealer's window, looking extremely fine and grand. The brass handles had also greatly improved in the interim.

To say that it is easy to detect such a fraud is preposterous. Both chest and pendants were genuine and of nearly the same period, and one cannot smell glue, which was the only modern part about this chest-of-drawers promoted to commode status. Only a high degree of technical knowledge, coupled with an almost microscopical examination, could detect such a "marriage," yet I have known "experts" with such a "flair" or "eye for the right piece" that they could detect a fraud of this kind in a moment—according to their own account. They could probably "find the lady" in the three-card trick worked by a professor in the art, in much the same manner, the only difference being that, with the latter, they would lose their own money. I can recollect one such "expert" (who only acquired wisdom two or three years ago, and

33

by the process which will educate us all one day) who expatiated on a lacquer cabinet which he described as "fairy-like" (whatever that may mean), and of the quality which the modern faker could never hope to imitate, while the man who had made it outright, and had only delivered it ten minutes before, stood by. He had not even had the time to take his departure! I must explain here that this cabinet was not marked as an antique; it had not been in the shop long enough to have acquired a ticket at all, but it was bought, then and there, as a genuine example of late seventeenth-century work, with the price to be fixed later on. The lady who was with the "expert" said she "simply must have it." She got it—and in more ways than one.

(7) Can the piece have been something else originally?

Here is the opportunity for the exercise of the powers of observation and deduction on the part of our budding expert. We can commence with the definite fact that the altered piece was, originally, not valuable as it is now, unless the alteration had been done for convenience, and with no intention of deceiving. It is impossible to give here more than a vague and general idea of what may have happened. A commode may have been a simple chest-of-drawers, a hanging wardrobe a press-bedstead, a Chippendale arm-chair a commode-chair with the "apron" cut away, a writing-desk a simple dressing knee-hole table with added or carved-up mouldings, a tripod table may be a "marriage" between a tray and the base of a pole screen, and I have known many other transmogrifications too numerous to be mentioned here. I can remember one instance which was large enough to be generic. At the time of the antique boom of 1919-21, when anything which was old could find a ready market, one enterprising individual had the brilliant notion of creating a vogue for the simple oak pieces from one of the Channel Islands, which were genuine for much the same reason that the side curls of Mrs. Gamp could not have been described as false. The venture failed, and a whole shipload of oak furniture, on similar lines to many of the Normandy or Brittany pieces, went begging for a home. It found one, *en bloc*, in a certain provincial factory, and was heard of no more for about a year, when, all of a sudden, the market was flooded with some of the most "genuine" Gothic and Tudor pieces I have ever seen. Unfortunately, no skill could turn French oak into *Quercus robur*, but that did not hinder the sale, and I know of one castle on the Welsh borders (in the process of being "restored" at the time) which was completely refurnished with Gothic pieces of the time. (By "the time" I refer to 1920, not to 1420.) It is surprising how far this shipload of furniture went. I found it everywhere. One house in Dorset was full of it, another in Warwickshire sent up a "collection" to London, and it sold extremely well. How much went to America I cannot say, but it was good enough for any "look-at-the-back" expert, as the surfaces were original as far as possible, and an old oak untouched surface is the most difficult thing to imitate. In short, the gentlemen with the "eye" and the "flair" were utterly deceived, although none of the pieces would have taken in a timber merchant or a cabinet maker of the old school.

(8) Has the piece been altered in any way, either by additions or repair?

This should be an easy problem, if the addition has been honestly made or the repairs frankly done, but I must confess that I am in favour of restoring a piece so that the repairs shall be invisible. That is not to say that I believe in the practice of restoring an entire piece on the basis of a genuine old screw, but I do not think, for example, that an old stone church of the fifteenth century should be "darned" with brand-new stone left in the same state as when it was taken out of the quarry. It is too much like patching a pair of black trousers with "shepherd's plaid."

This raises the interesting point, in equity, as to who is the faker; the one who makes outright or restores an old model to an unreasonable degree, or the dealer who sells it, at a high price, as an "untouched bit"? I leave this nice point to be settled by dialecticians.

(9) Is it the kind of thing which was made at the period to which it purports to belong?

Reduced to absurdity, this proposition can be understood at once. If a dealer possessed Queen Elizabeth's automobile, no one would believe it, even if it were smothered all over with Tudor roses. There are certain types of furniture which originated at certain definite periods, and are not found before. Thus the table on legs, as distinct from one of the trestle-type, belongs to the late sixteenth century and after; the bureau dates from 1665, about, the flat pedestal desk from *circa* 1725, the sideboard with urns and pedestals from 1765, and the self-contained sideboard, with drawers and cellarettes, from 1780 onwards. Thus a Queen Anne sideboard, or even a dining-table, is just as unknown as a Tudor motor-car. Similarly, a bedstead without posts and a canopy is unheard of until the nineteenth century, and upholstery begins, and very sparingly, in the reign of Charles I and does not become general until after 1680. Washstands (as distinct from wig or powdering-stands) are as unknown in the eighteenth century as bathrooms. Baptism must have been the one bathing experience of our Georgian ancestors, if the testimony of their houses and furniture is to be believed.

The desire of the faker to provide the exceptional, bordering almost on the unknown, often leads him into this undiscovered country, and hardly a year goes by without I receive a commission—usually from America—to procure the thing which never existed. Some of these gaps in English furniture and woodwork are difficult to understand. We can imagine why Chippendale, in his *Director*, does not illustrate a washstand, but why is there no example of a dining table? Also, while we find panellings of oak and deal and (very rarely) of walnut, why was mahogany never used for this purpose? It is the most reliable furniture wood in existence. These are some of the problems to which we can find no solution.

(10) Are the tools which have been used those of the period or are they of modern character?

Here the expert has to rely on technical knowledge, but a little intelligent study in a modern machine shop will be found of the utmost value. The indications of the use of a circular saw, or of an "overhand" planing machine or a "thicknesser," should be evident enough, and it is not difficult to see how regular are the marks left by the power-driven band- or fret-saws. Again, there are no gauge-indications left when the mortising machine is used, but the signs of the spindle-moulding machine are not so readily discernible, especially if the moulding be carved afterwards. All old mouldings were worked in one of two ways, either by the "scratcher" (see illustration), which must slightly undulate the moulding, or by the carvers' gouges outright. Taking the commode, here, I have tested the top moulding by a series of wax impressions, and the section is not the same anywhere; it varies with every inch. This proves that the carver must have worked the moulding at the same time as he carved the ornament, and I have found the same on more than one example. This trifling detail shows that one cannot be too minute in one's examination. The modern wood-carver has gouges, chisels and "parting-tools" of a kind which were unknown even in the late eighteenth century, and it is possible to detect the signs of their use in faked work.

There are other details, such as of screws, nails, brass-work, etc., which can greatly assist in the detection of the fake, so long as one bears in mind that these may be frank replacements. To substitute for old worn-out screws, in the hinges of the doors of an original Chippendale bookcase, others of Nettlefold's manufacture does not make the piece a modern forgery.

(11) Original state as compared with renovations.

This must be largely a question of degree, but the amount of such restoration must affect the market value. It is necessary, therefore, to be able to ascertain to what extent a piece has been so restored, and to have a definite idea as to the limitations beyond which the article ceases to be a genuine antique at all. Especially is this necessary with up-holstered furniture. One does not expect the original covering on a chair or settee of the eighteenth century or earlier (unless it have the original needlework or tapestry, however much that may have been repaired), and many are not very particular even if the frame, which the upholstery conceals, has been renovated entirely. This means, with a "stuff-over" piece, that one buys four legs, and often only two, as the back legs of an upholstered settee are of no great importance anyway. Where is one to draw the line? A friend of mine bought a pair of small settees from a West End dealer not so long ago, with cabriole walnut legs on the front and straight stumps behind. They were covered with fragments of old seventeenth-century tapestry borders. He paid quite a good price for them (nearly £1,000 for the pair), and when I questioned their genuine character the dealer coolly confessed that he had made them up from an old four-legged stool, adding the back legs and the frames from some old timber, and covering the pair with some pieces of tapestry border. In the face of this admission he regarded them as quite genuine, "for what they were," whatever that may have meant. I pointed out that his original stool must have been a fake, and I characterized the whole transaction as a swindle, but he refused to disgorge. I suppose even West End dealers must live, although, in this particular case, I failed to see the necessity.

The question of original state versus restoration will be treated at some length in succeeding chapters, so we can leave the matter here for the present.

(12) Are the wood thicknesses correct for the period?

It may not be generally known that the unit for all hardwoods in commercial use, other than fancy woods such as ebony, boxwood, holly and the timber from fruit trees, is the three-inch plank. If cut into boards, the purchaser loses the wood which the saw-cut takes away. With soft woods, deal, pine, bass-wood, poplar and the like, the timber merchant is usually a little more generous. In the trade, it is usual to regard inch boards as "holding up" 13/16th of an inch when finished, allowing 3/16th for cutting and "cleaning up," and lesser thicknesses are reduced in much the same measure. This custom appears to have originated after the first half of the eighteenth century, before which time the thicknesses of oak, walnut and mahogany were irregular. I have found mahogany table-tops of the early Georgian period "holding up" exactly one inch, which is not a present-day timber thickness at all. Allowance must be made for veneers, which, at this date, add nearly 1/8th of an inch, as the old veneers were often very thick. With shaped surfaces, such as a serpentine front to a drawer, these thicknesses have no standard, as these drawers are always glued up in layers, cut with the saw, and then veneered.

It is possible, in many cases, to detect modern-cut timber by careful measurement and calipering, and this is a point which should not be neglected.

(13) Is the construction of the period?

This is a wide subject, and involves extensive research especially with the early oak pieces. Sawn oak of the sixteenth century, when cut straight through the trunk, should be suspected. Tenoning and mortising were known in very early times, as the late fourteenth-century roof of Westminster Hall will bear witness, but almost at all times this jointing method was neglected by inferior workmen.

Dovetailing appears to originate, in England, towards the close of the sixteenth century, although it was practised earlier on the Continent. It would be interesting if one could trace the evolution of dovetailing, and draw a lesson therefrom, but this would only be misleading. Generally speaking, the fine dovetail is late, but the large coarse one is not necessarily early. So much depended on the status, education, and tradition of the individual workman and his shop. Thus, at all times, the mortise of the carpenter is carried right through the rail, with the exposed tenon wedged for extra security, but this is not the practice of the cabinet maker or the chair maker. With American chairs, even of the Chippendale type, it is quite usual to find the tenons of the seat rails carried right through the squares of the back legs, and often wedged. One is forced to the conclusion that the early Colonial woodworkers were carpenters by trade, rather than cabinet maker or chair makers.

Drawer construction of the various periods varies considerably. In the seventeenth-century oak pieces one often finds drawer-sides grooved on their outer faces, so that the drawer pulls out on runners. Dovetailing, where present, is invariably coarse, but more often the sides are nailed or pegged into rebates in the drawer fronts. Drawer bottoms are frequently nailed, but sometimes they are inserted into grooves in the sides. The custom of fixing grooved fillets to the sides in which the drawer bottoms run (usually with a quarter-round bead-finish at the top) is quite a recent innovation, possibly of about 1810-20. It is never found in genuine early work.

(14) Has the piece a history or a pedigree?

The point that a really notable piece cannot arise from nowhere, unless it has been made yesterday, is often neglected, but it is one of great importance. It is necessary to offer a caution here, when the provenance of a well-known auction-room is cited. "I bought that at

——'s auction-room, and it came from the —— collection. Here is the catalogue and the illustration of that piece." Apparently nothing could be more convincing, yet, in a Court of Law, not so many years ago, I was shown a piece which was covered by a catalogue description and illustration, the original of which I had actually bought myself at that sale, and had in my possession at the time. It is as well to regard all pedigrees in a sceptical spirit until some more convincing evidence than an auctioneer's catalogue is forthcoming. It is a wicked world, and he who would make a fortune out of high-priced goods bought at public auctions (where his prices are known to everyone who is interested) must both buy and sell an enormous amount in the year. It does not require an expert, but an actuary, to prove this point.

In conclusion, beware of the fine piece which is offered for sale in a country house, unless it can be definitely established that it has been a family possession for a number of years. There is a process, known to the trade as "planting," and, like other planting, it often brings forth fruit—to the planter.

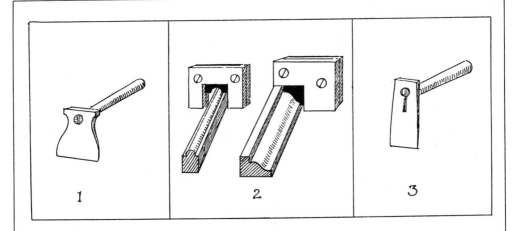

(1) The Veneering Hammer. This is not used in hammer fashion, but is held down by one hand and pressed from the top with the other, giving it at the same time a semi-rotary action, from the centre outwards, to squeeze out the superfluous glue to the edges. The glue is used thin and hot, as any overplus not exuded will contract and produce blisters later on.

(2) Moulding "Scratchers." Still used in hand-shops for shaped mouldings only. In a straight length they produce an uneven result, which is troublesome when the moulding comes to be mitred.

(3) The Chipper. The faker's tool, usually an old plane iron fixed to the end of a handle. It is not used like a chopper, but is drawn over surfaces and edges to simulate wear. The signs of its use should be patent to any observer.

Plate number Twenty-five

If the top, with its carved moulding, be examined carefully, and tested with wax impressions, it will be found that the moulding has been made by the carver, and not with the machine or the "scratcher," as it varies with every inch of its length. Carved mouldings of the eighteenth century were often made in this way, but with fakes they are usually "run" on the "spindle" and then carved. Plain mouldings, at all times, were made with the "scratcher," of course.

Plate number Twenty-six

CHAPTER VI

EARLY OAK FURNITURE AND WOODWORK

T is rare to find any early oak in original condition, that is, with the surface untouched other than by the wear and friction during the centuries. Apart from the fact that so much appears to have been painted over at later periods (possibly as a revulsion from the somewhat sombre appearance of the wood itself), it is doubtful if some, at least, was not decorated with colours at the time when it was made. This may not have been a general practice, but certain painted examples have persisted to our time where the applied decoration appears to be original.

With many historical examples, such, for instance, as the Bromley-by-Bow and the Clifford's Inn rooms in the Victoria and Albert Museum, not only have many coats of paint been stripped from the surfaces, but, what is worse, the wire-brush has been extensively employed, in other words, the faker's methods have been adopted in this stripping. The brush, with "bristles" of steel wire, is the tool which the faker uses to tear out the "meat" or soft parts from the surface of oak, leaving the harder medullary grain standing up. It is regrettable that the Museum authorities did not seek some other method.

This painting in many coats, and with lead colours, has had one decorative effect: it has turned the "splash figure," or medullary ray, nearly black. In the usual way this ray is lighter than the other parts of the wood, and age alone does not alter this relation. It is the lead in the paint which darkens the figure, and, at one time, this blackened figure could be taken as evidence that the surface had been painted, that is, until the faker found a method of darkening the ray without the necessity of painting first and then stripping. He achieves this by using the stripper without the painting, and these strippers—which are usually preparations of caustics—have another result: they bleach the surface of oak, and harden it at the same time, not by any means as original oak wears after centuries, but quite enough to deceive the unwary, especially those who are prepared to accept some "restoration" in qualification of their judgment.

Oak appears to have been originally finished in various ways. Often it must have been left bare, for subsequent waxing to produce a fine golden shade, or to turn grey where exposed to the weather. Sometimes, as we have seen, it was painted and stencilled with colours. At other times it was somewhat thickly coated with varnish. Those who are interested in examining these original states can be referred to the mantel in the "Feathers" Hotel at Ludlow, or the pew-ends at Ufford Church, or elsewhere, for the first, or to any of the barge-boards or other exposed timbers on the many half-timber houses which are to be found in so many of the country districts of England, for the second, that is, where these timbers have not been painted black or daubed over with what looks like tar, as on so many of the old buildings in Shrewsbury and elsewhere. The student will find imitation "timbers" painted on the faces of brick walls; anything to produce a cheap effect which is good enough for the average tourist sightseer. It is in East Anglia where original external oak has been left in its natural state, weather-worn, but not artificially "antiqued."

One of the finest examples which I know of original varnished oak is to be found in St. Mary's Hall at Coventry, in the fragment of the triple Guild Masters' throne there. Also, in the Mayor's Parlour is another Gothic chair, of lesser importance, but genuine and untouched, other than by a flagrant addition to the back and the loss of the boxing-pieces between the legs, and also one of the finest James I oak draw-tables in England, original even to the tusk-tenons of the tops.

It has been pointed out before that oak only case-hardens with the lapse of time. There is little merit in old oak once it is sawn apart or planed on its surfaces; once touched in this way it will warp, crack, and shrink almost as much as freshly-cut timber. I have known pieces of undoubted authenticity behave in the same manner when the overlying varnish has been removed. Especially is this likely when new varnish or polish is applied.

If it be the fact that oak furniture was painted over, in the original instance, at certain periods, it follows that this furniture is hardly ever found in this original painted state (which is certainly the case), and the expert has to determine which is genuine and which is spurious of two examples, both of which have been altered. This is a problem, but before considering it in technical detail it may be as well to examine the evidences for the former existence of this original decoration.

It is well known that many of the chancel screens of the mid-fifteenth century were painted in colours and picked out with gesso and gilding. Some have survived, in more or less original state, as at Ludham and Ranworth in Norfolk, and Southwold, Bramfield, Yaxley, and Eye in Suffolk. The Devonshire screens, as at Bovey Tracey, are also coloured, and, although much of this is later restoration, there is no doubt that they were originally decorated, and many more, which have been stripped to the bare wood, still exhibit traces of paint. The same is true of certain pulpits, and even the secular Coronation Chair in Westminster Abbey.

It is reasonable to assume that this decoration would inspire imitation in the homes of the wealthy, and that oak pieces would be similarly painted if only to accord with the gay costumes, both masculine and feminine, of the various periods. This is assumption, however, but it explains so much of the otherwise crude furniture of the latter part of the sixteenth century. If we imagine this furniture painted with colours and gold, much of this crudity departs. It is akin to judging a mirror frame from which the gold and the preparation have been removed; the underlying wood was never intended to be exposed in its bare state.

It is significant that, on the Continent, painting of woodwork appears to have been far more prevalent, in the Middle Ages, than in England. May it not be that in the former the colours have persisted, while in the latter they may have been stripped? We had a Puritan era in England, when the taste was for the sombre, and we know that many of the coloured church screens were deliberately defaced in Commonwealth times. We know also of painted altars which have been utterly destroyed, not only under Cromwell, but also by edicts of Edward VI and on other occasions.

There is another important factor to be considered. Furniture intended for painting and decoration would not be so highly finished as other pieces intended to be varnished or left in the natural wood. Thus, it is highly improbable that the Guild Masters' Chair in St. Mary's Hall at Coventry was ever originally painted, as it is fully elaborated in the carving. There is no room for paint, it would be like gilding the lily, but with much of the post-Dissolution Gothic, and the chip-carved pieces of earlier date, one can imagine that painting or gilding would be an improvement, would give a meaning to vacant spaces, and the crude carving might lose its primitive character if left to the gilder to prepare and gild. We shall see much the same thing at a later stage, when the subject of eighteenth-century mirrors is considered. One can conclude, at the present juncture, by pointing out that the trade of the "luminer" was an extensive one in the fifteenth and sixteenth centuries, mentioned often in records with expenditures for paint and gold, and this is highly significant as these accounts are often secular as well as clerical. In other words, these colours and gold were used in private houses, true, of the palatial kind, but where do the evidences remain at the present day from these periods?

In the early years of the seventeenth century we can see how elaboration in carving grows; there are no longer the empty spaces left, which, apparently, fulfil no function. Where the ornament is full, and conventional in character, there would be little incentive to colour, but where realism was deliberately attempted, as in the chest-front in the Victoria and Albert Museum, illustrated here, the inducement to colour must have been very strong indeed. At present, this piece is like a picture in monotone, and we can easily imagine, in the first years of the fourteenth century, that it would be regarded as a great improvement if an attempt were made to put the whole scene in natural colours, more or less. We know that this was done, as a general practice, in Germany and Italy at this, and later, periods. Often carving was superseded by raised gesso, which aims at a similar result, but by dissimilar means.

If it can be established that much of this early crude oak was originally painted, and that the colours have been stripped, it can be imagined that the task of segregating the original from the later fake is a formidable one, as, to take off paint, one has to adopt almost precisely the same methods as the faker uses to "antique" his pieces. Caustics, however, always leave traces of "salting" for many years, but with pieces which have been so treated a century or more ago this bloom of caustics or acid has disappeared long ago. It is lucky for the present-day expert that faking is of recent development. Had Gothic oak been well copied in the seventeenth century, it would be impossible to detect the copy now, if we assumed that the spirit and the traditions of the Gothic had been preserved at the same time—which is, perhaps, a somewhat large assumption. To the skilled craftsman, there is a spontaneity about an original work which the copy nearly always loses, although the latter may be the more perfect of the two so far as mere workmanship is concerned. The copyist cannot "let himself go"; he is there to copy, not to originate.

Unfortunately, this arkwright-made furniture is so crude that it lends itself to imitation, the only necessary condition being that the faker shall be a bad workman, which is not difficult of attainment, especially in these days. It must follow, therefore, that only by a close scrutiny of minute details can the fake be detected. That wonderful "flair" and "eye" for the genuine is of no use whatsoever with this arkwright-made Gothic. The purist and the cultured may say that, as furniture, its proper place is the refuse-heap, but apart from values, which may be purely artificial and misplaced, it is, nevertheless, a part of the history of English furniture, and, as such, must be respected, even if the artistic element be wholly lacking. Even this latter cannot be conceded. So long as any art-crafts are the literal expression of their creators (as distinct from slavish copies), they are interesting and worthy of attention, be the art ever so crude or immature. To me, the post-Dissolution Gothic is eloquent of a people divorced from its teachers, and groping in the dark for fresh inspirations, or for guidance out of a labyrinth.

The problem of the expert can be best apprehended if we take a cupboard, such as the one here (although any other example would do as well), and endeavour to trace its making as a forgery. It is a problem reduced to its simplest possible denominator, as there is little art, less construction, and still less design to confuse the issue. The one factor which has to be coped with is that of age. We commence, at the beginning, with the stack of oak or the junk heap. It matters very little if old oak beams be sawn open or new oak used; there is the difficulty of the old surface with each. Therefore, the faker seeks for old surfaces and old carcases, where possible. With the latter, he is not likely to find those of the actual period itself, so he has to chance anachronisms of construction, and that is the first thing for which the expert should seek. Obvious later additions or replacements, such as the iron strap-hinges, here he can ignore, for obvious reasons.

Applying the formula stated in an earlier chapter, he can begin with the question of nationality. This cupboard is English; it could not well be anything else. The wood is also English oak. It has been riven, and has been dressed up with the adze. Thus far, there is nothing to act as a guide. It must be obvious, however, that if this cupboard has been made up from old fragments (assuming that the surfaces are original) some new cutting must have happened somewhere. The door is one simple slab of wood, and it has shrunk, in consequence. Has this shrinkage been equal, as it should be? In other words, is the pierced panel in the centre, or is the apparent shrinkage really bad fitting? Are the nails which hold the fronts to the sides of iron, and are they perished? Are they modern nails, and, if so, do they replace others of iron or wood, and where are the signs of the original nails or pegs? Does the base show any signs of wear, and, if so, is it genuine wear and not imitation? Are the piercings made with the saw, and, if so, with what kind of a saw? Are there any sharp edges to the carving, and, if not, have these edges been deliberately blunted with the rasp, file, steel or stone? These queries must be all left to the student; the answer to the problem will not be given here.

Let us take another example where the date is in question. Here we have a standing cupboard which should be from the early years of the fifteenth century, but is, obviously, not only much later, but also a hodge-podge of various parts. It figures in the Metropolitan Museum in New York, and some excuse may be found on that account as American museum officials can hardly be expected to be experts in early English furniture.

If we divide Gothic woodwork into two classes, that of the carpenter and the arkwright respectively, it will be found that the former, at least, has certain hard-and-fast traditions. Where he can construct in

45

wood, as in the case of rood-screens with their lofts, he does so, and with great skill. The manner in which the heavy lofts are supported on, apparently, inadequate screens, with traceries and lights, is amazing. The medieval carpenter could calculate his timber stresses to a nicety, and the proof is to be found in the manner in which his screens and his roofs have persisted to our day. This constructional tradition he carried into pieces of furniture where much of the construction is really sham. Thus, in the Guild Chair at Coventry, while the real construction is adequate and sound, the panels of the back and the box-seat are of oak with an applied tracery pegged on. In larger work this tracery would have been built up with mullions and transoms, but here this is out of the question, so the former manner is merely imitated. The carpenter would never carve this tracery in the solid wood. In the chest in St. Michael's Parish Church (Coventry Cathedral) the tracery is again applied.

The work of the foreign artisan, half craftsman, half outlaw (owing to the stringent laws regulating labour at his period), is similarly noticeable. To have been able to work at his trade, in a foreign country where labouring strangers were the reverse of appreciated, he must have been exceptional, and in this quality his work is to be distinguished. Sometimes a pure designer or artist in wood, metal or stone, such as Torregiano, a metal-worker such as Cellini, more often (in England) a wood-carver, one sometimes find carpenters from France, Flanders and Germany executing work here, in English oak but in a foreign manner. Thus, the chest-front—which has never been made up into a chest—shown here is French in design, but the oak is English, proving that it was made in this country. The next chest is another Anglo-foreign example, and the construction of the Gothic front, with its applied crocketed balusters, is worthy of careful examination.

Reverting to the standing cupboard from the Metropolitan Museum, the first notable point is that while the carcase and the front are properly framed up, and in a manner which belongs to the seventeenth century (note the scratched beads, mason-mitred at the top and sides, and the chamfer below), the doors, with their chip-carved roundels, are solid slabs of wood, and in two the side rails are missing. The linenfold panels, also, do not line with the doors at all, they are neither the same in height nor in width. The top rail of the cupboard has been pared away to make a fixing for the meaningless piece of cresting which is applied to the front only. In an age where use-considerations were paramount, the three inadequate doors are especially noticeable. A little exercise of the powers of deduction will show that we have, here, several fragments which have been contrived into the one piece of furniture, and the whole construction cannot be earlier than the seventeenth century. Actually, although this cannot be indicated in a photograph, the cupboard is a fake of about forty years' standing. Had it been of more recent origin, the details, and their harmony, would have been more carefully studied.

From the same source comes the small post-Dissolution hanging cupboard or almory—sometimes known as a dole-cupboard. Allowing for the frankly modern capping and base mouldings, and the later iron furniture, this piece is original, and is interesting as illustrating the Catherine wheel which one finds so often at this date in woodwork. The Guild Chair at St. Mary's Hall (which has been referred to so often in this chapter), in its original triple state, may have had the same device, as the Coventry Guild of Clothworkers acknowledged St. Mary, St. John and St. Catherine as its patron saints. St. Catherine was popularly supposed to be the patron of philosophy, and her device is frequently found in early furniture made for college use.

This dole-cupboard, with its empty space, appears to have been intended for decoration of painting, stencilling or gilding. At a period when labour was cheap one can hardly imagine a piece such as this left in the bare wood with no other ornamentation than the two pierced panels in the door.

Chests were very important articles in the Middle Ages, not only intended to contain valuable things, vessels of gold or silver, linens (distaff-woven and, therefore, greatly prized), fabrics and vestments, but also to transport them from place to place, in the event of change of residence or threat of attack. The usual plan was to sling the chest between two sumpter mules. It is only during the seventeenth century that the chest became a permanent piece of furniture, and then it had developed into the standing cupboard, which permitted of orderly arrangement, on shelves, as distinct from the disorderly piling in the chest. The cupboard made to stand on the floor, as distinct from one hung on the wall (which was a definite innovation, and a direct evolution from the chest on short legs), originated in France—as the credence—late in the fifteenth century, but in England its advent was not until nearly a century later. The credence form, although rare, is not as unusual in England as one would imagine, as one often meets with chests where the stump legs have, obviously, been cut down. This can be detected by the fact that the front doors have been fastened up and a lid added. The latter would have been impracticable with the chest at its original height.

The next is an example which is, patently, a forgery. Here is crudity of the wrong kind. At no period were chests made in the manner in which this has been constructed. The ends copy the Gothic stools of the late fifteenth century, and the front is pinned to the sides in a manner which would burst it away with the slightest shrinkage. There are other indications of modern origin which are not apparent in the photograph, such as the timber and the construction of the top and the back.

It is only natural that, with pieces intended to be coloured, the woodworker should treat timber in the stone-mason manner. The two doors, from a clerical "aumbry" or wall-cupboard, shown in the next two illustrations, must have been painted originally, and the paint relied upon to act as a preservative for the wood. Here we have the work of the carver, not the carpenter or the arkwright. The usual hinges to doors of this kind were stout leather, not metal. The next is another door of this late Gothic period, probably from a buffet of the late fifteenth century, and shown here as it is to large scale it is almost possible to note how the oak has the appearance of having been painted, and for a long period.

Certain pieces of this pseudo post-Dissolution Gothic can be exposed on the evidence of a photograph alone. Thus the next is highly suspicious for three reasons. It purports to be a side-table—almost a sideboard, which is not a piece of the period at all—the front is pegged in the same manner as the chest shown before, and the oak is obviously cut from a beam, without quartering, and has split in consequence, and not so long ago. The cutting away of the front legs to house the "apron" is recent and has been done with modern tools. The wear on the legs is purely artificial.

Following this is a chest which is another obvious fake. Here the construction is of seventeenth-century *type*, but the detail is a hundred years before. Actually the piece is modern, made up on the basis of an old top.

There is one characteristic which belongs to all Gothic, that is, its geometrical basis of design. There is hardly a Gothic form, even in the Flamboyant period, which cannot be produced with the compass, working from one or more centres. I have said elsewhere that, given the compass in the hands of an intelligent designer of wood and stonework, the Gothic style would evolve again as a necessary result, even if it had never existed before. There is an infinity of variety possible within strictly geometrical forms, in the interlacing of circles and segments. Perhaps that is why one encounters what is known as "chipcarving" (where the designs are mainly drawn out with the compass or actually cut with the sharpened divider) at all times from the thirteenth to the fifteenth centuries. The tools used are so general, and so established, that the manner of this chip-carving was fixed; very unlikely to undergo any serious modification. Not only the arkwright but even the carpenter appears to have used this geometrical carving at all periods. Thus here is a typical chip-carved, carpenter-made chest, whereas the next is as unmistakably arkwright-made. The latter is of oak and elm, and, while the front is sawn, the back is riven. This admixture of woods is common with the arkwright, but rare with the carpenter. Both chests give the impression of being incomplete without polychrome painting, and in the second of the two traces of paint are still visible. The next two are of doubtful authenticity, and, in view of what has been said before in this chapter, the reasons for suspicion are left for the student to find out.

Turning from chests to tables, those of Gothic date hardly exist, with the exception of the examples at Penshurst and another—much restored —at Great Fulford in Devon. The English table begins with the trestle-form; it is not until the latter part of the sixteenth century—if as early— that the table on turned legs appears. The draw-table, where the under tops pull out on "lopers," with the centre top falling down when the others are fully pulled out, to make one level surface, is a seventeenth-century device, although there is one of this kind in the Victoria and Albert Museum, from Ilminster in Somerset, which the authorities claim to be of the first half of the sixteenth century, on what evidence it is difficult to imagine, as the entire construction is much later. The long tables in the Refectory of the Bablake Schools at Coventry, with their oak framings and elm tops, are late fifteenth century, and another, formerly at Cowdray Priory, and much smaller in size, is very little later in date. Oak tables of the sixteenth century are much rarer than one would imagine. There is a fine example in the old Vicars' Hall of Exeter Cathedral (in South Street), with Victorian top and capping rails to the stretchers, and another in the Drapers' Chapel in Coventry Cathedral with added feet to raise it to altar-table height.

The evolution from the trestle-form for tables and chairs to turned legs marks a more important development than one would suspect. It is not for another century that the woodworker dispenses with the stretcher-railing which ties his legs together. It will be found, through-out the entire history of English furniture, that the progression is always towards lighter construction, which is another way of stating that the maker learns to apprehend the possibilities of his material better. So long as a piece of furniture fulfils the function for which it was intended, excess of strength—with consequent clumsiness of proportions—is just as much a fault as the opposite extreme. Both fetter the designer.

The Elizabethan chair, following out this idea of excessive stability, is really a box with back and arms. It is not until the seventeenth century that the chair with turned legs begins to appear. It is also important to remember that the chair, in the sixteenth century, was a very important article of furniture, a seat of dignity rather than of comfort. The guest or visitor was not expected to occupy a chair, especially at meals, unless he, or she, were of great importance. This old-time dignity has survived, in a manner, to our day, where we refer

49

to "the chair" at meetings. Almost until 1660 the stool was the usual seat at table, a habit dictated as much by convenience as by any idea of comfort, as the trestle type of stool, such as the one here, could be piled away when not in use. The hospitality of the Middle Ages must have been most elastic, as the great trestle-tables, such as at Penshurst, or the long "refectory" table, as at Cefyn Mably, testify.

The importance of the chair is evident, as in Tudor times these pieces were always entrusted to the carpenter; it is rare to find an arkwright-made chair at this period. Stools may be primitive in construction (apart from the carved ornament, many of these Gothic stools might have been made by Robinson Crusoe on his island), but the chair is always properly framed and panelled. Many were dated and with the initials of the owner, as in the example in the Victoria and Albert Museum shown here. The box-seat fulfilled a function which can be imagined. In many country districts this form of the Tudor chair persisted right into the seventeenth century, as the one here, where the seat-rails have been pierced for cords or ropes, in much the same manner as with many of the oak four-post bedsteads. The type has also persisted in the fireside settles, now usually found in old inns, but more general in the Midlands than in the Home Counties.

Valuable as these Tudor chairs are, they seldom come within the purview of the faker, as here he can have no old basis on which to work. He has to construct outright, and old timber, especially when it has to be entirely reworked, helps him very little. The surface of old oak, particularly when it has been extensively used, as in the case of a chair (a piece which would hardly ever be painted over), is more like polished stone, or old alabaster, than wood. This is a surface condition which the faker cannot even begin to imitate, as there are no margins for any "restoration" theories. Chairs constructed in the Tudor manner would not be likely to become decrepit, and the necessity for resurfacing must have been remote. Therefore the faker leaves Elizabethan chairs alone, as he has also the problem of provenance to get over, and the barrier is formidable. With court cupboards and the like he is not restricted in anything like the same manner, as they are supposed to be plentiful (as they are, in a way), and pedigrees do not offer the same difficulties to a really sturdy liar.

The subject of Tudor and Gothic oak is a very wide and difficult one, all the more so as few genuine examples exist for comparison and instruction. There is also more later copying, especially in the seventeenth century, than one would suspect. Only a trained expert can differentiate between the original and the old copy. A first-rate knowledge of timbers, details and methods of construction is indispensable, and for these qualities there is no substitute. If Gothic details could be accepted as proof of Gothic date, the matter would be simple indeed, and we might almost accept the Houses of Parliament as fifteenth century instead of nineteenth. The late Percy Macquoid certainly accepted the Ockwells credence as Gothic, and gave it coloured-plate prominence, as such, in his book. A good workman could have told him that it dated from the latter years of the seventeenth century at the most, and possibly was later still, but workmen cannot be experts—because they are workmen.

The fifteenth-century oak Guild Masters' Chair (a fragment), from St. Mary's Hall, Coventry.

The complete end, on the left, has the Plantagenet Lions of England. The end on the right has the Elephant and Castle, the arms of the City of Coventry, and is incomplete below the seat level.

Plate number Twenty-seven

Right

Oak Chair of the late fifteenth century with boxed-in seat (boxings missing) and modern extension to the back.

Below

Oak Draw-table of James I period (from Charlecote) which is original throughout. The squares of the legs have been worn down, the stretcher railing now resting on the floor.

Plate number Twenty-eight

The oak Coronation Chair in Westminster Abbey. This is four-teenth-century work, and the chair has been painted in colours and gold originally, of which only vestiges now remain.

Plate number Twenty-nine

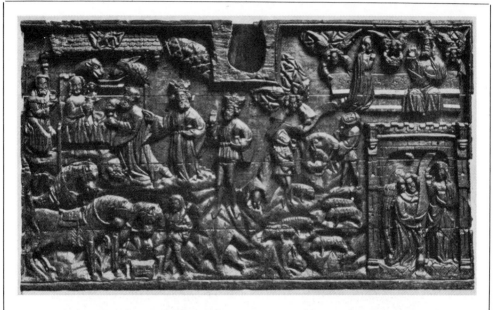

A carved oak Chest Front, where the realism of the design suggests that it was originally painted in colours.

Oak Cupboard of post-Dissolution type but of doubtful authenticity.

Plate number Thirty

On the left an oak Cup-
board which is an obvious
hotch-potch of fragments,
with late reconstruction.

Oak Chest in Coventry Cathedral. An example of a
carpenter-made piece with applied tracery.

A Chest Front which has never been made up into a
chest. French in design, the oak is English, and was
probably the work of a roaming French
carver in England.

An oak Chest of French design in English oak. Typical
carpenter-construction of early sixteenth century. Note
how the crocketed buttresses are applied to the front.

Plate number Thirty-two

Oak Dole Cupboard or Almory. With the exception of the cornice and base, which are frankly late additions, this piece is original post-Dissolution. The plain flanks to the door suggest that this cupboard was originally decorated in colours.

Oak chip-carved Chest; a modern fake. The construction is not of the period, and the entire chest is made up from straight-sawn oak. The appearances of age have been produced with caustics and the wire-brush.

Plate number Thirty-three

Two Doors from an oak almory or dole cupboard; first years of the sixteenth century. An example of semi-realism in carving which is found at all periods where early details are freely used in late work. The general character suggests that these doors must have been originally painted in colours, possibly with some gilding or silvering. There is no attempt at framing or other construction, but in this instance it is obvious that the wood-carver, and not the carpenter or the arkwright, has been the artisan.

Oak Door from an early sixteenth-century English cupboard. Reproduced here to large scale to show the marks left by the strap hinges, and the texture of the oak which has the appearance of having been painted and stripped.

Plate number Thirty-five

An oak Side Table of pseudo-post-Dissolution Gothic. The whole type-conception is not of the period to which this table purports to belong. The construction, or lack of it, is similar to that of the chip-carved chest illustrated a few pages previously. The oak is cut from the beam, without quartering, and the apron-front is pegged to the legs and has split in consequence, and in recent years. The "wear" on the legs has been produced by the aid of the "chipper," a well-known tool of the faker, made by screwing an old plane iron to the end of a wooden handle. A piece such as this is demonstrable as a fake from a photograph alone.

Plate number Thirty-six

An oak Chest purporting to be of the early sixteenth century, but made up of incongruous details on the original basis of an old top. The construction is imitated from that of the later Stuart period, but the pierced panels, with the device of the Catherine wheel, are of a type of a century before. With the exception of the top, the whole chest is modern, with signs of age imitated in the clumsiest possible manner.

Plate number Thirty-seven

Oak Chest with elm front and top. This admixture of woods suggests
colour decoration, and traces of painting are still visible. The work
of the arkwright, *circa* 1500.

Oak chip-carved Chest of late fifteenth century. The work of the
carpenter. Note the construction of the ends and compare with the
chest above.

Two oak Chests of doubtful authenticity, referred to in chapter VI.

Plate number Thirty-nine

Oak Table of trestle type from the Refectory of the Bablake Schools, Coventry. The type of the fifteenth century.

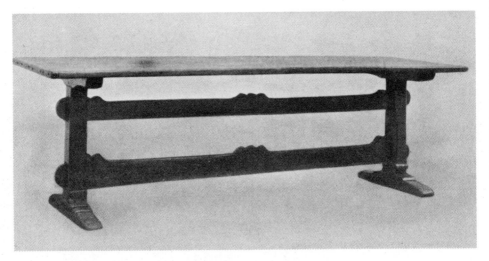

Oak Table of trestle type from Cowdray Priory. These trestle tables were put together with wedges so that they could be taken apart and stowed.

Oak Table from the Vicars' Hall, Exeter. Late sixteenth century.
The top and the cappings to the under-rails are Victorian.

Oak Table from the Drapers' Chapel in Coventry Cathedral. Late
sixteenth century. There is a curious foreign influence in this table
which one finds in the work of Lancashire and Cheshire at this date.

Oak Stool of the late Gothic trestle type made without stretchers to facilitate piling or nesting when not in use.

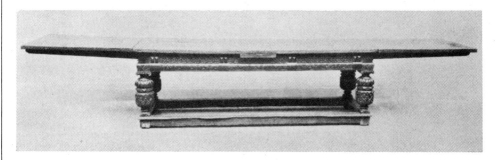

Oak Draw-table of the seventeenth century, from the Metropolitan Museum, New York. The tops are pulled out to show the "lopers" or runners underneath. It is instructive to note what American steam heating has done to the tops of an English oak table.

Plate number Forty-two

Right
Tudor type Chair, but of later date and country make. The seat has been pierced for cords or ropes to support a cushion in place of the usual wood seat.

Left
Typical Tudor Chair, dated 1574 and with initials I (or J) E S. The usual box form with back and arms, generally with the box open at the back.

Plate number Forty-three

Right

Late sixteenth-century (*circa* 1590) box type of oak Chair, probably of Lancashire origin. The carving of the back panel shows a pattern more general in seventeenth-century chairs than those of earlier date.

Left

Fine State Chair, carpenter-made, of early sixteenth century (*circa* 1520), with Gothic detail from earlier and foreign sources.

Plate number Forty-four

CHAPTER VII

OAK PANELLINGS AND WOODWORK

HE initial difficulties in a book such as this have been pointed out in the first chapter. If a fake be really good it has exactly the same appearance, in a photograph, as a genuine piece; in fact, it need not be a clever forgery in order to conform to this condition. If we take the catalogue of a modern furniture manufacturer, one who reproduces from the antique with a fair knowledge of detail and proportion, and cut out any single illustration, it will require a clever—or a foolhardy—man indeed to be able to state, positively, whether the picture is a reproduction or an antique. Its presence, together with many others in a catalogue, will tell him, of course, but this is extrinsic, not intrinsic information.

If the illustration of a frankly modern reproduction, as such, tells us so little, what can one hope to glean from the photograph of a fake with artificially simulated wear all complete?

Again, if this book is to concern itself solely with details of surface conditions, details of design, workmanship and the like, one chapter will be merely a wearisome repetition of another. There is one important weapon of anachronism in the detection of the thing which in type is much later than the period to which it purports to belong. It has already been pointed out that Queen Elizabeth's motor-car cannot be genuine, with any amount of royal crowns and Tudor roses thrown in, just because it is a motor-car, but it occurs to very few that many less pronounced anachronisms than this do turn up, in the antique world, almost every day, certainly every week. To detect these at a glance, and to waste no further time on them, implies a good knowledge of what was and what was not made at the various periods, together with a close acquaintance with the constructional methods of the same dates, and this implies a corresponding knowledge of the historical side of the subject. Really, an erudite book on English furniture, which deals with this aspect of the matter only, is just as valuable a guide to the student-expert in this respect (if not more so) than a book of this character, with one stipulation: that the author shall not have illustrated misleading fakes, or later copies, as genuine pieces of their periods. This condition, however, is hardly ever fulfilled; I know of no single historical work on the subject of English furniture and woodwork which does not illustrate fakes, my own among the number. It requires, very often, a long and close acquaintance with certain pieces to be convinced that they are later copies, or outright fakes of a high order, and when one has to write a book illustrated with upwards of a thousand examples, scattered all over England, this close association with each is, manifestly, impossible. I have relied, in the main, in this book, on photographs of pieces which I have regarded as genuine years ago, but where later knowledge, or closer acquaintance, has convinced me are spurious. With the obvious fake I have little concern; this does not require an expert for its detection; a removal man will often be enough for this job; certainly a country carpenter can offer a final opinion.

Many will remember the famous—or infamous—Shrager furniture case which figured in the English Courts in 1923, where furniture was sold to the unfortunate plaintiff, in this action, at massive prices, but which afterwards realised the prices of bad second-hand goods at a well-known London auction-room, with the trade in attendance and in force. I was the principal witness for the unfortunate Shrager in this action, and my evidence was rebutted by the leading lights of the antique world, whose testimony in turn was contradicted in an unmistakable manner by the subsequent auction prices. I mention this nauseous affair here only for one reason. I was accused, at the time, of "putting the cat among the pigeons," and "giving the show away," but, actually, the first suspicions were aroused in the mind of Adolph Shrager by a local carpenter at Westgate, who pointed out that many of the pieces were so obviously made up that they could not be all that Shrager (or the vending dealer) represented them to be. The points which this seaside carpenter made were fully upheld at the trial, and especially after. Actually he knew more than all the defendants' experts, or he was more unbiased—which may be nearer the truth, perhaps.

This chapter deals with Gothic Tudor and Stuart oak panellings, and can hope to do little more than to point out what should be obvious anachronisms. The "genuine oak room" was a very profitable field for the faker until a few years ago, and his efforts, of that time, still exist to confound the expert. A complete room which will sell for thousands of pounds is much more lucrative to make and to sell than, say, a Gothic chair about which some awkward questions as to origin may be asked. The provenance of an oak room can be so easily manufactured. There was the famous Shrager panelled room which came from "Royston Hall." Actually there was no "Royston Hall," and there never had been. The room began and—as far as its genuine character went—ended, with a few odd scraps of panelling taken out from a dairy in Royston. I knew of another house—or rather a yeoman's cottage—in the Midlands from which no less than six rooms came—including a Long Gallery—but where no single apartment was anything like large enough to have contained a single one, not even the smallest. One is reminded of Mark Twain's tunnel which ran through a mountain and stuck out one hundred feet at the top and four hundred feet at each end, or many of the secret passages "which led to the neighbouring Abbey." There is one, at Lyme Park, in Cheshire, which begins on the first floor—at least so I was told! When I heard of it I was reminded of the schoolboy's account of the making of a cannon. He said they took a hole and then cast metal round it!

Wainscotings of wood—oak or deal—in private houses or palaces do not begin until the first years of the sixteenth century. That is not to say that the art of panelling and framing was not known before. Chancel screens of the early fifteenth century have panelled bases, as a rule, but in the important houses of that date the walls were either in rough stone, plastered brick, or oak timbers with "wattle-and-daub" between, sometimes masked with arras tapestry or "painted cloaths." Occasionally the plaster of the walls was decorated with somewhat crude paintings, and these were not as rare, originally, as one would imagine. Covered with later panellings, or hidden behind coats of whitewash, these old wall paintings were effectually concealed, and many houses must have been demolished with their presence not even suspected. It was due to the researches of the Curator of a small unimportant museum—that of Saffron Walden, in Essex—that some of these old wall decorations were discovered and preserved. Needless to say, these paintings are difficult to forge, as commercial propositions, other than *in situ*, as one has to remove the entire plastering of the walls to get them away. In the house itself there is the difficulty of provenance; their origin has to be veiled with the mists of time, and the faker is usually in a hurry—that is, if he pay his rent with respectable regularity.

Wainscoting appears to have commenced, in secular houses, as a kind of close-boarding, similar in principle to modern matchboarding. There is an extremely rare example, from West Stow Church, in Suffolk, now in the Victoria and Albert Museum, where butt-jointed flat boarding is covered, on the joints, with pierced and carved tracery. It is decorated with painted ornament, parts of which appear to be original. It is the only example of true Gothic wainscoting I have ever seen of unmistakable fifteenth-century date, and coming from a church is not as valuable, for our purpose, as it would have been had it originated from a secular house.

The introduction of true domestic framed panelling almost coincides with the dawn of the Renaissance in England, which can be placed at about 1510. In the carving of the panels we have three distinct devices adopted: the linenfold, the curved-rib, and the Italian conventional floral patterns, often with central cartouches. The latter became very popular in France in the reign of Francis I, and the style is often incorrectly known as François Première. It coincides, in point of date, with the linenfold and curved-rib panel in England.

I have traced the genesis and evolution of the linenfold in another book,* and it may be instructive to summarize here. Let us commence with a brief dissertation on the character and peculiarities of timber, oak in particular, due apologies being tendered for being elementary.

Wood shrinks across its width, never in its length. Framings of early wall panellings are narrow, as a rule; it is the wide panels which are, therefore, liable to shrink. Riven oak, being split on its natural cleavage lines, will stand better than sawn, but split oak is, naturally, irregular and uneven on its faces, and framing demands accuracy, or the whole flank will be "in winding." With Tudor and Stuart panelling (the era of the small panel, the large panel will be considered later) the styles and rails are always sawn; the panels are generally riven, and their thicknesses are very often uneven. It should be noted here, among other points, that faked oak wainscotings usually have sawn panels.

A split panel, without joint (hence the small area in nearly all old panellings) and dubbed smooth on the face side only, either with the adze or the plane (both tools appear to have been used indiscriminately, according to the district), will stand, but owing to the fact that it must be thin to permit of its insertion in the framing grooves, it is liable to buckle, especially in damp weather, as moisture causes wood to swell. A solution of the problem was sought by the device of making the panel thicker and bevelling or chamfering it on the back. The vertical chamfer would allow of the insertion of the panel in the grooves, but at the sides only. At the top and bottom it would be too thick, especially in the centre, where the ridge resulting from this chamfering was thickest. The obvious thing to do was to work a step, or rebate (sometimes known as "rabbit," for some obscure reason), of the depth of the framing groove, at the top and bottom, although this, naturally, involved an overhang of the central rib above and below, but being at the back of the panelling flank, this did not matter very much.

Later on this chamfering device (the value of which in stiffening the panel was appreciated) was transferred from the back to the front, and here a problem presented itself. The top and bottom overhang mattered very little at the back, but it became serious when transferred to the front. Various attempts were made to overcome this defect, which was serious, as damp, lodging on the upper projection, attacked the oak at

* *Early English Furniture and Woodwork* (1922).

its most vulnerable point—the end-grain. Sometimes lateral chamfers were added, which was, perhaps, the most satisfactory method of all, but the desire for ornament led the old woodworkers to give the chamfer a decorative form, hence evolved the linenfold, so-called from its resemblance to the folding of stiff parchment rather than soft linen, although, in the Vicar's Hall at Exeter, the folding of soft fabric is deliberately attempted.

It follows, therefore, that the earlier a linenfold panel is the less it is "linenfold" at all. In some examples (such as the bedstead-end shown here) the overhang is still allowed to persist, but in the more usual form the folds are shown in decorative projection, cut away at the top and the bottom. With close-boarding, after the modern "match-boarding" fashion, it was found that the linenfold device masked the tongue-and-groove joints, that is, if no shrinkage took place. There is an interesting linenfold close-boarded dado of this kind in the Guildhall of Lavenham in Suffolk, a rare example now, probably because this close-boarding was not prized in the same manner as panelling, and may have been treated as waste rubbish at the time of any demolitions.

The diagrams here shown illustrate the development of the linenfold, and they are reinforced by illustrations of actual examples in case the idea should obtain that only a wild theory has been ventured.

The stiffening of the panel was also accomplished in another way, by the "Vine" or "Parchemin" device, which I prefer to call the "Curved-rib," as being the more exact term. Here is decoration based on a definite useful purpose, that of making the panel stouter in order to minimize the shrinkage or tendency to buckle.

Using the weapon of anachronism referred to at the outset of this chapter, one can be reasonably certain, judging by a photograph alone, that the panelling flank shown there does not belong to the Gothic period in spite of its detail. Actually it was made in 1859. Of the other nine examples illustrated, two are not true to type. It matters little here that none of the nine are original examples; in detail seven belong to their period, but in the two just referred to the upright panels are too tall for their date, and the smaller square panels have carved details which are never found in English wainscotings at all, neither in the sixteenth nor the seventeenth centuries. The flank, with door and interior porch, is French, and may be original, but it illustrates the marked distinction between English woodwork of the sixteenth century and that of France.

Many of the localities of England had their distinctive styles of wainscoting, especially during the first half of the seventeenth century. In Wales and the Welsh bordering counties the panels were nearly always unusually large, with heavy-sectioned mouldings separately mitred in.

This is true also of Lancashire and Cheshire, in an even coarser degree. Somersetshire and Devonshire produced rich and refined woodwork, with carefully chosen timber, and carving executed with taste and skill. The same may be said of Norfolk and Suffolk.

Elaborate panelling is proper to wealthy districts, as one would naturally expect. The rich merchants who traded in textiles with the Low Countries panelled their walls with oak, carved and often inlaid. The commerce between north-western Devonshire and the Americas was lucrative, in fact, a keen rivalry existed for many years between Barnstaple and Bideford. Then the district fell on lean times and the houses fell into neglect, and, even within recent years, many of the fine panellings disappeared.

Rich woodwork is rare in Kent or Sussex (Rye offers the only exception, perhaps, and natural conditions, such as the receding of the Channel, extinguished the glory of this former southern seaport), and also in Essex. We know little of London houses as so many were destroyed in the Great Fire of 1666. One finds the remains of great hall screens even in what are now labourers' cottages, and even in parts of the poor county of Kent, so one may assume that rich woodwork was the rule, rather than the exception, in the closing years of the sixteenth and the first half of the seventeenth centuries.

After about 1650 waiscotings were fixed by nailing to battens, or "grounds" secured to the rough unplastered walls, but before that date it was quite customary to nail the framings directly on the stone or brick, and as walls were seldom built straight or plumb, the panels gradually warped to the irregularities of the wall itself. In houses of timber, shrinkage of the wood, or subsidences in the fabric, probably accentuated the original unevenness of the walls, and it is not unusual to find a flank of panelling bowed or warped several inches in ten or twenty feet. How far even massive beams will bend under great strains, and over a long expanse of time, may be noted in the case of many of the oak wall-plates of timber houses. One notable instance can be seen in the Old Siege House at Colchester.

The old makers of panellings were never exact, and wainscotings purporting to be of the early seventeenth century, where the framings are straight, both vertically and laterally, should be suspected. Panels of sawn oak are very rare at his period, and it was not until the era of the large panel, that is, after about 1675, that the saw began to be freely used, coupled with glue-jointing of the panels themselves. These large-panel wainscotings will be considered, in detail, at a later stage.

The difference in the cost of constructing a panelled room in the old way, as compared with the modern method, is considerable, much more so than one would imagine. Where a maker can cut his framings on the circular saw, mould and groove them on the "spindle," get his panel-wood in proper thickness from the timber yard, run his linen-folding on a cutter in the cutter-block of an "overhand" planing machine, and even make his tenons and mortises by power, he can produce infinitely cheaper than where he has to use the hand-saw for his cutting, the "scratcher" for his mouldings, the "riving-iron" for his panel stuff, and the carver's chisels for his linenfold. If there is one distinction, in labouring conditions, between the seventeenth and the twentieth centuries, more marked than any other, it is in the fact that, in *circa* 1625, the labour charges constituted only a fraction of the total cost, whereas in *circa* 1930 they are the principal item.

It may be remarked that, considering the great prices demanded for these "genuine old" rooms, the sum should allow for the necessary outlay to construct in the old manner, but one forgets that the actual maker of bogus panelling does not get this reward. He sells to a dealer who is under no misapprehension as to what he is buying, and there is considerable competition in his trade. It is the one who fits up the room and manufactures a pedigree, who inserts costly advertisements in periodicals, and who maintains an expensive staff of salesmen, who expects not only the lion's share of the profits, but almost the share of the entire menagerie.

The expert should remember this, that behind the romantic story of so-and-so "Old Hall," or the "Haunted Chamber" in such-and-such Grange, is really a commercially made room, and here he will find his knowledge of old and modern manufacturing methods invaluable. Only—he must not be in a hurry; he must be content to look for, apparently, insignificant indications, which will tell him whether panellings are old or modern fake, and if he possesses the "eye for the right thing," or have any delusions about this quality, he had better get rid of that "eye" before he starts on the job of the expert. Perhaps that was what the well-known text really meant: "If thy right eye offend thee, pluck it out and cast it from thee." It is the other eye, the one which notices signs of the power-saw, the planing machine and the moulding "spindle," which really matters, and while one would think this was an obvious platitude, it is so frequently ignored—perhaps because it is so obvious.

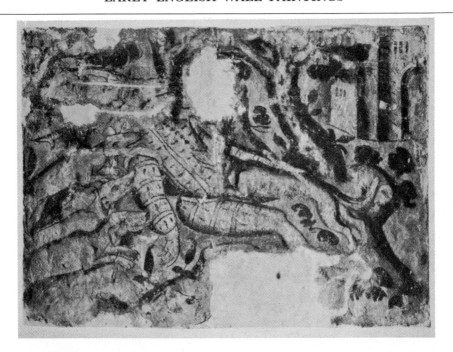

Wall Paintings on plaster from a house at Stodmarsh, Kent (now demolished). The story of Diana and Actæon.

Plate number Forty-five

Plaster Wall Paintings of the late sixteenth century.

Plate number Forty-six

English Wall Paintings on plaster. *Above*, Painted Frieze of 1640;
below, Wall Panel. Late sixteenth century.

Plate number Forty-seven

Oak Wainscoting from West Stow Church, Suffolk, now in the Victoria and Albert Museum. Composed of butt-jointed boarding with applied mullions and pierced and carved tracery. Late fifteenth century. Although the colours have been restored in places, many traces of the original pigments remain. While it is probable that this wainscoting may have been put to other uses, in the church, than the one for which it was made (as an altar frontal, for example), it is doubtful if it was intended for clerical purposes at all originally. It may have formed a part of the wainscoting of a small room, probably in a clerical house.

Plate number Forty-eight

Left

French linenfold Screen with interior porch. Early sixteenth century. The similarity between this and the English examples which follow show the close relations which must have existed between the two countries.

Right

Close-boarded linenfold Wainscoting from Lavenham Guild Hall. This is put together in a similar way to modern matchboarding.

Plate number Forty-nine

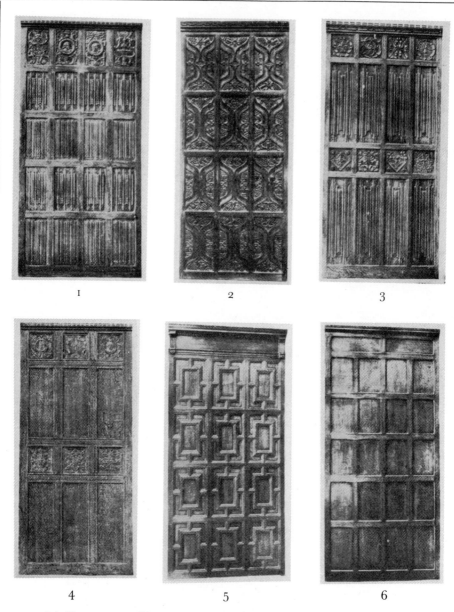

1

2

3

4

5

6

(1) Four stages of linenfold, varying, with Renaissance panels above.
(2) Four stages of varying curved-rib or "vine" panels.
(3) Two stages of tall linenfold panels, alternating with late Gothic.
(4) Tall plain panels with square panels with Tudor devices.
(5) The "strap" or "inner-frame" panelling of the seventeenth century.
(6) Small panels in "scratched" and chamfered framings. Seventeenth century.

1

2

3

4

(1) Alternate long and short panels with applied mouldings, carved frieze and brackets. Type of the Bromley-by-Bow room.
(2) Two stages of inner-frame panels, with interlaced arches between, gadroon below and inlaid frieze above. Type of Lyme Park.
(3) Heavily moulded panels with applied mouldings; carved frieze. Type of the Welsh bordering counties.
(4) Panelling of 1859 showing curious jumble of details, French and English.

Three varieties of Linenfold with curved rib panels above. Early
sixteenth century.

Plate number Fifty-two

Left. Panelling and pilasters with carved frieze from a house at Exeter. Now in the Victoria and Albert Museum. *Circa* 1600.

Right. Four stages of Linenfold of identical pattern with machicolated cornice.

Plate number Fifty-three

Above, Linenfold back of settle with interlaced capping and crocketed
finials. First half of sixteenth century.

Below, Linenfold bedstead-end, showing rope-holes for mattress.
Middle sixteenth century.

Fragment of an oak Great Hall Screen from the Old Manor House, Brightleigh, N. Devon. Extensively restored, but useful to show original variations of the linenfold with shields and tracery above.

Plate number Fifty-five

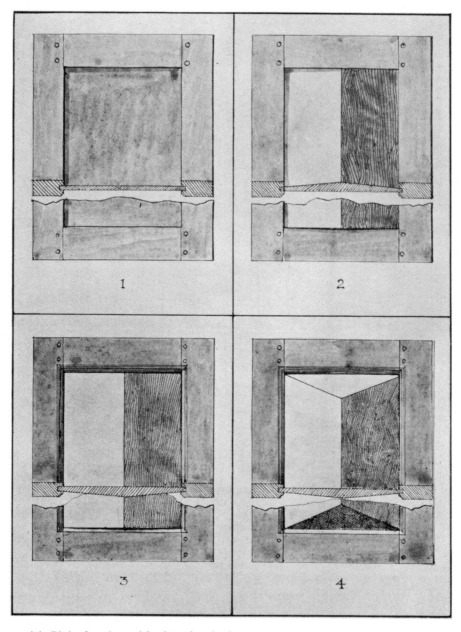

(1) Plain framing with chamfered edges.
(2) Plain panel with stiffening rib at the back.
(3) The stiffening rib at the front, with overhang top and bottom.
(4) The stiffening rib chamfered top and bottom to get rid of overhang.

Plate number Fifty-six

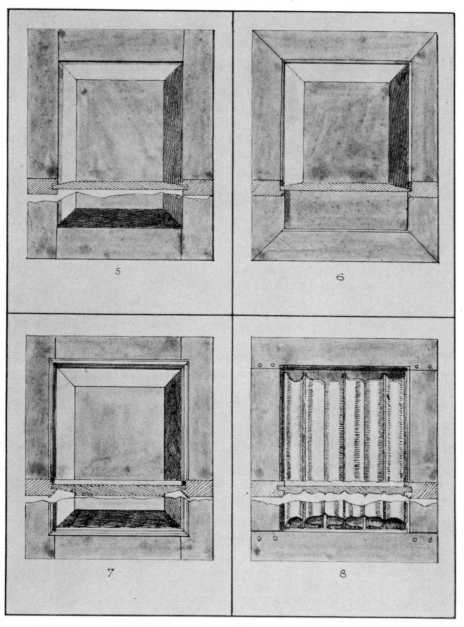

(5) The panel chamfered at the back and grooved into framing.
(6) Panel chamfered at back, fixed in with separate beads.
(7) Panel chamfered on the front; the "fielded" panel.
(8) Linenfold panel which develops from the foregoing.

Plate number Fifty-seven

(9) The carved or mason's mitre. (12) Shaped mitre.
(10) The joiner's mitre. (13) Tenon and mortise.
(11) Half mitre. (14) The "shouldered" tenon.

Plate number Fifty-eight

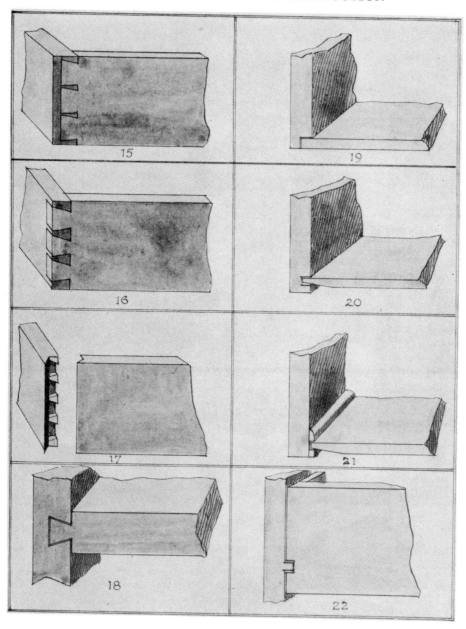

(15) The "cover" dovetail.   (19) Drawer bottom rebated.
(16) The "through" dovetail. (20) Drawer bottom in groove.
(17) The "mitre" dovetail.   (21) Drawer bottom in slip groove.
(18) The "slot" dovetail.   (22) Drawer on runner.

Plate number Fifty-nine

An example of a cleverly designed pseudo-Renaissance
room which can be demonstrated as belonging to a recent
date from the photograph alone. It is full of fine detail,
all the same.

A fine oak room, dated 1617, formerly in a house in Cross Street, Barnstaple, Devon. The Overmantel bears the initials, P.D. and E.D., of the original owners, Pentecost and Elizabeth Doddridge.

The room from Barnstaple as re-erected in another house in the town. The doors are modern. Pentecost Doddridge was a wealthy merchant of Barnstaple in the early years of the seventeenth century.

Plate number Sixty-two

CHAPTER VIII

OAK FURNITURE OF THE SEVENTEENTH CENTURY

T is the common idea that walnut superseded oak as the English furniture timber in 1660, and that any oak pieces, of any distinctive age, must be prior in date to the Restoration. Like many popular conceptions, this is far removed from the truth, other than in a very general sense. Oak remained the constructional wood, for carcase-work and the interiors of drawers, throughout the walnut years, and for almost the whole of the mahogany period. This must imply that oak was kept in stock in factories or in timber yards, and, consequently, there was every reason why it should still be used, sporadically, for furniture. Not only is this the fact, but many of the typical walnut models, such as the well-known carved and caned Restoration chairs, were made in oak quite frequently, especially in the Midland counties and in the west.

It is as well to point this out here, as, with the oak furniture of the Stuart period, later copies are not infrequent, and one has to clear them out of the way before one can concentrate on the two main issues, of the genuine piece and the fake, respectively.

We are not troubled, in the case of this Stuart oak, as we were with the Gothic and the Tudor, by stripping of earlier painting of the surfaces, whether original or later. It is practically certain that seventeenth-century oak furniture was never decorated with colours or gold at the period when it was made, nor was it a general practice to do so afterwards. Such plain surfaces as we find are obvious foils to others which are carved. It was an age of rich ornament—as the costumes of the period indicate, in a way—and not only was carving lavishly employed, but inlay as well. It would be interesting to trace the origin of the taste for elaborate ornament which occurs and recurs at certain dates, apparently irrespective of historical incidents. The fashion for plain things in the home during Puritan times may be true of costume, partly true of silver, but it is not true in any way of Commonwealth furniture. There are plain Cromwellian pieces, but there are also rich ones, and the same can be said of all other periods. It is the obvious inference that some preferred the plain, others the ornate. The furniture of the wealthy would, as a rule, be ornamented, that of the poor, or less wealthy, of a simple type. We find rich and expensive marqueterie in the short reign of James II, but also in that of William III, spread over a period of thirteen years. Side by side with this (not succeeding it, as so many have imagined) is the taste for plain walnut, in all stages from the simple flat veneering to banded veneers, inlay of "oyster pieces" or parqueterie, right up to the marqueterie itself. It is only by a process of artificial isolation that one can segregate the simple walnut furniture from the highly decorated.

It is reasonable to expect, therefore, that seventeenth-century oak furniture is, more or less, in its original condition, that is, as it left the maker's hands, plus the surface acquired by upwards of three centuries of use, wear, waxing and friction, minus reasonable restoration and repairs. The amount of the last must be left to the discretion of the expert, and where such "restorations" have been of such kind that they alter the character, or materially add to the apparent value of the piece itself, the furniture in question cannot properly be classed as an antique at all. These surface conditions apply to furniture, but not necessarily to the panellings of the same, of a slightly later period, for reasons which will be given subsequently.

The wire-brush is the most evident tool of the faker, and there is no reason why it should ever be used for old oak furniture. With panellings which have been painted, and are fixed *in situ*, it is a quick, but bad, method of stripping. The signs of its use are obvious. After it has been employed the surfaces of the oak are in ridges, which can be felt with the finger. It tears out the softer parts of the wood, leaving the medullary ray projecting. It matters very little if it has been used on a genuine piece or a modern forgery; it is better to class both as fakes and to pass them by.

Stuart oak was frequently varnished in the original instance, and a good deal was done subsequently and at various periods. Evidently varnishing must have been, at times, the *sine qua non* of successful restoration. On the other hand, shellac polishing was never done, and should be regarded as highly suspicious. I have found, also, many pieces, some genuine, where a bitumen varnish has been used, where the bitumen has caused the varnish to turn nearly black, to craze and to pustulate. Such varnish can be carefully removed with alcohol; the scraper or the wire-brush, in fact any sharp-edged or abrasive tool, should never be employed.

Oak surfaces, with the years, case-harden, especially if waxed, and acquire the surface of stone, soapstone or old alabaster, after a long period of time. This surface the faker attempts to imitate with caustics, which bleach the wood, and subsequent varnishing. Remembering that the faker is in a hurry, as a rule, and the dealer also (both may have to wait an "antique" time for their money), and knowing that varnish never dries stone-hard for some years, it is possible to detect recent surfacing by placing a milled-edged coin in a white handkerchief, and rubbing the surface with the coin edge. None but an extremely hard face will stand this test.

When one buys old oak furniture, while original condition is highly desirable, the price is really paid for construction. The piece may have been resurfaced, it cannot possibly have been reconstructed. It is here where the question can be pertinently asked: "Has it been altered or 'improved' in any way?" One may be reasonably sure that any addition or alteration has been done with an idea of enhancing the market value, therefore it is the details which make this value which should be scrutinized, such as carving, inlay and the like. If the article be unusually small or large, and if its price is governed by these exceptional dimensions, then one should ask the question, mentally, has it been extended on the one hand or cut down on the other? Thus open buffets, if original, are costly things, and "angle buffets," that is where the upper stage has a central cupboard with splayed sides, are more valuable still. Granted that the wood-surface and construction are all old, has the splay-sided cupboard been added from another piece, and partly reconstructed in the process?

It is always wise to suspect really elaborate oak pieces, unless they are authenticated by an unquestionable pedigree. One may find the large apples at the bottom of the basket, but they are much more likely to be at the top. Similarly, the really outstanding oak examples are, or should be, known. They are extremely valuable, and are not likely, in consequence, to be hidden away in cellars, lumber-rooms or attics. It is the business of the expert and the dealer alike to know every outstanding piece of furniture anywhere in England. Examples are not so numerous as to render this impossible, but the outright fake, or the "improved" piece, which has originated from some obscure workshop, and not so long ago, must be unknown, necessarily. The work of nearly every factory has a definite "handwriting," and when piece after piece turns up with the changes rung on the same, or similar, details, suspicions should be aroused. To many, unacquainted with original surface conditions or constructional details of the various periods, oak furniture is the easiest of all to fake. I have seen massive oak bulbous legs thrown from a fourth floor to a stone pavement below in order to get the genuine "Tudor" cracks, and to maltreat furniture in other ways is not difficult. I always regard a good oak fake as the most difficult of all to detect. Compared with it, walnut, mahogany, satinwood and lacquer are easy. One should beware of the piece where the dealer informs you that he has "just rubbed it up a little." It is surprising what a little "rubbing up" will do in the way of stimulating productivity.

Stuart oak furniture does not exhibit any great variety in function, as pieces were usually made for definite purposes, not as mere ornament or for "occasional use," which I have found, as a rule, to mean for no use at all other than to look "pretty," or the reverse. It is possible to make a list of pieces of the oak period thus:

Wall Furniture.
>   Court Cupboards.
>   Open Buffets.
>   Angle Buffets.
>   Cupboards.
>   Chests.

Floor Furniture.
>   Draw Tables.
>   Gate-leg Tables.
>   "Refectory" Tables.
>   Chairs.
>   Settles.
>   Bedsteads, four-post.
>   Bedsteads covered with fabrics.
>   Bedsteads enclosed, with panelled roof or ends.

Anything in the way of writing-tables, desks (for writing), bureaux or secretaires are practically unknown.

Exception must be taken here to walnut, marqueterie, lacquer or needlework pieces, as they do not come into the oak category, although they may belong to the oak period.

To recognize English furniture of the seventeenth century by its localities of origin is valuable knowledge to the expert, as it explains so much that is, otherwise, incomprehensible. Thus the spindle-back of the Yorkshire chair, the detached panel of Lancashire and Cheshire, the distinctive peculiarities of Warwickshire, Shropshire, Somersetshire, Devonshire and East Anglia are noticeable at a glance, once the eye has become accustomed to each. In this respect, English oak furniture has a kinship to Persian and Caucasian rugs. One examines a typical Kouba, Ladig, Ghiordes, Khorassan, Saruk, Feraghan and Kula carpet, and takes in the differences in the design of each, only to find another selection, from the same districts, utterly different, at first, and positively unrecognizable. It is only after a long acquaintance with Persian rugs that one begins to see, not identical patterns, but certain characteristics in common. Actually no two Feraghans, for example, are ever exactly alike, yet, after a time, no one will confuse a Feraghan with a Herat or a Bijar. Similarly with Yorkshire or Lancashire chairs, for instance, each example may differ from another, yet there is something in common with them all. I have illustrated patterns of the various districts of England here, but that is not to say, by any means, that an example which differs from any shown in these pages may not have originated from the same locality.

This introduces another important aspect of the problem, one which is difficult to explain in text, and still more difficult to show in illustration, and that is the separate character, of ornament and construction, which belongs to each county at this period. Where one finds constructional methods, choice of woods, and details which belong both to Norfolk and Warwickshire in the same piece, one has every warranty to reject that piece as a later copy or, much more probably, a recent fake. It must be obvious, however, that in problems such as this a little knowledge is a very dangerous thing. I am peculiar in this respect that I would rather see fifty fakes accepted than one genuine piece condemned. Later knowledge may rectify the errors in the former, but a condemned antique is seldom rehabilitated. It is an example, lost to us, from a stock which is very far from plentiful.

There are three major divisions in the woodworking trade during the oak years of the seventeenth century: the carpenter (or joiner), the furniture maker (it is, perhaps, too early to refer to him as a cabinet maker), and the chair maker. It is advisable to keep the work of each segregated, as we are dealing with three separate trades, each with distinctive traditions. Even up to 1660, or later, the joiner still splits his "panel-stuff," planing it on the exposed face, but dubbing it with the adze behind, while the furniture maker saws his wood. The chair maker is the more advanced of the three, in following and originating new fashions, and he uses the lathe to a considerable extent, which tends to beget new possibilities. The uses of turning, in the sphere of the furniture maker, are limited to legs of tables and applied split-balusters, and it is doubtful if the lighter forms of oak tables were not the work of the chair maker. The large bulbous legs of long tables and the balusters of standing cupboards hardly ever show the same precision in the turning as chair legs, and when bobbin-turning and spiral-twisting came into vogue, in the years just before the Restoration, the chair maker's turner far outstrips the furniture maker's. The truth is that the former uses the treadle-lathe, the latter the pole-lathe, a much more primitive affair. In the massive bulbous legs and balusters of tables and cupboards one can often notice the signs where the wood-carver has helped out the turner, as the thicker the piece which is turned the greater is the power required. In the pole-lathe this must be direct; in the treadle-lathe it can be obtained by gearing down (a loss in revolutionary pace but a gain in power), and the amateur can get a good idea of the amount which is required if he "chucks" a ten-inch oak square in a modern power-driven lathe and attempts to "rough it out" with the wood-turner's gouges. He will not wonder why the Stuart turner did his part perfunctorily, leaving a good deal for the wood-carver to finish.

Constructional methods vary considerably with the three trades referred to here. The joiner still pegs his tenons, and joints "dry," that is, without the aid of adhesive, while the furniture maker begins to rely on glue more and more, until, in the era of veneering which sets in shortly after 1660, glue, or other adhesive, becomes an absolute necessity. The clock maker begins to import his cases from Holland, with finely sectioned mouldings and veneered surfaces, and from these the cabinet maker begins to learn a good deal of the methods practised on the other side of the North Sea. Later on he gathers still more from actual Dutch makers who follow William the Stadtholder to England, and there had been some percolation of Low Country ideas before, when Charles II left the Netherlands to ascend the English throne.

The chair maker, once established as a distinct trade, soon became the most progressive of the three, both in his methods and his assimilation of foreign ideas. Much of this must have been due to two factors: a chair is, in its nature, not a costly thing to make, and could be soon produced; and, secondly, many would be required in the one house, as compared with other furniture. The maker of chairs, in consequence, would have a much greater output than his fellow craftsmen who confined their attentions solely to furniture or panellings. There is still another factor, the effect of which may have been greater than one would suppose. A chair is used continuously and hardly; any constructional weaknesses or imperfections would tend to develop faults very quickly, whereas wall-furniture would be used, if at all, in quite another way. Providing that drawers opened and closed easily, and cupboard doors did not stick, the carcase construction itself would be subjected to no great strain other than on the rare occasions when the piece was moved from place to place. On one occasion I defined perfect furniture construction thus: that a piece should be put together, and stand without the aid of adhesives—and Stuart oak, as a rule, very nearly conforms to this definition.

Evolution of ideas and quantity of output have a necessary relation. He who makes much, especially by hand, must learn more than he who makes very little. That accounts for the progressive character of the chair maker, considered as a trade. This development trend is away from the unnecessarily massive towards the adequate only. Economy in the use of timber alone would dictate such a tendency, also, with pieces which had to be moved about, such as chairs and stools, a cumbersome one would be at a disadvantage compared with another of lighter make. Another necessary condition was that a chair should stand firmly on the floor, and not tip backwards if the sitter leaned back with any force.

It is a curious and noticeable fact, with the evolution of all furniture, that practical conditions tend to gradually become submerged by the dictates of fashion, but there are periodical recurrences in the direction of the former sound traditions, and then away again, as succeeding fashions get their grip on principles. Progress is, therefore, always pendulum-fashion, alternate progression and retrogression. A typical Stuart chair is sound both in principle and construction. It stands firmly and immovably. The same may be said of the early Restoration chair, where walnut is substituted for oak. Then comes the taste for the high back, with the greater leverage it affords, until we get the absurd tall-back chairs of the James II period, faulty alike in construction and in principle. Some return to sanity follows in the years of Anne, although here the use of veneer often hides a multitude of constructional sins, until, in the early mahogany period, we are back again into solid construction and sound tradition. The further developments in this pendulum evolution will be traced at a later stage in this book.

If one takes the pains to visualize a piece of Stuart oak at the time when it was new, with all details perfect and all edges sharp, it must be obvious that its present state is the same, only plus wear, accidents, and some restoration. Wear is the principal point to which attention should be directed, as it is the one which the faker nearly always overdoes; he puts imitation signs of wear where none could have occurred. A large table with stout legs and stretcher-railing underneath is a good example in illustration of this point. It is obvious that no sitter would take up a position with his feet on either side of a large bulbous leg, for example, but in no other way would the top of the under-railing be worn right up to the squares of the legs themselves, yet, if one examines a faked table of this description, this artificial "wear" is carried all along the rail. It is unnecessary to labour this point by stating where signs of usage should exist in every piece. It is sufficient if one accept a piece of oak furniture as having a definite purpose (as it has, in nearly every instance) and goes through the pantomime of putting it to that purpose. One can then be reasonably assured where the signs of wear should be, and where they should be absent. This leads to another point; in the case of a buffet or standing cupboard, where the base would receive bad usage, almost as a matter of course, by kicking, blows while cleaning, or damage due to damp when the floor is washed, it may be as well to concentrate the attention on this part to see if the signs of wear are adequate, and, if not, to turn the piece upside down to see if the base has been replaced entirely. It is surprising to the collector (but not to the restorer) to see what wrecks are many of these oak pieces in their "original condition," and to what extent restorations may go. It is often akin to "restoring" a shirt to an "original" button. One hears of Persian rugs, at a death, being cut up into pieces and divided among the members of the family (which was often the fact); but I have seen the top part of a buffet in the one house and the lower stage in another, often miles apart from each other. Often they never come together again, and in this case the temptation to a "marriage" is sometimes very strong. Better, perhaps, a marriage of two parts which did not originally belong than an outright fake of an upper or a lower stage. One has original work in the one, but only gross deception in the other. One finds these "marriages" throughout the whole of English furniture and woodwork, and many of them are highly ingenious. Unfortunately, the portions of two pieces, not made together, will rarely "marry" without some alteration to the one, and often to both, and it is for the signs of such alteration that the expert must look.

With pairs or sets, chairs for example, there is always the probability that some of the set may have been produced at a later date, to "make up," in the common phrase. One would think that an exact copy should not be difficult to produce; actually, in the absence of the original templates and "jigs," it is by no means easy, especially in later commercial days. Here a line goes wrong; there a proportion is faulty, too large or too small. One should never forget that, with an original set of chairs, where the shapes are cut from the same moulds, there is no reason why one should differ from another, and every reason why each should be the exact counterpart of the other. This is true of oak, walnut, mahogany or satinwood furniture, and at all periods. It is not so true, perhaps, with the very early work, where primitive tools would engender differences, naturally, nor with that of the faker who is conditioned by the old basis on which he has to commence. Here is where the expert who has schooled his eye to a wise discrimination has the advantage of the one who relies on "instinct" or "flair," and has never trained his at all, or reinforced his mind with knowledge or by the use of the faculties of observation and comparison.

Oak Bedstead from Saffron Walden Museum. Early sixteenth century. The tester is missing. The extreme rarity
of these early beds, not only actually, but in mention in
inventories of the time, coupled with their foreign character, suggests that they may have been imported from
France. They were certainly not usual pieces, even in
wealthy houses.

Plate number Sixty-three

Enclosed oak Bedstead from Queensbury, Yorks, now in the Victoria and Albert Museum. Middle seventeenth century. The bedstead of the better-class yeoman. Owing to the draughty, badly warmed and ill-ventilated rooms of the period, protection from the cold was of great importance even at the price of stuffiness.

Plate number Sixty-four

Oak four-post Bedstead with panelled tester complete, from Astley Hall, Chorley, Lancashire. The rich type of the seventeenth century, one remove only below the fully-draped bedstead of the palace.

Plate number Sixty-five

Fully-draped Bedstead, complete with head and foot curtains, head-board, back-cloth, valances and plumes. Victoria and Albert Museum.

Plate number Sixty-six

Draped Bedstead with moulded and shaped cornice covered with material, and head-board to match. Victoria and Albert Museum.

Plate number Sixty-seven

Draped Bedstead in velvet and bullion appliqués. Note
the elaborate cornice and head-board. The palatial type.

Metropolitan Museum, New York.

This shows the state in which many of these original oak Buffets are found to-day. It is obvious that, like long-case clocks, they must have passed through a long period of neglect, and the lower stages, the "pot-boards," would be the first to suffer. This piece was found in two stages, divorced from each other.

Plate number Sixty-nine

Open Buffet of two tiers, in oak and walnut. Victoria and Albert Museum. This piece dates from the opening years of the seventeenth century, and is unusually early for the type.

Plate number Seventy

Oak two-tier open Buffet of early seventeenth-century type. The tops are thin, in separate boards, and often run from back to front with the end wood on the front. The bulbous balusters with Ionic caps are of the usual type in these pieces.

Plate number Seventy-one

The type of angle Buffet, with central door and splayed sides; open below to the usual "pot-board." Original angle buffets are rare and valuable, but fakes abound. This is one, although it may look genuine enough in the photograph.

Plate number Seventy-two

Oak Buffet elaborately inlaid with various woods. The heraldic beasts supporting the top stage are most unusual. The deeply recessed and gadroon-framed doors are pin-hinged in the usual manner of the period.

Plate number Seventy-three

Oak Buffet inlaid with various woods and with "diamond"

appliqués of bog-oak.

Oak Buffet inlaid with ivory, bone and mother-o'-pearl.

The type of the last years of the Stuart Dynasty.

Oak standing or "Court" Cupboard in three stages. Type of the Welsh-bordering counties, and known as a "Tridarn." The cupboards of Shropshire, Worcestershire, Cheshire and Lancashire are nearly always very wide in proportion to their height.

Plate number Seventy-six

Oak standing Cupboard in three stages, but all enclosed.
It has eight doors with iron hinges. The pin-hinge was
rarely used outside of East Anglia. This cupboard is of
Shropshire origin, of the first half of the
seventeenth century.

Plate number Seventy-seven

Oak Court Cupboard of East Anglian type. There is a good
deal of tradition in this design, more than one would expect at
a cursory glance. The lower doors, panelled with two upright
and one horizontal panel, achieve the maximum strength.
With the exception of the top, all other mouldings are on
the front only, thereby obviating mitres which might have a
tendency to burst apart and fall off with any shrinkage.

Plate number Seventy-eight

Oak Court Cupboard of East Anglian type. This is a fake, and, even from the photograph, the over-elaboration everywhere should arouse suspicion. The arcading of the doors is a feature often found in East Anglian chairs; rarely in court cupboards, and never to this extent.

Plate number Seventy-nine

English oak Credence, known as "Sudbury's Hutch." Perhaps no oak piece in England has a better authenticated pedigree (apparently) than this. It was given to St. James' Church, Louth, Lincolnshire, by a vicar named Sudbury (hence the name), who was Incumbent of the Parish from 1461 to 1504. The hutch was "repaired" in 1586 and in 1666, and it is fairly obvious that in this 1666 "repair" the whole hutch was re-made, using only the three original doors, which are of the closing years of the fifteenth century. Otherwise it is a seventeenth-century piece in every respect.

Plate number Eighty

English oak Chest with Gothic front. This is an instructive example, one of many to be found in small English parish churches. It must be obvious that the one who carved the front never made the chest. We know that there were several edicts against the use of stone altars in churches, in the reigns of Henry VIII, Edward VI and Elizabeth, and none have survived the destruction which followed. Stone altars must have had each its own carved wood reredos above, and these would not be destroyed under the edicts. What has become of them? I suggest they are to be found in the elaborate fronts of otherwise crude clerical chests.

Plate number Eighty-one

Above. A fine Chest of Charles I period, with strong Renaissance character in the carving, suggestive of an earlier period.

Below, right. An oak Chest of Connecticut origin, showing the traditions carried to New England by the early settlers.

Below, left. Another New England Chest. The feet have been restored.

Yorkshire.

Yorkshire.

Lancashire.

Plate number Eighty-three

Lancashire.
East Anglia.

East Anglia.
Shropshire or Somerset.

Plate number Eighty-four

Long six-leg oak Table with underframing, usually
incorrectly known as a "refectory" table.

Oak Table with draw-out tops, known as a "draw-table."
If this illustration be carefully studied there will be evidences apparent of wear in the wrong place. Note, there
is no injury to the overhanging bases to the legs.

Plate number Eighty-five

CHAPTER IX

THE LARGE PANEL IN ENGLISH WOODWORK

F the technical reader can project himself into the period when the large panel first appears in English woodwork (*circa* 1675), many of the difficulties in the solution of the problem itself will disappear. We have seen, hitherto, that the joiner or the carpenter kept the area of his timber within certain strict limits, in order to minimize shrinkage. Panellings were designed not only where the panel width was kept small, for very good reasons, but where the height was similarly restricted. The reason for the latter was, that with riven wood it was much easier to keep a panel of twenty inches, or less, in height, of approximately equal thickness, but with a tall "pilaster" panel one could never be certain, with splitting, that it would not rive away to a "feather-edge" at one end, and thus be useless for its purpose.

The large panel does not evolve, that is, it does not begin small and then grow gradually in area; it appears suddenly, and in full-blown form. Obviously, there must have been some influence at work which dominated the craftsman, and it must have been that of the architect, who, at this period, was adding interior decoration to his sphere. In this, beginning with Inigo Jones in the reign of Charles I, there ensued a period of stagnation for nearly seventy years. The Banqueting Hall in Whitehall, as an essay in the Palladian manner, is practically unique for its date; it is not until long after that the classical style comes into its own. The large panel in woodwork belongs to this classical revival, and there is not the slightest doubt that it was initiated by the architects Wren, Kent, Vanbrugh, Brettingham and their school.

Let us now imagine a group of craftsmen, whose knowledge, training, and tradition had all imbued them with a respect for the proper seasoning of timber, and its liability to shrinkage, warping or buckling in large areas, being suddenly confronted with a design of large-panel wainscoting as at Ramsbury Manor (*circa* 1685), the dining-room at Belton, or some of the rooms at Drayton, both of about the same date, or at Dyrham Park some fifteen years later, and being powerless to offer any effectual criticism. It has been said that no man can know what he can do until he tries; even the gouty squire jumped a five-barred gate when an infuriated bull was after him, but here it was not only a question of doing something which had never been done before, but inventing new methods to do it. The jointing of edges was the first problem, as even if wood could have been procured of the necessary width, a large panel would be certain to shrink, warp and crack. Actually, if these large panels are examined (as in the Clifford's Inn Room in the Victoria and Albert Museum, for example) it will be found that boards have been sawn apart, in widths of not more than six or seven inches, and each alternately reversed before glue-jointing; a method of security which has never been superseded since. It is only when panellings of red Memel deal began to replace oak that boards were used in greater width. Of course, the cutting of oak "on the quarter" would, in itself, limit the width of the staves to be jointed, but even here the oak boards are kept narrower than quartering conditions actually demanded.

It is difficult enough to induce a trade, fettered by ages of tradition, to change its ideas, but when a change of method—even the invention of new methods—is demanded, in addition, one can see how involved the problem of the large panel must have been at the time. Luckily for the innovators, the fashion arose just at the right time. The former solid oak had given way to the veneered walnut at least ten years before, and veneering involved both new tools and novel operations. A veneer can be laid by means of the "hammer" (see illustration), the sandbag (for shaped surfaces) or the caul. With all three the idea is to exude the surplus glue, leaving the adhesive layer as thin as possible. The erroneous, but popular, idea that glue will stick anything has been pointed out before. It will be referred to again when the veneered walnut furniture is dealt with, as the expert cannot know processes too well. The knowledge enables him to detect apparently insignificant signs which are Greek to the layman.

We have seen that the carpenter of the Tudor or Stuart periods avoided the jointing of boards wherever possible. That the art was known, even in much earlier times, is certain. Many of the pictures on panels, even from the early fifteenth century, are on jointed boards, and it is seldom that the joints are found opened. It is probable that casein, or "cheese glue," was the adhesive, but this is not half the battle. No wood edge-joint will adhere if the joint-faces are not absolutely true, straight, and "in square." To achieve this demands not only skill but also tools of precision. With screw-cramps it is possible to force together the edges of two boards not accurately jointed, but after a few months, or even a year or two, the joint will fall apart again. On the other hand, if the edges are perfectly fitted, no cramps are required. It is a common practice, in shops, to rub two joints together, and the result is far more permanent than with a bad joint where cramps are used. There is a natural cohesion between two perfectly fitting surfaces, even when no adhesive is used at all. Place two sheets of plate glass face to face and notice how difficult it is to separate them. One has to overcome fourteen pounds of air-pressure to each square inch on the one face only, with no countervailing pressure on the reverse side; that is the secret.

To plane the edges of two boards (if not more than one or two feet in length) straight and "in square" is not difficult, but the problem becomes much greater when the length is increased to six feet or more. There is a natural tendency, with a long heavy plane, to "dip" at the ends, producing a bowed edge in its length, which is fatal to good jointing. It is far better that the opposing edges should be slightly concave rather than convex. They must be strictly "in square" in any event. To overcome the difficulties of this operation, the "shooting board" (see illustration) was devised, where, if the plane be kept flat on its bed and impelled from its centre (the "iron-hole"), the edge must be straight and "in square." The workman tests the result with the straight-edge and the square to make certain, but with the shooting-board the operation of edge-jointing is robbed of a good many of its terrors for the amateur.

In theory (and in practice also) no gluing is ever perfect, as glue contracts all the while, from the hot fluid state to the cold and thoroughly hard condition, a change which may take many months to accomplish. No matter how thin be the glue layer (and one can now understand that the thinner it is the better), the slightest contraction of the adhesive must weaken the joint a little, and this little may be serious. Actually, the operation of gluing is more complicated even than this. With the use of the screw-cramp, or handscrew, and hot liquid glue, the latter is forced into the pores of the grain on either side, and, when cold, acts as a number of double-pointed nails holding the two faces together. But these "nails" are connected, at their centres, by the thin layer of the overplus glue, and if this be so thick that the necessary contraction is serious, *the nails break at their centres* and become useless. The perfect glue (which has never been invented yet) is one which will not contract in drying, and as with loss of heat contraction is inevitable,* an adhesive which can be used cold would be nearer the ideal. There is one on the market, Croyd glue, which very nearly conforms to these conditions, to such a degree, in fact, that in the directions for its use cramping or other pressure is expressly interdicted. In America, at the present day, the hot glue-pot is unknown in wood-working factories.

In the later years of the seventeenth century, and for more than two hundred years afterwards, glue was crudely prepared from the boiling down of glutinous substances, such as the hooves of horses. Actually, in substance, human and animal hair, nails, hooves, horns, and even

* There are only two substances known which expand when hot, and again when the temperature falls to freezing point: water and bismuth.

certain shells are very alike. Thus tortoise and turtle shell, in the natural paper-thickness layers, will cohere into, apparently, solid slabs if immersed in boiling water and forced together in the press, and without any adhesive between the laminations. The apparently solid back of a tortoise-shell hair brush, for example, will fall apart again into thin layers if boiled in water, as many have discovered to their cost during ill-advised cleaning processes.

With crude glue, liable to excessive contraction on cooling, perfect jointing was impossible, and this may account for the fact that, in large panel woodwork, deal which was intended for painting rapidly replaced oak which was left in the natural wood, with only varnishing or waxing. Beginning in *circa* 1685, it is rare to find these large-area panels, in oak, much later than about 1700. It is not that jointing in deal was more effectual than with oak (although this is true, in a measure), but, with the former, coating with lead paint was the rule, and this paint not only acted as a protection against the atmosphere, but permitted also of the stopping of open joints with putty. Only such a necessity could have dictated the later painting of oak panels, a fate to which so many succumbed at a later date. The idea that this subsequent painting was intended to lighten the sombre appearance of oak will not bear examination; oak is not a dark wood unless it is stained and varnished, or allowed to become dirty, and time and light has a tendency to bleach rather than to discolour it. In addition, the wood was valuable and prized at all times, and one could hardly expect that quartered and figured oak would be painted over other than for a very good reason. This is not far to seek. Given a panel-shrinkage which would leave open gaps, cracks not only unsightly but also harbouring-places for dirt and vermin, grant a construction where the panel was fixed between immovable bolection mouldings (and even if these were removed and the panel-gap closed up, the result would be that the panel itself would be too narrow, besides being an expensive and a troublesome operation), and it will be seen that paint and stopping must be the easy solution, and once painted (where stripping, *in situ*, would be very costly) the panelling would be treated in the same way again and again. When the Clifford's Inn Room was taken down for re-erection in the Victoria and Albert Museum by the authorities more than a dozen coats of paint were stripped off. Examine the room in its present habitat, note the superb quality and figure of the oak, and one must admit that only dire necessity would dictate such later painting, or utter vandalism, yet these old Inns of Court were not governed by vandals. On the contrary, the benchers take the most meticulous care of the property in their charge, and always did.

This later painting of old oak panellings, which was the rule rather than the exception, and the original painting of those of deal or pine, means that hardly any of these rooms have come down to us in their original state, and as the paint has, too often, been removed by the faker's methods of the wire-brush and stripper, the problem of the expert is a formidable one indeed. The difference between an old room which has been taken down and stripped and another which has been juggled together from indiscriminate scraps is often very little indeed. This is true alike of the large and the small-panel wainscotings of the seventeenth and eighteenth centuries. There are many ways, however, by which the made-up room can be detected, but these are by no means of placard size. First, there is the lack of cohesion in the design, due to the faker being conditioned by his existing scraps of panelling, and their arrangement. Secondly, there must be some recent details, carvings or mouldings where the signs of the use of modern tools should be evident. Of course, some rooms have been made outright from old wood; there was quite a flourishing industry in these some twenty years ago, which still persists, I believe, and here the faker is not fettered by existing old materials. The modern tool, however, is still his pitfall, if he is to make commercially, and, it must be repeated here, the faker rolls up no fortune; it is the dealer who basks in the thousand-per-cent patch.

I have already referred to the famous, or infamous, Shrager case which figured in the Referee's Court in 1924. One of the prize exhibits there was the celebrated "Royston Room," which was alleged to have come out of Royston Hall. I have illustrated two views of it here, and it was highly endorsed by the defendant's experts at the time. One even went so far as to describe it as "utterly genuine." Actually there never was a "Royston Hall" at all, and the basis of the room was a few odd scraps of old panelling (afterwards all resurfaced during the reconstruction) taken from a dairy at Royston, and used up. The upper stage of the panelling, the central carved frieze panels, the door and the chimney-piece, overmantel and stone lining were all new, rather an unfair proportion of modern work for an original "old room." The sum of £1,972 was charged for the room, including its adaptation and fixing, and, without recollecting the exact figures, I remarked at the time that the dealer's profit was more than half of this total. It should be noted that the maker could not be described as a faker, as I understand the term to imply a deceiver, and the dealer who sold it as a genuine "Elizabethan" room (which it could never have been, in any event) to the unfortunate Adolph Shrager could have had no delusions on the subject, as he saw it being made, and on more than one occasion. So much for the rewards of faking, which I define here as a sale under false pretences which may have little or nothing to do with the actual making of the fake thus sold. It is as well to be clear on this point. A club may be a handy weapon, but if one swing it indiscriminately it may strike the wrong person.

The references to this "Royston Hall" room (which certainly never came from such a "Hall," and which was conclusively shown in the evidence to be very largely made up), as stated by the late Sir Edward Pollock, in his judgment,* are worth quoting here verbatim (the italics are my own): "The only point about it was, was it Elizabethan? Un-*doubtedly it was Elizabethan,* and undoubtedly it was a most beautiful job,† and everybody thought it was a most beautiful thing when it was put up. I have not the slightest notion why it was called the Royston Room,‡ but, as I say, *it is absolutely immaterial; why it was called Royston Hall I do not know; whatever it was thought to be does not matter the least in the world.*"

Comment on the above is superfluous.

The problems which confront the expert who has to examine these old rooms differ very little in the case of the large or small-panel wainscotings. They may be stated, briefly, thus: (1) Is the room in its original state, and, if not, how much has it been re-adapted, and on how many occasions? If it is not in its original habitat, and if the new room has not been specifically built for the old panelling, including the doors, windows, and chimney-piece (a very unlikely contingency), it is practically certain it has been adapted once, at least. As it is, obviously, impossible to cut a room in the same way as a yard of calico, as doors, windows, or mantels must come in anything but the right places, it follows that any refitting must involve extensive alterations. Once the expert has made up his mind as to the character and extent of these, he can segregate such necessary new work from the old. A faked room is practically *all* new construction, and never had any original habitat, as a room.

(2) Has the panelling been painted at any time, has it been stripped subsequently, and, if so, how?

(3) If removed from the original house, has the necessary alteration to the new surroundings ruined its original character, wholly or partially, and, if the latter, to what extent?

This must be largely a matter of opinion, but an instance may be cited in the case of the well-known oak room in Curat's house at Norwich. If one examine this on the skirting level, the remains of an original arcading will be seen, which has been cut away to get the

---

* The whole judgment was afterwards upset both by a Divisional Court and later by the Court of Appeal.

† The word has more than one meaning.

‡ Other people had a very good notion.

panels into a room lower than the one for which the woodwork was made.

A caution here may be necessary. Distrust all local legends and "old wives' tales." I have seen so many oak and deal rooms which I have been assured, ostensibly on the best authority, are in original *situ*, but where the signs of later cutting and adaptation are obvious. There is one in Sparrowe's House in the Buttermarket at Ipswich which has evidently been very largely altered, and two mantels and some of the panelling in the "Feathers" Hotel at Ludlow are also not original to the house. The Long Gallery at Lyme Park in Cheshire is partly of oak and partly of deal, the remainder of the original panelling (very ignorantly cut about and with considerable additions) being in the drawing-room on the floor below.* In Lyme Park it is not surprising that some such alteration should have taken place, as the 1603 house of Sir Piers Legh was entirely rebuilt by Leoni in *circa* 1725. That Leoni could have retained the panelling is possible, but he could hardly have preserved the Long Gallery itself, although Lady Newton, in her book on Lyme Park, appeared to think this a possibility!

Oak case-hardens when exposed to the air, as we have seen, but the same process goes on when it is painted. In addition, the lead in the paint turns the medullary ray dark, almost black. True, the faker has found a means of imitating this darkened ray, but the steel-hard surface of original oak (which some quality in the paint intensifies) defies his efforts to reproduce. Of course, if old panels be stripped with the plane or the scraper, then all the integrity departs, but if the ordinary methods of paint removal are resorted to, oak panelling of the seventeenth century, or earlier, is, or should be, unmistakable. The same applies to deal, which was always painted originally, and was intended to remain in this state.

It must be remembered that the fashion for "stripped deal" rooms is not thirty years old. Red deal bleaches, possibly by the exclusion of the light, when it has been painted, and the signs of early stopping with putty or white lead are evident, when the paint is removed, and cannot be imitated. It is not necessary, however, for the expert to pay more than a passing attention to such details; the faker has still a stock of old painted deal on which he can draw for his "new-old" rooms. It is the construction which matters, and whether the design of the entire room be coherent, whether it looks as if it had all been made at the one time. Of course, if the room be in original *situ*, no expert knowledge is necessary at all, but a warning must be given against pedigrees, however plausible, not substantiated by exact evidence. I have learned to distrust these pedigrees thoroughly, and the more plausible they are the

* See *Early English Furniture and Woodwork*, Vol. I, p. 273.

more I become suspicious. I have found, in some forty years' experience, that they are easier to fabricate then the pieces to which they purport to relate. The latter do require skill, taste, facilities and opportunities; a lively, if dishonest, imagination is all that is necessary with the former. It is, after all, only the romantic imagination of an author such as Stanley Weyman put to commercial uses.

MADE-UP OAK AND DEAL ROOMS

HERE is an easy and lucrative field for the faker. He has only one difficulty, that of provenance, and this is easily overcome. Genuine panelling, in fragments, is to be found in country houses, formerly of some state and consequence, but now reduced to the level of labourers' dwellings. It is simple enough to promote one of these to its former dignity for the purpose of selling a bogus room, and there is the further avenue of escape, the house of note which has been pulled down long ago and has disappeared. Genuine panellings have been found under these conditions, so why not a few more! Unfortunately, like other good things, the tendency is to overdo them, and given sufficient demand—and credulity—it is truly surprising how these "old" rooms begin to multiply. Perhaps soil and conditions are both ripe for a good crop, alike of rooms and "collectors."

[*Facing page* 76

On this and the facing page are two views of the "cele-brated" oak room from the mythical "Royston Hall," which figured in the English Courts of Law in 1923-4.

(See chapter IX.)

Plate number Eighty-six

On a genuine (?) basis of a few odd scraps of panelling found in a dairy in Royston, this room was evolved and sold. In any case it could never have been earlier than 1630, if genuine, but it was upheld as a "genuine Elizabethan" room.

Plate number Eighty-seven

The development towards the large Panel. Oak panelling from St. Botolph's, Colchester, Essex, of *circa* 1660. A comparison of the panels with the detail of the architrave will show that the former are unusually large in area although still without joint.

Plate number Eighty-eight

The Clifford's Inn Room, now in the Victoria and Albert Museum. Of English oak, with enrichments of Barbados cedar, this room was put into the old Inn of Court by John Penhalow, a Cornish gentleman, in *circa* 1686. For his expenses, Penhalow was granted a lease of his chambers "for a term of three lives." In this room the large area of the panels has necessitated jointing. When bought by the Museum, the room was covered by numerous coats of paint (possibly applied because of the shrinkage of the panels and the opening of the joints), but all this has been removed and the rich figure of the oak exposed.

Plate number Eighty-nine

The Clifford's Inn Room. The Mantel. Above the over-mantel are the arms of Penhalow quartering Penwarne.

The Clifford's Inn Room. Details of the two doors and

window recess.

Room of red Memel deal from 5 Great George Street, Westminster, London, S.W. Now in the Victoria and Albert Museum. *Circa* 1750-60. At this date mouldings and enrichments were all carved, as composition ("carton-pierre") was only introduced by the Brothers Adam some twenty years later. It is rare to find wood cornices to these deal rooms; they are usually of plaster.

Plate number Ninety-two

CHAPTER X

WALNUT FURNITURE FROM 1660 TO 1700

NGLISH walnut (*Juglans regia*) is not an indigenous tree. Tradition says that it was first planted at Wilton Park by the Earl of Pembroke and Montgomery in 1565. It is native to Persia and the Himalayas, but it must have been known, and used, in Italy and France at a considerably earlier date than in England, as the sixteenth-century furniture in both these countries testifies, unmistakably.

It is well known that timber tends to vary in different soils, and over a long period of time, and, although walnut may have begun with the Persian and Himalayan variety in Europe (assuming that it exhibited no variation in the East), by the middle of the seventeenth century, if not earlier, walnut in Europe could already be classed into five distinct categories at least, leaving out, for the moment, any sub-species. These are:

Spanish,
Low Country, the Rhine valley, and part of Austria,
French,
Italian or Ancona,
English.

We can ignore here the *Juglans nigra* of America, as it does not concern our subject. With the English walnut, also, we can omit any mention of burrs or other freak growths, as they are peculiarities which have nothing to do with the main species itself.

When it is remembered that, in the final analysis, the question as to whether walnut is of English or Low Country growth may determine the nationality of a piece, especially with furniture made in the last two decades of the seventeenth century, it is highly desirable that the expert should make a profound study of walnut and its varieties. Added to this, if the faker be careless enough to use American walnut, for example, in the making of his "Stuart" furniture (and I have known slips just as bad as this, as the faker has by no means the profoundest respect for the present-day expert), then the presence of such timber may be taken as conclusive evidence of recent manufacture. It is unlikely, also, that

French, Italian or Spanish walnut would be used in England during the seventeenth or eighteenth centuries, although, with work of an earlier date, it is unwise to be pedantic in this respect. Thus, the famous room from Rotherwas, in Herefordshire, which came into the market some twenty years ago (a typical example of Welsh-bordering-county panelling of the early seventeenth century); the timber must have been imported, either from the Pyrenees or Spain itself. I have seen exactly the same wood used in Andorra and the Carcassonne country.

English walnut is a milder timber than oak, easier to plane and to carve. It is finer in grain, and will take a friction-polish readily. Naturally pale when new, it darkens to a deep brown on exposure, or if oiled, but, if varnished, it may bleach to a lovely golden shade. That, however, is the action of light on the varnish itself, a fact which should not be forgotten, as to re-surface this early walnut is to spoil it, as a rule. It is a mistake, however, to imagine that the Restoration chair maker (who used the timber in the solid, as a rule) invariably selected walnut for his work. Overlying varnish, or an amalgamation of wax and dirt, over a long period, often disguises the underlying wood itself. I have found sycamore (*Acer pseudoplatanus*), plane tree, and cherry used indiscriminately for many of these Restoration chairs. With the furniture of the same period (other than oak, which was still used to a much greater extent than is generally supposed), where it was usual to veneer flat surfaces, such as the tops of tables or the fronts of drawers or cupboard doors, walnut was nearly always employed, with bandings or "herring-bone" lines of the same wood. At a slightly later date the fashion set in for the use of freak growths or unusual methods of veneer-cutting, such as the cross-cut saplings known as "oyster-pieces." From these to a regular patterned parqueterie, and so to definite inlay and marqueterie, is an easy and regular progression, the development of which will be considered in the next chapter.

Walnut is not as strong and tough a timber as oak, and, as the Restoration models are invariably of lighter construction and proportion than those of the earlier years, it is not surprising to find many evidences of old or recent damage and repair. Could one have guaranteed that broken furniture had been promptly mended, no great harm might have resulted, but a broken top rail of a chair-back, for example, must often have been allowed to lie about in a lumber-room, and to get lost. The result, at the present day, is that, in many instances, these fine Restoration chairs are found with cresting-rails or stretchers of late date, and generally of much cruder workmanship. The job of mending the broken chair must have been entrusted, very often, to the local jobbing carpenter. In examining such a piece, therefore, I make it a definite rule to scrutinize each part with the utmost care, as a Charles II chair with eighty per cent of ignorant Victorian addition is hardly a bargain at any price.

These chairs were nearly always caned in the seats and backs, but it is extremely rare to find the original caning. It is regrettable, but true, that this was often an integral part of the construction itself, in the sense that a chair relied, for its stability, to a considerable extent, on the permanence of its caning. The era when constructional principles were sacrificed to design and fashion had already begun in *circa* 1660, although English furniture had not yet reached the depraved state which it attained some twenty-five years later.

At no period in the entire history of English furniture were fashions in a more fluid state than in the forty years from 1660 to 1700. Changes succeeded each other with bewildering rapidity. This is unfortunate, in a way, as if it were possible to illustrate what was made at various periods, and by implication to exclude what was not, it would be of considerable assistance to the expert. This is impossible, however. One has to rely on intrinsic, rather than on extrinsic, evidences.

It would be incorrect to describe the spiral or the twist as an innovation of this period, but the invention of the slide-rest, as an adjunct to the turning-lathe, certainly dates from *circa* 1660, that is, the mechanical method of producing a result formerly attained only by hand with the aid of the chisel, file and rasp. If one examine the twisted legs and balusters of the Cromwellian oak period (to say nothing of an earlier date) it will be seen that this spiralling is entirely hand-fashioned. Perhaps that may account for its comparative rarity before 1660, and its popularity after.

It is instructive for the student to see the slide-rest at work in a wood-turner's shop, but a brief description of its principle may suffice here for the present. Take a round ruler, for example, and centre it in a lathe, and allow it to revolve slowly. Place a pencil against the ruler, and the result will be a ring. Now move the pencil from one end to the other, and the result will be a spiral, provided that the ruler revolve slow enough to prevent a complete ring being made anywhere, or the pencil be moved along quickly, which has the same result. Substitute for the pencil which marks, a tool which cuts, and you get a modelled twist, one which may require finishing by hand, it is true, but where the actual marking and spacing of the spiral is accomplished mechanically. If the cutting operation be protracted, and the cut be made deep enough, the result will be an open (or "double-bine") spiral, such as one would get if two sticks of soft macaroni were twisted together.

A good deal may be learned from an intelligent examination of original late seventeenth-century twisting, where the slide-rest had not reached the perfection to which it afterwards attained. There are minute points which are not present in the later fake, where the work is done with the modern perfect slide-rest. Here is an example of the signs of ancient methods, as compared with modern, much more apparent than with other tools such as planes, saws or chisels.

With all the furniture which has been considered, up to the present stage, it has been possible either to enhance the value of a simple piece by the addition of carving or to make up one from another, to promote a chest to the status of a credence, for example. There are no such possibilities with these late Stuart chairs. They are nearly always carved to the decorative limit, and it is obviously impossible to make a chair from another piece, although I have known of a single stool (and that was a fake) which formed the only "antique" portion of a pair of "guaranteed genuine" settees. The fakes with which one has to deal are outright forgeries, as a rule, sometimes containing an authentic cresting-rail or a stretcher, but more often new throughout. Walnut is a wood very liable to the attack of worm, and very few know that a worm-eaten piece of timber, if placed in a dark and slightly damp place, together with walnut or beech furniture, in the month of February, will very successfully infect the lot before June is out. There is no necessity to employ a "worm-hole" maker, even if such an individual ever existed, which is doubtful. For those who will trust a worm, implicitly, yet will doubt the word of any dealer, it is as well to know this, even if their early confidence be somewhat rudely undermined.

In the fine Restoration chairs there is considerable spontaneity and vigour, both in the design and the carving, but there are many where the execution falls far below this standard. It is these specimens which the faker usually selects as his models, trusting to the mere worship of the antique, real or bogus, to cover a multitude of sins. As Spencer remarked, "Only by repeated iteration can alien conceptions be forced on reluctant minds," and the statement must be made again that there is no merit in antiquity without quality. It matters very little if an egg-box be old or new, the value is much the same, excepting, perhaps, that the new one will be the more reliable for the successful transport of eggs. With these Restoration chairs, the first things to study are the design and execution; if these are poor, then it matters very little if the chair be old or new; one should pass it by.

At no period in the whole history of English furniture does construction become debased, at the dictates of fashion, to the same extent as with the chairs from 1680 to 1700. If we admit the sham of veneering, which, like wallpaper, can hide a multitude of sins, then the cabinet maker of the same period is not nearly as guilty as the chair maker. It is the outstanding characteristic of the oak chair that it was not only stoutly made, but it was also constructed on sound principles. The back is framed, the legs braced by side-rails and stretchers, and the arm supports are prolongations of the front legs. The early Charles II models have the same good principles, but these do not persist for long. After a few years we find the cresting-rails of the backs no longer tenoned *between* the outer balusters, but dowelled or spiked *on top* of them. A little later and we get the seats similarly dowelled on the front legs. It is little wonder that nearly all these later Stuart chairs are found in a more or less repaired state to-day.

Side by side with this imperfect construction goes rank bad designing. The earlier oak chairs invariably stand firmly on the floor, a quality due partly to their weight but still more to their design. In the short reign of James II not only are chair-backs disproportionately tall, but there is also no countervailing outward splay to the back legs, with the result that the chair will fall backwards with the least pressure on the part of the sitter. After 1690 this unfortunate tendency appears to have been recognized, and chair designs improve, somewhat, but it is not until after 1700 that they become logical again.

These criticisms do not apply to the furniture of this period, which is usually fine in design and detail. Allowing a concession in favour of veneering (in itself a sham), there is a marked improvement in this walnut furniture as compared with the oak of the earlier years. Mouldings, in the oak period, are nearly always crude in section, but in the walnut years we first get genuine classical sections. How much of this improvement may be due to the influence of architects, or how much to traditions imported from the Low Countries, it is difficult to say. It is certain that fine sections are first found on the cases of "grandfather" and bracket clocks (of which the earliest specimens were made in Holland to the orders of the renowned English clock makers such as East, Clement, Quare, Tompion and Knibb), and it is reasonable to suppose that the inspiration for this classically moulded furniture may have originated from the same country.

Oak remains the usual carcase-wood almost throughout the walnut period. Occasionally, but very rarely, pine was used instead, but drawer interiors, in English pieces, are always of oak, and, in Dutch examples, often of deal or pine. It may be accepted, almost as a general rule, that a drawer, the front of which is veneered with walnut or pine, and where the sides and bottom are of the same wood, is of Low Country origin. In German work of the same date white beech was used instead, and in French pieces walnut was often employed in the solid, which appears never to have been done in England.

Veneer is largely at the mercy of the underlying wood. If a top shrink, then the veneer will crack. It is also an axiom in veneering (the result of long experience) that to keep a top straight it is necessary to veneer it on both sides, even if the reverse side be not visible at all, *and with veneers of equal thickness.* A top with saw-cut veneer on the one side, and knife-cut on the reverse, will warp and become concave on the side which has the thickest veneer. If the top be so fixed that it cannot "cast," it will crack instead. In the early days of veneering, in the late Stuart period, this secret had not been discovered, and veneers were laid on the upper or exposed faces only. An endeavour was made to minimize this warping tendency by using a milder timber, such as pine or poplar, for the beds of veneered tops, or the falls of secretaires, but it is rare, at the present day, to find an original piece of Stuart walnut veneered furniture which has not warped or cracked at some later period. Unfortunately, it is impossible to repair a gaping crack in veneer without visible and unsightly patching. Veneering methods, and the pitfalls for the beginner, will be explained fully in the following chapter which deals with the marqueterie furniture of the same period.

The original finish of this walnut furniture was always a clear oil varnish; shellac polishing is a discovery of more than a century later. With the necessary restoration or patching referred to above (which may be quite recent), it is not unusual to attempt to resurface the piece with this shellac, or "French" polishing, so the presence of this is not necessarily an indication of modern manufacture. It must be remembered, however, that with old walnut furniture the grain of the wood is always filled with dust and wax, and, if not stripped with the scraper, the surface is generally covered with anything from minute abrasions to positive bruises. It is as well to examine these closely with a magnifying glass, as they should be present in the larger numbers where the use has been greatest. These are the little points where the faker trips. A swinging drawer handle, for example, will always strike the front in the same place, but gently, unless it be used in the manner of a door-knocker. The faker generally fixes *his* handles, and then drives the backs into the drawer front with a blow of a mallet—with a very different result, as a rule. It is the most difficult thing in the world to imitate genuine age and wear in furniture, once the expert knows exactly what to expect, is not lazy in his examination, and not prone to stultify his better judgment.

With this walnut furniture, as distinct from chairs, a good deal of alteration, with consequent improvement in market value, is possible, but as the same applies, in the same way, to the marqueterie pieces as well as to those of plain walnut (perhaps in greater degree, as the marqueterie furniture is considerably more valuable), the consideration of these "improvements" can be deferred to the next chapter.

For the one who aims at furnishing a home as well as making a collection, there are, in my judgment, no more charming examples to be found than these simple walnut pieces of the last forty years of the seventeenth century. They have the additional advantage of not being unreasonably expensive, which is a consideration to many, if not most of us, in these days.

THE following illustrations of walnut furniture, from 1660 onwards, show the radical alteration which takes place in designing at this period, a change due more to the use of a new and different wood than to any novel fashion. Walnut, owing to its texture and figure, engendered veneering almost as a matter of course, whereas to use oak in veneers (other than with the pollarded varieties or other freak growths) would be a manifest absurdity. In contradistinction to oak, which was invariably used in the solid, for furniture, it is rare to find solid walnut used other than for chairs, or the legs of tables, the latter of which could not be veneered at all. On the other hand, carcase-work, table tops, drawer fronts, or doors are never found in the solid in the English walnut years.

Top, left. Simple twist-turned Chair, commencement of Restoration, where the lathe-twist is a novelty.

Top, right. Fine walnut Chair of late Charles II period, with Flemish scroll on legs and arm supports.

Bottom, left. Typical early Charles II Arm-chair with loose cushion and tassels; stretcher of well-known amorini type.

Bottom, right. Early Charles II Arm-chair, showing preponderance of twist-turning everywhere.

Top, left. Charles II Arm-chair, with oval caned panel in back, and unusual cresting rail.

Top, right. Flemish influence in the feet of the front legs, and turning substituted for twisting.

Bottom, left. The new fashion of the Flemish C-scroll used here to excess.

Bottom, right. The type of Charles II Chair which is frequently copied and forged.

Two elaborate walnut Arm-chairs of the later Restoration years (*circa* 1675), which are instructive as showing the strong similarity between models at this date, and indicate how plentiful were the products of the chair maker as compared with the maker of furniture. The development from the earlier types is shown by the front stretcher, reinforced by the flat cross, or X-stretcher, tying the four legs together. The dissimilarity between the two models is enough to suggest two distinct makers.

Plate number Ninety-six

Left

The utmost degree of elaboration in these walnut Restoration Arm-chairs. The front legs are in caryatid form with Flemish scroll front feet; front stretcher of amorini type but unusual detail.

Right

Arm-chair where the Flemish scroll is of double-C type. A curious detail is where the three splats in the back are flat, but simulate twist-turning. A type often copied but seldom forged for various reasons.

Plate number Ninety-seven

Left

A fine tall-back Chair of 1685, of good and rare detail, but showing the debasement in construction and principle which took place at this date. This chair is very unstable, as the leverage of the high back is enormous. The seat, also, is only pegged on the front legs instead of being framed between them.

Right

The single and double C-scroll used to excess in the first years of William III. The bowed front stretcher is of Spanish type.

Plate number Ninety-eight

Left

Elaborate tall-back walnut Arm-chair of James II type, with caryatid front legs and arms finishing in lions' heads. A type frequently forged.

Right

James II tall-back Chair showing the development of the cup-turned front legs which marks the early Orange years. Here can be seen, distinctly, how the seat is pegged on the front legs; a bad constructional detail. Also the want of stability, owing to the high back, and the small backward spread of the rear legs will be remarked.

Plate number Ninety-nine

In spite of the differences, the details in common in these Chairs should be noted for reference.

The details to be noted are the completely framed backs with caned panels, the cup-turned legs and flat X-stretchers, indicating a date after 1689.

Plate number One Hundred and One

The three important Chairs above show the type that was often made in sets, and the needlework coverings (which differ on each one) illustrate the taste for gorgeous fabrics which was characteristic of the years from 1685 to 1700. Here, also, we have the Flemish double C-scroll used wherever possible, and this indicates that the device was new at the period when these chairs were made.

Charles II married Catherine of Braganza, and during his reign influences from Portugal and Spain permeated English craftsmanship. In this table the construction, of end-framed trestles tied together with ogival straps of forged iron, is Spanish, and the piece can be taken apart and stowed flat, a device never adopted with English furniture. The spiral turning, which is a definite lathe twist as distinguished from a fashioning by hand, may have inspired English craftsmen, both from the points of view of design and method. In seeking for design-sources, this foreign furniture is often very useful.

Plate number One Hundred and Three

Typical walnut twist-leg Table of Charles II period. The top is veneered with "oyster-pieces" of walnut and olive wood.

Walnut Tables showing foreign influence. *Above* is a typical Low Country table with open "double-bine" twist. *Below* is an English table made under Dutch influence.

Typical walnut Cabinet on spiral-turned stand of 1670.
The doors and drawers inside are veneered with "oyster-
pieces" of walnut and laburnum, edged with cross-cut
sap laburnum. The brasswork is typical and original
throughout.

Plate number One Hundred and Six

Typical walnut Table of the early Orange years, *circa* 1690. From the close similarity in details between these tables and chairs of the same period, it is probable that they were the work of the chair maker rather than the former. Note the cup-turned legs and flat wavy stretcher, and compare with some of the chairs in the preceding pages.

Plate number One Hundred and Seven

[Plate number One Hundred and Eight was not used]

CHAPTER XI

MARQUETERIE FURNITURE

O detect the difference between old and modern spurious marqueterie often demands a high standard of technical equipment. Original marqueterie is rare and valuable, and being nearly always a mere decorative adjunct, we have to consider how it can be employed by the faker for his own material advantage.

Perhaps one ought to begin, as before, by substituting the wood "dealer" for "faker," but here it is often the dealer himself who is taken in. Given an old and quite genuine plain walnut piece—a small table with a drawer, for example—where the veneer of the top stretcher and drawer-front has been removed intact (which can be done with a rag saturated with linseed oil and a hot flat-iron) and used as the ground for floral inlays, and then re-veneered, it is by no means easy to detect the addition; certainly it demands an equipment which few dealers, with their general but superficial knowledge, possess. Yet to pay genuine marqueterie-price for such a beautified piece must be a bad investment. However well it may be done, no matter how difficult it may be to detect, there is always the man who has done the work in existence, and he is under no delusions. It is curious how such knowledge becomes diffused, after a while. Where I have had reason to suspect any marqueterie furniture (which happens in more than fifty per cent of the examples I see) I always prefer to find out the particular marqueterie-cutter responsible if I can, as, in card parlance, "one peep is worth two finesses." Nor is this as difficult as one would imagine. Marqueterie is a dying art in England, as it has not been in vogue with modern furniture for many years. For a while it had a spurt with the front panels of upright pianos, but this has died down again. I doubt if there be one hundred marqueterie-cutters left in the British Isles, and not one quarter of this number could cut marqueterie in the antique manner, in a way which would deceive anyone with the slightest knowledge of old furniture, so the sphere of enquiry is narrowed considerably.

It must be understood that I am not impugning the skill of the remaining seventy-five per cent of the trade, but the cutting of marqueterie in the antique way implies more than skill, and this will be

85

better understood if the various processes are technically described and illustrated, which it is proposed to do here.

Marqueterie is an inlay, of course, but all inlay is not marqueterie. The inlaying of one wood in another (more often one veneer in another) may be done in one of three ways. First, there is an assortment of wood in patterns, similar to the laying of a wood-block or parquet floor. This is parqueterie, and is rather an arrangement than a proper inlay. Secondly, there is an inlay of lines and bandings where the channels for their insertion in the ground veneers are made with the gauge or "scratcher." Circles, in like manner, can be inlaid with the cutting-divider or the boring "bit and stock." Thirdly, there is true marqueterie where both ground and inlay are cut with the marqueterie-saw.

There is really a fourth subdivision, a branch of true marqueterie, where the pattern only is cut with the saw and then chopped into the solid ground, usually with a pointed knife and a small hammer. Nearly all Tudor and early Stuart inlay was done in this fashion, and in the days of my youth, when a vile fashion came into being for inlaying veneered mahogany pieces of the Hepplewhite and Sheraton periods, we used this "knife-and-hammer" method as a matter of course. I have seen many fine plain pieces of the best period of Hepplewhite ruined in this way. With the necessary scraping and glass-papering which the inlay demanded, followed by "French" polishing, went the fine old light-bleached shades and the lovely original textures. It was not an occasional adventure either. I knew of one workshop (curiously enough, in an old disused church in Bloomsbury) which sent one vanload, at least, regularly every week to one firm not a thousand miles from Baker Street. That, however, is forty years ago, and sins have been forgotten in that time, but the mystery has always been, to me, what has become of all this stuff? Occasionally, but very rarely, I come across one of these "beautified" pieces, but, in these later days, no one has the impudence to put them forward as "antiques," which they are, in reality, and to a far greater extent than many of the "museum bits" which I see on every hand. There is nothing more utterly worthless than the thing of an obsolete fashion; perhaps it reminds one too much of the sins of one's youth.

Marqueterie begins with a design, which is carefully drawn out on paper and then "pricked," that is, each line is finely perforated by an instrument similar in principle to the modern sewing-machine. When the "pricking," or master-pattern, is completed, it is placed over a sheet of plain paper, and the design is "pounced" with fine bitumen powder from a "dolly" or pounce of coarse rag, through which the powder will escape if the "dolly" be beaten lightly on the pattern. This pouncing would smear if left as it is, but the powder-line is burnt into the paper by placing it on a hot plate and bringing it nearly to the scorching point. Several such patterns are taken, one being reserved for the ground veneer, the others for cutting up for the inlays.

The marqueterie-saw cannot cut a single veneer layer without the risk of breakage, so four, as a rule, are pinned together with headless "veneer pins," with an outer layer on each side of waste wood to take the "rag" of the saw. A glance at the illustration of a marqueterie-saw in action will show that the bow of the saw-frame must limit the area of the veneer which can be cut, so with a balanced pattern, the ground veneer of a table-top, for example, the design is cut in two halves or four quarters, the divisions either covered by the inlay itself or jointed together with a wavy line. The inlay woods, which may be stained in various colours, are cut in small packets of six or eight layers at the one time, each packet having the appropriate portion of the design pasted on the upper surface, as a guide to the cutter.

From this impossibility of cutting a single veneer at a time, and as there may be no repetition in the whole design (which was usually the case with old work), it follows that, with packets of eight layers (allowing two for waste), not only are six complete patterns cut at the one operation, but there is also the wood of the ground, which falls out in the cutting (the "counterpart" as it is called), which is also not thrown away. With a complete unbalanced design, and in woods of many colours, there is no counterpart other than with the ground veneer, which is worthless, but with a balanced design, where the ground is in walnut and the inlay in holly, for instance, allowing for the cutting of six usable layers, and the entire pattern in two halves at the one operation, we get three originals and three counterparts. It is as well to bear in mind that no single marqueterie piece of this kind can be unique, unless we are to suppose that the cutter throws all these "undercuts" and "counterparts" away, which is highly improbable.

Having cut both ground and pattern, the next job is to assemble them in order, and the method is to glue the ground and inlay-pieces on a sheet of paper, to keep each in position. There is another operation which may come before, that of shading. With inlay of light woods, box or holly, it is sometimes desirable to get the effect of modelling on leaves or flowers, and this is done by taking the piece between tweezers and dipping it into hot silver-sand, which scorches the part immersed to a deep brown, fading away into the colour of the veneer itself. This shading, or sand-burning, was extensively employed in the case of the laurelled bandings which one finds, not only with the early marqueterie, but the plain walnut also.

The cutting of some of this early marqueterie is amazingly intricate. The favourite flower at this period was the carnation, and here each petal, with its serrations, is outlined with the saw. More than a century later, when the taste for marqueterie revived with the Sheraton school, this elaborate cutting was dispensed with, its place being taken by engraving, where the veining was cut in with a fine V-tool (the graver) after the first polishing, the engraved lines being then rubbed in with black shoemaker's wax (heel-baw), and the polishing then completed. This engraving, however, is never found in the early work, and it is doubtful if the art was known, in relation to marqueterie, until about 1770.

The marqueterie veneer, with its adhering layer of paper, being completed, the next operation is the laying on its bed, and here there are several pitfalls for the inexperienced. It must be remembered that the art of the marqueterie-cutter appears to have arrived, in a full-blown state, from Holland; there are practically no "prentice" efforts in English furniture. The cabinet maker, however, had still to learn many of the secrets of laying.

The marqueterie panel is first turned over, paper side downwards, and the surface scratched with the "toothing plane" to afford a key for the glue. The bed—the top of the table, for instance—is then "toothed" in the same manner. To the amateur, glue is an adhesive which has to be used hot; in its cold state it will not stick. To lay a veneer, it is necessary to cramp it to its bed with a thick flat board (the caul) and handscrews. Using hot glue, the caul and the screws must be applied as soon as possible, but the time, however short, is long enough to cause the heat of the glue to expand the veneer, which is then put down in a state of strain. Contraction goes on for months, as the imprisoned glue dries very slowly, being excluded from the atmosphere, but sooner or later the veneer shrinks and cracks. There is also a tendency for the edges of the crack to curl up, and a panel in this state cannot be restored, other than by the removal of the veneer. The protecting paper, on top, having been removed for the "cleaning up" and polishing, the marqueterie veneer, when so removed for restoration, will fall to pieces, and, with the contraction which has taken place, it is probable that the pieces of inlay will no longer fit. In practice, it is quicker to throw the faulty panel away and to make another, but this is only possible if the "prickings" are available.

The workman's method of laying a veneer (a secret which was not discovered for some time) is to allow his glue to get quite cold before the veneer is placed upon it. The headless veneer pins are used to help it in position, allowed to project, as they will enter the soft wood caul, and when this is removed can be withdrawn with pliers. The caul is made very hot, placed on the veneer, and then handscrewed into position, pressure being applied to the centre first, to squeeze the glue to the outer edges. By the time the heat has penetrated through the veneer to the glue below, and liquefied it, the screws are in position, and no expansion with subsequent contraction takes place.

Owing to the bad habit of laying veneers on the one side only of table tops (which was nearly always done with the old examples), these are rarely found in a perfect state at the present day, and restoration must involve some re-surfacing. The result is that so-called "original surfaces" are practically unknown with English marqueterie of the late seventeenth century. One valuable indication to the expert is, therefore, absent. It is exceedingly difficult to describe the indications which remain. There are qualities both in the design and the cutting, but these are, necessarily, minute, and are apparent only to those with long technical experience. The marqueterie-cutter's saw, in its guides, with the "chops," which open and close by foot pressure, to hold the veneers while being cut, and his seat at the end (the "donkey," as it is called), have hardly varied at all in two hundred and fifty years. It is true that marqueterie saws are now often driven by power, fret-saw fashion, but these are hardly ever used for "antique" work, so do not concern us here. The "bubbling" or blistering of the old work (which is not general) can be imitated by the use of the hot iron. Illustratively, there is absolutely no difference between a good marqueterie fake and a genuine piece, and to any but the highly trained expert there is very little more in the articles themselves. Fakes abound, therefore, which have the appearance of being far more genuine than many restored originals, yet it is possible, with long experience, to detect the spurious, and at a glance, almost. Nearly every marqueterie-cutter can do the same, even if he be "only a workman," but, perhaps, if the shoemaker does not know all there is to learn about leather, who remains?

Marqueterie appears to begin about 1670, and the fashion persists to about 1705, being revived again, sporadically, at intervals throughout the whole of the eighteenth century. One can trace a regular progression of types. Beginning with a somewhat crude inlay of stars (in some examples the star-fish appears to have been adopted as a model), in the second stage we get gaily coloured woods (generally of dyed holly or sycamore), also white and green-stained ivories, with the jessamine flower and leaves preponderating as decorative motives. After about 1685 marqueterie becomes more sober in tone, and closer in design. Perhaps the last phase is the finely scrolled inlay of holly, box, sycamore or almond-tree in a ground of walnut, sometimes of laburnum or striped ebony. There is an alternative method, which runs parallel with this late scrolled marqueterie, where the inlay of dark wood (usually walnut) is in separate panels of holly, surrounded by a bed of walnut, thus

89

making a double counter-change. This inlay in panel was probably devised by the marqueterie-cutter himself, as the small panels were found to be much more manageable on the saw than large sheets which had to be cut in halves or quarters. At the same time the "all-over" marqueterie was still made, usually with laurelled "herring-bone" borders outside to frame the entire pattern.

It is inevitable that, as the art developed with the demand, new and more economical methods of cutting should be discovered. It is the great difficulty with the marqueterie-cutter that, while he can only cut a minimum of four veneer layers at the one operation, with safety (which, in the ordinary way, would produce four separate patterns and four counterparts), while only one or possibly two may be required, as a rule, but there may exist the greatest objection to the remaining two or three being sold elsewhere, to say nothing of the counterparts. With a pattern cut in four quarters there would be no original overplus (although the counterpart would still remain), but very few designs will lend themselves to this quartering. The fine scrolled marqueterie was often balanced in the pattern, which would permit of the cutting in two halves simultaneously, which was, probably, the reason why it came into vogue, as fashions nearly always originate from the makers, rarely from the general public. In a further stage of this economical development it was found that if the inlay and ground were cut *at the one operation*, not only would wastage be eliminated, but the result would be far greater accuracy in the fit. One can test this by a simple experiment. If a pattern be drawn out on white paper, and if to this a black sheet be pasted on the edges and both cut with the scissors at the one time, no matter whether the drawn pattern be well or badly cut, the black pieces will fit into the white (and vice versa) exactly. If we examine much of this late seventeenth-century scrolled marqueterie very carefully it will be seen that this plan of double cutting has been followed. Where the scrolls are bad in line (and it is unthinkable that they were drawn in this way on the master-pattern) they still fit the ground veneer exactly. Some writers on the subject of English furniture, unacquainted with this trick, have commented on the greater exactness in the cutting of marqueterie after 1680, but, in reality, the work is much more careless than in the earlier years. Curiously, the first English marqueterie, the star patterns, also permitted of this double cutting, which the all-over or coloured inlay of jessamine flowers and leaves, or the later sober-coloured carnation marqueterie, did not. The change from the one to the other is some evidence, in itself, to show that the simultaneous cutting of ground and inlay had not been discovered at this date, and an examination of the work itself will show that the two must have been cut separately.

Marqueterie neither precedes nor succeeds plain walnut in the chronological arrangement of English furniture. The two develop side by side, the one probably catering for the desires of those who preferred colour, the other made for people of quieter taste. Both have their uses in a scheme of decoration, if used sparingly and with discrimination. Like everything else, both the plain walnut and the marqueterie can be overdone. I have found that the most successful results can be obtained by an admixture of styles and woods, plain walnut, marqueterie, lacquer, mahogany, and even a little sycamore or satinwood. One has the charm of variety, which is the salt of life. When I am told (usually by ladies) that "my room is entirely in Queen Anne," I usually know what to expect: a monotonous result which may be true to style, but is true to nothing else.

Above. Pricking the master pattern.
Below. Cutting marqueterie.

Plate number One Hundred and Nine

Above. Putting marqueterie together.
Below. Sand burning or shading.

Plate number One Hundred and Ten

Example of marqueterie in panels of holly inlaid in walnut. The panels have been cut in pairs, as each stage differs in detail.

Plate number One Hundred and Eleven

Inlay partly made with the saw and partly jointed with the plane
(parqueterie).

Plate number One Hundred and Twelve

Marqueterie being the cutting of one veneer into another with the saw, and parqueterie being the arrangement of a number of pieces to form a pattern (jig-saw puzzle fashion), this arrangement, where sapling slices are put together partly by jointing and partly with the saw, may be said to bridge the parqueterie and the marqueterie arts.

Plate number One Hundred and Thirteen

Above are two cabinets of very dissimilar design, where the marqueterie of one is the counterpart, or "fall out," of the other. One is

dark inlay in light panel in walnut, the other is light inlay in dark panels. The ground of both is formed of walnut "oyster-pieces."

Plate number One Hundred and Fifteen

The name "seaweed" is often incorrectly used to indicate scrolled marqueterie. In this piece, especially in the top, seaweed is closely imitated.

The inlay here is of walnut in a ground of almond tree banded with sand-burnt laurelling. *Circa* 1695.

Plate number One Hundred and Seventeen

An example of floral inlay of various woods in a ground of small
laburnum "oyster-pieces."

Plate number One Hundred and Eighteen

Example of floral inlay of various woods in background in panels
double bordered with (*a*) sand-burnt laurelling and (*b*) "oyster-pieces."

Plate number One Hundred and Nineteen

Although very similar in general design, the differences in detail in
these cabinets are significant. In the central front panels in the
cabinet on the right, the design is cut in two halves, one half partly

Plate number One Hundred and Twenty

counterparting the other. In the one on the left there is no marqueterie inside other than on the central door, and the inlay on the
front drawers differs not only on each stage but also with each panel.

Plate number One Hundred and Twenty-one

An inlay of coloured woods and also white and green-stained ivories in a black panelled ground. The first type of marqueterie as it appears in England.

Plate number One Hundred and Twenty-two

A cabinet veneered with walnut and inlaid with scrolled marqueterie of holly. The two pilasters on the central door, produced entirely by inlay with no projection, was a familiar conceit at this period.

Plate number One Hundred and Twenty-three

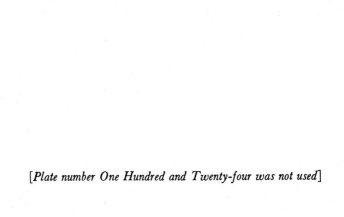

[Plate number One Hundred and Twenty-four was not used]

CHAPTER XII

LACQUER WORK

HE subject of lacquer is both involved and intricate, and it may be as well, at the outset, to get the subject into some form of order. We can commence with two main divisions: furniture which has been specially designed for lacquering, and without which it would be incomplete, and other pieces where it is only used as an adventitious decoration, and where the design would not suffer if the article were finished in paint or plain polished wood. The well-known Charles II square cabinets are examples of the first, and the fretted furniture of the Chippendale period of the second. So much for the first classification. There are others even more important.

The art of the lacquer-worker originates from China, from whence it appears to have spread to Japan, Korea, Hindustan and Persia, and, through the medium of the Dutch and English trading companies, to Europe, especially to Holland, northern France, and England. The true Oriental lacquer is the gum from a native tree, *Tsi*, which is applied in the semi-liquid state as it is exuded from the tree, but which hardens on exposure to the air. There is a good deal of mystery about Chinese lacquer, as there is about many other of the decorative arts of that country. Take quite a commercial product, one of the small rock crystal bottles, painted with scenes, *from the inside*. Here is a material almost as hard as a diamond, yet through a hole less than an eight of an inch in diameter some instrument is inserted which hollows out the interior of the bottle to tissue-paper thickness. (It is obvious that, if glass be painted on the reverse side, the design will radiate from the front when it is moved from side to side, according to the thickness of the glass itself.) Having accomplished this miracle, the artist then inserts his brushes, through the small hole, and paints his scenes from the inside, and, naturally, in reverse, and the manner in which the work is performed permits of no error. How is this done? No European ever appears to have seen the operation in progress. One thing is known, however, that lacquer artists, both in China and Japan, work in a very high temperature, probably to prevent premature hardening of the gum. Once it has dried, it will resist such solvents as pure spirit-of-wine, which will attack all European paints and varnishes, even if centuries old.

Excluding the works of Persia and Hindustan, and massing that of China, Japan and Korea together under the generic title of Oriental, we can make two other broad divisions, namely, the Eastern and the Western lacquer. Further classification is possible, with both, into flat, raised or cut lacquer, ornament in polychrome or plain gold, or into colours, black, red, yellow, buff, gold, brown, blue, green, and other shades.

To enter into the question of the age of this Oriental lacquer is beyond the scope of this book, and is a vast study in itself. It must be remembered that the Chinaman has, at all periods, imitated or faked his own work. Thus the "six-marked" blue-and-white Ming porcelain was extensively imitated in the early Manchu period. Probably, at the time when it was made, the Ming pieces had the greater value, or were more in demand, which may be the same thing. Certainly, at the present day, the K'hang H'si imitations of the Ming realize, by far, the bigger price in the market, which amounts to the curious state of the fake being more valuable than the original.

It is possible to recognize true Oriental lacquer not only by the drawing and the execution of the ornament, but also by the perfection of the ground. I regard the Chinese or Japanese lacquers as infinitely superior to anything produced in Europe, but it does not realize the same prices, for some peculiar reason perhaps known to collectors or the trade. Some of the square cabinets, mounted on English carved and gilt wood stands, which appear to have had a great vogue from 1665 to 1685, are Chinese or Japanese, possessing all the perfection of detail and workmanship of those countries, yet I have known of several where the fine Oriental work has been obscured by a dirty varnish in the attempt, probably, to make it look English. I had the task—or the pleasure—of stripping one of these "Anglicized" Chinese cabinets some years ago, and I can remember my delight when the beautiful lacquer ground was exposed again.

These Oriental square cabinets are either of Chinese or Japanese origin, and the former are to be preferred, as not only the more valuable, but also the finer in execution. In one detail it is easy to differentiate between the two. The Chinaman habitually sits on a chair, the Japanese on the floor. The one, therefore, has a view-point from eighteen inches to two feet higher than the other. Japanese furniture, in consequence, is always dwarfed, and where these square cabinets have either a cut-out plinth or stump feet they are of Japanese origin. It is as well to examine the under side of these Oriental cabinets to see whether the feet have been cut away, with the idea of passing them off as Chinese.

The English cabinets of this type copied the Oriental originals as faithfully as possible, but the quality is never so high. The hardware, on the other hand, is of stouter metal and more sharply chiselled in the chasing. There is a great difference between Oriental and English brasswork which should be studied by the expert. There are many examples of both in the Victoria and Albert Museum which can be examined and compared, and no illustration or explanation here can describe these differences.

With pieces of furniture made specially for lacquering, such as these Charles II cabinets on gilded stands, if the expert satisfy himself that the wood and construction are of the period, he may be certain that the lacquer itself cannot be a later addition. With others, especially of the Chippendale period, where the lacquer is by way of being an alternative finish, he has no such guarantee, even of the age of the piece itself, as lacquering hides a multitude of things—and sins.

English lacquer—so-called, as, in even the finest, the ground is prepared with paints and oil or spirit varnishes, and is, therefore, not true lacquer at all—varies in quality from the highest down to a mere daubing of paint with the addition of some crude ornament in gold or base metal. It must be evident that the cruder a "work of art" is, the more easily can it be imitated, and the less worthy it is of being collected. I prefer to exclude all this rubbish. It matters very little, if at all, whether it be old or new. My advice has always been to fix a definite standard of quality and to ignore everything below it. Whether rubbish be old or new, where it be over-restored or not, can matter very little. It is not worth while wasting time on it in any event.

The restoring of really fine lacquer examples is of considerable importance, however, especially where this has been necessitated by extensive cracking of the underlying wood. It is evident that a piece which has been restored all over is exactly in the same category as one which has been originally plain and lacquered entirely at a later date. Here the distinction between the genuine and the spurious is very fine indeed. New lacquer—to give it a complimentary name, as it is nothing more than paint and varnish—will not stand the test of rubbing with a white rag dipped in spirit-of-wine or methylated spirit. The colour will come off on the rag almost at once. It is true that old English lacquer will not stand up to the same test, but a considerable amount of rubbing will be necessary before the colour moves. Much depends on the elasticity of the term "lacquer." I have known of some who would almost apply the name to a black-painted street door.

The furniture productions of the seventeenth and eighteenth centuries, in England and elsewhere, were always the work of skilled craftsmen or artists, but lacquer-work seems to have been, in many instances, a polite occupation taught in young ladies' academies. Much the same may be said of needlework of the late seventeenth and early eighteenth centuries, but here the standard of skill appears to have been much higher. In lacquer, the difference between this 'prentice-work and that of genuine artists is very marked, and the former should appeal only to those to whom mere antiquity hides every blemish. Fine English lacquer is well designed and beautifully executed, as a rule, but the same may be said of the fake, where the degree of skill is usually very high. It is impossible for English lacquer to persist, in a perfect state, for a hundred years or more, and the piece which looks patently new should be suspected. I have before me the catalogue of the Shrager "collection," where a pair of cream lacquer cabinets on silvered stands were sold on May 2nd, 1924, for £147. They appeared in court, and were endorsed, by at least one "expert," as "utterly genuine," with the additional remark that they were of a quality which no modern lacquer-worker could imitate at the present day. I stated they were modern commercial articles, worth, at trade prices, £85 each; £170 the pair. The auction price did not endorse my estimate by £23. I have illustrated one of these cabinets here.

They were charged to the unfortunate Shrager at £1,250, which must have represented quite a working profit. Similarly, a pair of "William and Mary red and gold lacquer stools," for which £250 was charged, but which I valued at £20, fetched £27 6s., in spite of the catalogue description. They were endorsed, in court, as genuine, equally with the other "gems" in this collection.

A real knowledge of old English lacquer-work can only be obtained by long and patient examination of accredited pieces. The provenance of houses, however famous, should be discredited unless one can ascertain that pieces have been there for many years. Why any example, bought at random in the trade, and quite recently, should promptly become genuine immediately it enter the front door of this Hall or that Grange I, for one, utterly fail to understand, but the superstition is more widespread than one would imagine. I have often been accused of having "fakes on the brain," but if the paper currency of England, for instance, were known to be eighty per cent counterfeit, perhaps the inhabitants would also get spurious money "on the brain." Nor are the proportions, stated here, in any way exaggerated, with regard to English furniture. Considering that many large faking factories are working at full pressure, and have been doing so for years, it is a pertinent question to ask, what has become of their productions? They do not sell as new, and one does not find them in the second-hand market. Where are they? I am afraid I must leave the reply to "collectors." Who else remains?

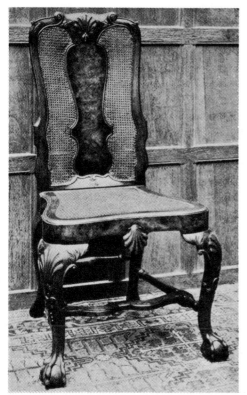 

Lacquer furniture in England can be divided into two classes; that which was specially designed for the work and which would be incomplete without it, and other pieces where lacquering is simply an adventitious decoration. With chairs, it is rare to find lacquer on other than models of the Queen Anne period, similar to those above. The usual colours were black, red, green and yellow, and the ornament is rarely, if ever, polychrome.

Plate number One Hundred and Twenty-five

Oriental Cabinets were frequently mounted on English carved and gilt stands. The independent stump feet on the cabinet above show that it is of Japanese origin, and was never made to be elevated on a stand at all.

Plate number One Hundred and Twenty-six

Typical English square Cabinet in the Chinese manner, mounted on
a carved gilt stand. Charles II period. The original stands of these
Restoration cabinets often resemble each other very closely, showing
that the area of production must have been severely localized
at the time.

Plate number One Hundred and Twenty-seven

Black lacquer Cabinet on carved gilt stand. The design of the double stretcher should be compared with those on the chairs of the 1690 period.

Plate number One Hundred and Twenty-eight

A fine green lacquer Cabinet on stand of 1690 period. It was bought in Sussex, sent to America, bought back and re-exported to England within one hour of its arrival in New York.

Plate number One Hundred and Twenty-nine

A comparison of these two Cabinets is instructive in showing not only
a strong similarity in design, but also in the lacquer patterns. The
former might indicate a localized sphere of manufacture, but the

Plate number One Hundred and Thirty

latter may be accounted for by the fact that teachers of the "art of lackering" may have roamed from place to place with portfolios of patterns and designs.

Plate number One Hundred and Thirty-one

A section of a Table Plateau in lacquer on a brown
ground with tinsel border and silver rim and feet. The
workmanship is European (probably French, although
the silver rim is English) and of the finest quality and
execution. It is painted to be observed from either side,
as a table plateau should be.

Plate number One Hundred and Thirty-two

Square Cabinet in incised polychrome lacquer (known as "Cut" or "Coromandel," and, in the early eighteenth century, as "Bantam-work," Bantam being the name of an old trading station of the Dutch East India Company in the East Indies). The English nationality of many of these incised lacquer cabinets and screens is doubtful; they were probably made in Holland and imported into this country at the time.

Plate number One Hundred and Thirty-three

Plate number One Hundred and Thirty-four

ON Plate 134 is one of a pair of yellow lacquer Cabinets from the Shrager case of 1923. They were described by one of the defendant's experts as "utterly genuine" and "fairy-like." The pair were sold to Shrager for £1,250. Evidence was offered, at the trial before the Senior Official Referee, that they were bought in Barcelona, but no purchase price was stated, and neither an invoice nor a bill of lading was produced. I condemned them as modern fakes (which they were, as I saw the stands in the process of making in a kitchen in Charlotte Street, Fitzroy Square) and I valued them at £85 each; £170 the pair. At the subsequent sale at Puttick and Simpson's rooms they fetched £147 the pair, on May 2nd, 1924. They were bought at this price by the late Lord Leverhulme, and came with his collection to New York in 1927, where I refused to catalogue them. I considered them too "utterly" anything but genuine. They were sold in New York, in separate lots, and one returned to England later.

It is possible that the other now ornaments some American "Collection".

[Plate number One Hundred and Thirty-six was not used]

CHAPTER XIII

NEEDLEWORK AND STUMP-WORK

HE art of the needle plays an important part in the history of English furniture, whether as coverings for chairs and other upholstered furniture, for caskets, mirrors and the like, or for bed or window hangings. In reality, needlework falls into three categories quite naturally, namely, cross- or tent-stitch (whether petit-point or gros-point is only a matter of size of stitch, not an intrinsic difference at all), stump-work, and appliqué, which includes crewel-work as well. Considering that this book has been written, in the main, with the idea of pointing out the difference between the old and the new—the antique or the spurious—we can see that with needlework, which is the stitching of wools on canvas, we have only the design and the colourings to guide us. The wools and the canvas, the making on the tambour frame, have all remained exactly the same since the seventeenth century. Stitching from a master-pattern, transferred to the canvas in much the same way as with marqueterie-cutting, every shop must have its stock of designs, which, whether large or small, must still be limited. In practice, of course, the needleworker copies old patterns, as a rule, so one clue is lost, at least.

With a good needlework studio, the stock of wools is very large, as many as one thousand different shades being held at the one time. These colours have also been improved very much of recent years. The days when the needleworker resorted to the "Berlin wool store" have gone, other than with the merest amateur. There remains the fact that age softens and mellows crude colours, but the faker is equal even to this, and with caustics and acids he "fakes" the tones of his wools, and, incidentally, rots his fabric at the same time. Petit-point needlework, where the mere pressure of the finger is enough to cause a rent, should be suspected at once. With proper treatment, fine-stitch needlework is practically everlasting. In point of durability, it is superior even to loom tapestry.

In much of the old needlework, even making due allowances for the mellowing of age, the colours of the wools were finer than at the present day, and, what is still more important, the needle was pulled tightly with each stitch. Old needlework is harsh to the touch, due, perhaps equally, to this tight stitching and the flattening inevitable in wear over many years. These, however, are qualities which have been appreciated and imitated by the needleworker (who is not necessarily a faker) in recent years. The fact remains, nevertheless, that needlework which is soft and woolly to the touch is always modern. There is, also, an indefinite crudity about the old work, even in the finest examples, which is very difficult to imitate. Where silk has been used, for the very fine stitches, it is never found in a perfect state if the old piece has been subjected to any wear whatsoever. Silk will even perish if the piece be kept in a drawer for many years, although the colours will not fade, of course.

With very tight stitching there is the tendency to slightly raise the pattern above the surface, as if it had been padded or "stumped." Age will not flatten this, as all surfaces tend to wear equally, more or less.

To appreciate all the various stitches which are used by the needleworker, old and modern, it is a good exercise to take a sheet of paper ruled into tiny squares, and to draw in the possible stitches with a pen. There is the vertical, the horizontal, and the two diagonals to commence with, each taking up four squares only. Then one can miss one or more squares, and get the long stitch known as Congress or Burgundian. The next stage is to superimpose one stitch on another, and it will be found that the art admits of almost infinite variety. The stitch can be varied also in size as the work proceeds, and this is arbitrarily classified as "petit-point" and "gros-point" respectively, with no definite line of demarcation between the two.

If no attempt at acid-faking be made, it is not impossible to recognize the work of various factories by the colours of their wools. Pinks and reds are especially noticeable. A large admixture of colours not only means a costly stock of wools, but also expensive work, as each colour and shade has to be carried on a separate needle.

It is practically impossible to find any original "petit-point" needlework of the late seventeenth or eighteenth centuries which has not been put to some purpose, whether tacked down as an upholstery covering, put on a straining-frame as a panel to a pole- or banner-screen, or pasted down on the top of a card table. With the last named it is as well to beware of needlework where the pattern is composed of representations of cards. I have seen many tables with these tops, but either the tables themselves were deliberate fakes or the needlework had been added in recent years. Card tables with original needlework top are exceedingly rare, of any kind, and for the good reason that they were used for play, and, in the eighteenth century, for very high stakes. Apart from the fact that a card-player would not care to have his attention distracted by any patterns on the top, there is the further objection that representations of actual cards could easily be used for cheating. It is something like marking a pack, in a different way.

If old needlework can be removed from a chair, a panel-frame or the top of a table, there should be indications on the back or edges which should show its age. The actual canvas on which the design is worked may also afford some evidence, as if the faker use old canvas (which he does, nearly always), it is often of a kind which has been used for some other purpose, the signs of which should be evident. As the minimum size of the stitch must be governed by the mesh of the canvas, it was usual to patch this in the places where fine work was required, as in the faces or hands of figures.

Costumes of the figures are some guide in determining the age of needlework, but only of the genuine old pieces, for obvious reasons. It is remarkable how the currency of costumes persists at the various periods. Thus, in Biblical scenes (which were very often selected) it is not uncommon to find King Solomon and the Queen of Sheba both in the costumes of the Stuart period. With loom-woven tapestries there are no such anachronisms, as a rule, but this is due to the fact that tapestry weaving was always a definite trade or profession, practically free from the amateur status of much of the needlework of the time. The latter is in much the same category as the well-known samplers which kept our great-grandmothers out of mischief—presumably.

Stump-work appears to have been a domestic art to an even greater extent than "petit-point" needlework. Here the design is padded, and helped out with pencilling or painting. Faces and hands of the miniature figures were often carved from wood, sometimes coloured, more often covered with satin and pencilled. I have seen tiny real pearls used for necklaces, and mica to imitate the glazing of windows. The miniature figures are actually clothed with removable garments, as a rule, and the costumes are generally true to the period of the work itself. Charles II stump-work is nearly always mounted on a ground of greenish cream satin, nearly always of a shade very difficult to imitate at the present day. Not only are the figures and other subjects sewn down to this satin, but the stitching is nearly always prolonged over the ground in fine tendrils and scrolls, sometimes with tiny sequins added for further effect.*

It is only natural that this delicate satin should perish with time, and it is rare to find stump-work of the seventeenth century on its original ground. If the work be removed and put down properly on new satin, not much harm is done, as this is only a reasonable restoration, but, while the main subjects can be detached, the fine scrolls and tendrils

* I have even found a design which had been worked in "petit-point" as a preliminary measure and then completely overlaid with later stump-work.

are a part of the ground itself, and can only be copied on the new satin. Very often they are left out entirely, with the result that the whole subject has a disjointed appearance. A stump panel where the satin has been glued or pasted down on its wood bed is practically ruined; it can never be restored satisfactorily.

This stump-work appears to have been made in the form of panels or pictures, very often as presents to commemorate marriages (where the happy pair figure in the centre), as coverings for small caskets or workboxes, or as decoration for mirror frames, usually in conjunction with half-round mouldings of tortoise-shell. It was also used, in conjunction with other needlework, for the ornamentation of the gauntlets of the Cavalier period. Examples of these are now exceedingly rare.

Stump-work, when found at all, may be original or restored, either well or badly, but it is practically all genuine. Modern commercial considerations, cost of labour, and lack of proper training render the faking of the work almost impossible. With "petit-point" it is quite another matter, as there are several well-equipped factories in England, to say nothing of Belgium or France. There is quite a school in the neighbourhood of Rouen, but its work is markedly French, both in design and colouring. Needlework was used extensively as furniture covering during the reigns of Louis XIV, XV and XVI, alternating in favour with the tapestries of the Beauvais, Gobelins or Aubusson factories. It was also in vogue in Holland at the same period.

The art of the needleworker is wide and varied, but it is proposed to treat of one other phase only, that of appliqué. The simplest form of this is the sewing of one material (velvet) down on another (damask), edging the pattern round with a roping of unspun floss silk, oversewn. From this to the more elaborate forms, where all other kinds of stitchery are employed, is only a progression; yet some of the elaborate headboards and testers of the important Carolean beds are marvels of skill, ingenuity and patience, especially the latter. I have illustrated one here, which begins with a board and mouldings of wood, on which is laid a covering of quilted satin, and the whole surface then worked over with the needle, in stitchery and ruching. The curtains of a bed such as this would be similarly elaborate. It is almost unnecessary to point out that objects such as this are free from the attentions of the faker. To reproduce such a bed as this (even were it otherwise possible) would cost far more than it would ever realize in any market.

The art of the needleworker appears to be extremely ancient in England, especially in the case of ecclesiastical vestments. There is a stole and maniple in Durham Cathedral which dates from the late tenth century, and with appliqués of velvet, enriched with bullion, there are many examples from the fourteenth century or before, which are known.

Bullion embroidery appears to be the earliest type of work with the needle in England. Sometimes actual gold threads were used (which have the drawback of cutting the basic material); more often the gold was spun, with an admixture of silk, into yarn. Where the actual metal has been used, it is rare to find old work which has not been restored or repaired.

"Petit-point" needlework is also fairly ancient, as an art, several examples of the sixteenth century being known. The designs usually contain figures in the costumes of the period, and the general appearance of Elizabethan needlework is that of an imitation of tapestry. The latter has a definite rib, while the former has the tent-stitch of tambour-work, so the difference is really marked. Some confusion has resulted from the attempt, in many cases, to restore tapestry with needlework. There is an example in the Victoria and Albert Museum, a cover belonging to Lord St. John of Bletsoe, which is labelled "needlework," but is really tapestry, somewhat extensively repaired with the needle. There are definite examples of English needlework carpets, where the stitchery is coarse—even beyond the limit known as "gros-point"—and this was known, in the seventeenth century, as Turkey-work, and was used for cushion coverings or the seats of oak chairs of this date. Actually the machine-made, so-called "Brussels" carpets achieve the same result, with the carpet loom and frame, as these old needlework carpets made on the tambour. The great distinction between pile-carpet weaving (apart from the warp and the weft) and needlework made on the frame is that with the carpet each strand has to be knotted, as when the loops of every stitch are cut, or "shaved," the work would fall apart. With needlework each stitch is tight round its canvas thread, and one stitch reinforces another.

To go beyond the tambour or the embroidery frame to the loom would be to enter into fabrics such as silks, damasks, brocatelles, velvets, and so on to loom tapestries. Even then, the progression to hand-made carpets would be an easy and a natural one. It is better to stop with the needle and its uses, and even then crochet and crewel-work, and many of the other branches of embroidery proper, have had to be neglected.

For the expert, it is better to devote attention to dates rather than to look for forgeries. The method having remained unchanged for four hundred years, it is difficult to detect the subtle difference between, say, Elizabethan work and that of the next two centuries, where the attempt has been made to copy the original patterns, both as regard design and colouring. The knowledge is indispensable, however, if one is not to make costly mistakes. With old appliqués on velvet there should not be the same risk, as velvets prior to the seventeenth century are unmistakable—or should be. Velvet-weaving is not only a great art, it is also a great labour, especially when the pile is both extremely tight and short, and the day has departed, more or less, when anyone will pay the price of a weaver working for a whole week to produce less than six inches of a twenty-one inch velvet. Dyeing, in these days of aniline colours, is also practically a lost art, and it is to be feared that these fugitive modern dyes are fatal to permanence in needlework wools, or with the colours of damasks and velvets. In the last resort, a chemical analysis of the threads of wool or silk may be valuable as a definite criterion of age, or, at least, of modern origin.

The needleworker at the tambour frame.

Plate number One Hundred and Thirty-seven

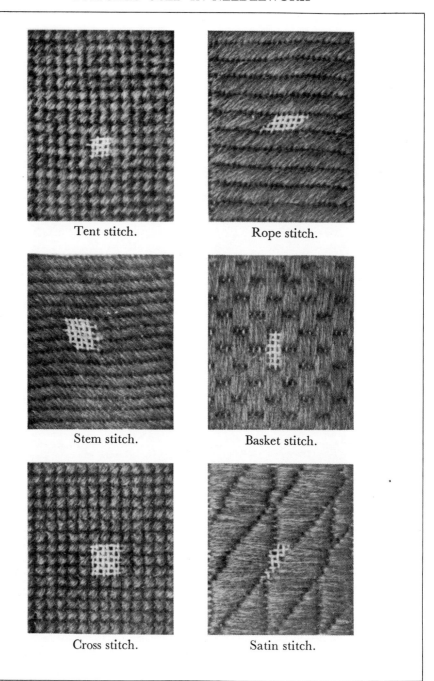

Tent stitch.

Rope stitch.

Stem stitch.

Basket stitch.

Cross stitch.

Satin stitch.

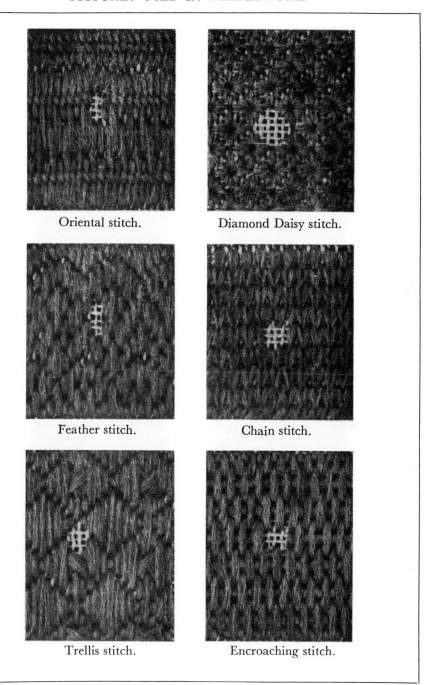

Oriental stitch. Diamond Daisy stitch.

Feather stitch. Chain stitch.

Trellis stitch. Encroaching stitch.

Plate number One Hundred and Thirty-nine

Needlework pictures of the eighteenth century. Above is a
representation of Daniel in the den of lions.

Plate number One Hundred and Forty

Two large Needlework panels of the Elizabethan period. Biblical subjects were nearly always selected for these panels.

Plate number One Hundred and Forty-one

Needlework pictures of the late seventeenth century.

Plate number One Hundred and Forty-two

One of a set of mahogany Chairs of the Lion period (*circa* 1735) covered in fine-stitch petit-point needlework of wool and silk.

Plate number One Hundred and Forty-three

Above. A gilt Settee in ruby-ground needlework.
Below. A picture by Peter Breughel copied in the central panel
of the settee.

Stump-work Mirror in tortoiseshell frame. Charles II
period. These mirrors appear to have been made as
marriage gifts as a rule.

Front and back of a Charles I work Casket.

Plate number One Hundred and Forty-six

End views of the Casket on left-hand page.

The top of the Casket on the previous pages. The work is
nearly all in long "drop-stitch."

Plate number One Hundred and Forty-eight

These Mirrors were obviously made to commemorate marriages. This can be seen from the devices. They are generally framed, externally and internally, in tortoise-shell, although walnut is sometimes used instead.

Plate number One Hundred and Forty-nine

Many of these pictures are monuments of patient industry. In these two the tiny figures are fully clothed, each garment made by the needle, no plain fabric being used anywhere. The necklaces of the ladies are real pearls.

Plate number One Hundred and Fifty

A needlework Cabinet with the work on a ground of
cream satin. Every stitch known to the needleworker is
to be found in this cabinet.

Plate number One Hundred and Fifty-one

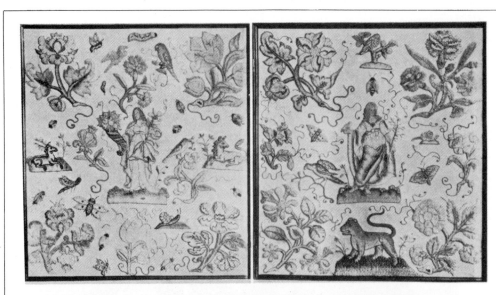

Sides and top of the Cabinet on the preceding page. On
the left is Peace with the dove and the sprig of myrtle. On
the right is Plenty with the cornucopia. On the top are the
figures of Mercy with the lamb and Justice with the scales.

Plate number One Hundred and Fifty-two

Above. The interior of the Cabinet, drawers of pollarded elm framed
with mahogany.
Below. The central panel enlarged. This is the finest possible stitch,
forty-eight to the linear inch.

Plate number One Hundred and Fifty-three

The Head-board and Tester of an elaborate bed draped entirely with needlework on a quilting of satin. Bullion thread is extensively used.

Plate number One Hundred and Fifty-four

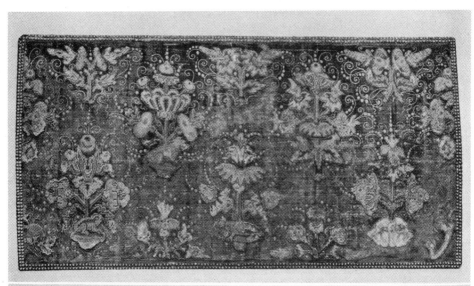

A large Coffer covered with red velvet and ornamented with needlework in appliqué.

[Plate number One Hundred and Fifty-six was not used]

CHAPTER XIV

QUEEN ANNE AND GEORGIAN WALNUT

HERE is one outstanding detail in English furniture which marks the dawn of the eighteenth century, and that is the smooth cabriole leg. Beginning, in a tentative form, some years before, and undoubtedly a detail borrowed from Dutch sources, it reaches its full perfection in the period from 1700 to 1705-8.

Very few appreciate all the factors which contribute to the making of a smooth round cabriole. The finished result owes practically nothing to an existing templet, or, rather, the lines of the original pattern are obliterated in the making of the leg itself. The shape is first drawn out, in profile, and transferred to a thin board which is cut out with the saw. This is the templet. The usual cabriole has two "ear-pieces," or brackets, which connect it to the seat framing. Invariably these are glued on, in order to economize timber, as to make these in the one piece with the leg itself would mean a square of wood at least two inches thicker than is really necessary. The timber being cross-grained at the ear-pieces, these would be exceedingly liable to fracture if cut from the solid.

The timber-square, of sufficient thickness to take the entire shape of the leg, minus these brackets, is first marked out from the templet, and then cut with the saw, in profile, *and the one way only*. To cut it the other way, and thus to produce a square-sectioned cabriole only, the pieces which fall away from the first cutting are put back again, to form a "saddle" for the second shaping, for it is impossible to cut this otherwise, as the first profile will prevent the leg from being held flat and firmly enough on the bench for the second operation. The result of both cuttings is a square-sectioned cabriole, *where the outer edges* conform to the shape of the templet. As, to round the leg, it is necessary to take away those edges everywhere, with the single exception of at the "knee," it follows that the original sketch of the leg itself, which aims at the delineating its finished form, does not agree with the templet, which sets out the profile, but with the necessary allowances for the subsequent rounding of the leg. The final result has to be achieved by the eye of the workman; there is no other guide. With the modern vertical carving machine it is possible to fashion six legs from the one pattern, at the one operation. There are six revolving cutters (something like a boring

103

"bit"), and one central dummy (with a rounded point in place of the cutting edge) which follows the lines of the pattern and acts as a guide for the cutters. By this method, no preliminary sawing is necessary; the six legs are fashioned directly from the squares of wood. These machines, however, are rare in England (they are plentiful in America), nearly every shop preferring to fashion these cabrioles in the old manner, the only concession to modern commercialism being the substitution of the power-driven band-saw for the old hand bow-saw. The subsequent fashioning, with the spokeshave, the rasp, file and glass-paper, effectually removes all indications of the saw, excepting, perhaps, on the under side of the separate brackets or ear-pieces.

The greatest skill and a discriminating eye are necessary for the making of these smooth cabrioles, as there is no mechanical guide. The initial square-cut leg is some indication of the final result, but where nearly all the edges have to be pared away, it is evident that, even with a finished model, it is easy to go wrong if the eye itself be at fault. An examination of old examples will show not only the 'prentice efforts which were made before the final perfection was attained, but also the many attempts which were devised to get round these difficulties. Thus in provincial chairs, especially those of Midland origin, the cabriole is often left in the square-cut form. In others the leg is "collared," rounded below the collar only, with the square-section left above. A good English cabriole is delightful, shapely and dignified, very different from the legs of Dutch chairs and tables, which are nearly always over-shaped—bandy in fact. The trade of the furniture maker had already become specialized enough, in the first years of the eighteenth century, for certain workmen to have concentrated on the making of cabriole legs. This stage of perfection did not appear to persist for very long, as it was found that carving could be used to hide a multitude of blemishes, and we get the decoration of knees and ear-pieces, and the claw-and-ball, paw, and leaf-covered feet, all of which, ornamental as they may be, minimize the skill required in the making of the plain smooth cabriole.

It is in this walnut period that a closer relation between the chair maker and the cabinet maker begins to become apparent. This is noticeable in the identical character of certain details in chairs, settees and stools, and in other furniture as well. Thus we have the cabriole, the plain club- or "spade"-foot, the claw-and-ball, the leaf-covered foot and the paw appearing in a somewhat definite order, both on tables and chairs, and even on wall-pieces such as cabinets and the like. The new fashion may have tended to draw the two trades closer together. With the ball-and-claw foot on chairs, settees and stools, but with no other furniture, we get the device of the eagle's head, which, perhaps, was the logical addition to the claw-and-ball. That both are attributable to Chinese sources is to be suspected, as English fashions, in the first quarter of the eighteenth century, were in a fluid state, liable to take impression from anywhere. At a somewhat later date we get the lion-mask as an adjunct to the paw foot, but more often in mahogany than in walnut furniture.

Another innovation of this walnut period, which may be said to begin from *circa* 1695, is the "drop-in" seat for chairs and settees, where the upholstery is on a separate frame, placed loosely into a rebate in the seat itself. This method, dispensing as it does with all trimmings of braid, gimp or fringe, may have been dictated by motives of economy, and was certainly introduced from Holland, where it had been in use for some time previously. It has the advantage, from our present point of view, in baring much of the construction which fixed upholstery conceals. There is such a thing as replacing simple legs on an old chair with others of a more elaborate character. I have seen this done on many occasions, and propose to refer to the subject, both in text and in illustration, in a later chapter. With the drop-in seat the junction of the leg-squares and the seat-framing can be studied from all angles, and should be of great assistance in the detection of the "improved" old chair or settee.

A word or two as to old upholstery may be of service at this stage. The webbings of the seventeenth and eighteenth century were very similar to those which the saddler uses at the present day, and for faked upholstery these old saddlers' webs are generally selected. Without possessing the tensile strength of the modern grey web, they are much stouter and more durable in use, allowing of a better fixing to the rails. On these webs a coarse hessian is fixed, then the horse-hair, and lastly the final calico and covering. The coil-springs of the present-day upholsterer were utterly unknown even in the last years of the eighteenth century. They were used, but were still a novelty, less than seventy years ago. While giving greater comfort to the sitter, they are a dubious advantage over the old method, as they have a tendency to wear the webs below and the canvas above, and to break the cords with which they are laced together, and this damage cannot be repaired other than by stripping the seat to the frame again.

I have had opportunities of examining a number of specimens of original upholstery from the last half of the eighteenth century, as there was quite a practice made, some thirty or more years ago, of having upholstered furniture from this period renewed. I have seen chairs and settees which were actually designed by the Adam brothers, and made under their supervision, taken into the shops and stripped for re-upholstery. I mention the Adam work here, to show that I am not forming a judgment on rubbish. It is a good reply to those who maintain that furniture of the eighteenth century, both in quality and workmanship was much finer than anything produced at the present day, that I found many of these Adam chairs, from notable houses, had been "filled" with tow or similar rubbish, horse-hair being used very sparingly, and nearly always of poor quality. If I had to name the age when materials were at their best (pure white curled horse-hair for the seats of chairs, for example), veneers of the finest figure, and workmanship of the highest and most painstaking kind, I should say, unhesitatingly, the early-Victorian. Yet in this era of fine production both the designs and general proportions were monstrous.

Among the many innovations of the first decade of the eighteenth century we get the hoop-back fully developed in chairs accompanied by broad veneered central splats, and also the coupling of two or more chair-backs to form a settee. One problem here appears never to have been solved in a really satisfactory manner. To join the two inner balusters of a back, two legs would appear to be necessary to prolong them to the floor, yet two legs, at about one inch apart, would look absurd, so the plan was adopted of finishing the two balusters on the back-seat rail, and centring one back leg, only, between them, which is in the nature of evading a problem rather than solving it. Later on, in the mahogany years which succeeded the walnut period, another device was adopted, of making the entire settee-back in the form of one wide chair, with outer balusters only, and multiplying the splats between them. This method interdicted the use of a central leg, either on the back or the front, and was far from satisfactory, as the seat-rail always had the appearance of sagging, or, at any rate, the liability to sag.

There are many familiar articles of furniture which do not appear to have been made at all in the years from 1700 to 1725, unless every example has disappeared since. Walnut dining-tables are unknown, side-tables are rare, and, when found, nearly always have tops of marble. Wardrobes in the same wood are exceedingly scarce, and the sideboard itself (in the modern acceptation of the term as a piece of furniture with cupboards and drawers) does not appear much before 1775. Walnut chairs of the 1700-25 period (but not later, as walnut was used alternatively with mahogany for many years after this) do not seem to have been made in sets, from which, together with the absence of the walnut dining-table, we can assume that the older Stuart furniture had not been discarded in the days of Anne and the first George for use in the dining-room.

To a student of English furniture, these gaps in types must be apparent, but that does not deter many "collectors" (especially from the United States) from asking for these unobtainable articles. At the same time it must be borne in mind that the faker has often supplied the deficiency. Sets of Queen Anne chairs, dining-tables and sideboards of walnut, and other unknown pieces, are not unknown to *him*, and one is frequently called upon for an expert opinion on such articles, where the slightest knowledge of English furniture and its development should tell the owners that no such opinion is necessary. Yet there is always the desire to possess that which no one else has, and the idea that one may unearth the unique example, which will always lead a certain type of collector into such a trap. The faker reckons on this weakness in human nature, and he is rarely far out. It is a thickly populated world, and you can usually swindle most people *once*.

It has already been stated that walnut is a wood very susceptible to the ravages of worm, and some account of this pernicious little animal may be of service. *Xestobium tesselatum*, to give him his full title, begins life as a wood-boring worm, and ends it as a winged beetle, one of the *Anobiid* species. This beetle lays its eggs in a crevice or crack in timber, selecting, if possible, a dark and unventilated spot, and the worm, as soon as it begins its life, starts to tunnel through the wood, absorbing and excreting the wood-dust resulting from the boring. Eventually it almost reaches the surface, leaving the merest skin of timber between its burrow and the outer air. Passing then through the chrysalis stage, it changes to the beetle, which hammers its way out. This is the so-called "death watch" beetle, the sound of which can be heard in many old timber houses. If the worm makes a mistake, and leave the remaining skin of wood too thick, the beetle dies in its burrow. If, on the other hand, the worm itself actually emerges, the metamorphosis to chrysalis and from thence to beetle does not take place, and the worm soon dies. *In any event, either the worm or the beetle leaves an emerging hole, never a furrow.* It follows, therefore, that any *worm channels* in a piece of furniture are evidences that the wood must have been attacked by worm before the article was made, and that a tool like the plane must have exposed the furrows. There is, of course, the remote possibility that worm-eaten wood may have been used originally, but this is not likely, for two reasons. In the first place, the ravages of the wood-worm were known in very early times and were always regarded as defects. Such timber would be rejected, in consequence, at any time when *new furniture was being made*.* Secondly, with pieces made outright, with no attempt at spurious antiquity, timber would be used from the plank or the board, opened and cut with the saw and finished with the plane. It is very rarely that the worm attacks timber in the raw state, and rot in growing trees is never the ravage of *Xestobium tesselatum*, so far as I know.

On the other hand, there is every incentive for the faker to use worm-

* Every "antique" was new once!

107

eaten wood where possible, especially for pieces intended for those to whom the presence of worm-ravage is unquestionable proof of antiquity. I have known of old beech bedstead rails used for chair frames which were riddled with worm, and, although some cutting was necessary to reduce the bulk of the timber (cutting to length did not matter very much), great care was taken to saw the wood only on the surface which was to be covered with the facings of the rails. I am speaking here of a conscientious—or, shall we say, a highly rewarded faker? He is *rara avis*, however, and with the usual run of these craftsmen, worm-eaten wood is frequently planed over and the worm channels exposed. I prefer to reject such pieces, where these furrows appear, without further examination. To kill the worm in wood is a much more difficult operation than many imagine. To attempt to reach it through a worm-hole is hopeless, as he is not at home. No liquid is volatile enough to reach it in its burrow; and to kill only a few out of many is mere waste of time. The liquids sold as "worm killers" are one and all quack remedies. During the restoration of the great roof of Westminster Hall, it was found that only a virulent poisonous gas was at all effectual, and to use this without danger a gas-mask and a "dope chamber" is necessary. It is, emphatically, not a job for the amateur.

Old upholstered walnut furniture nearly always requires to be re-covered (unless it have the original covering, which is very exceptional), either because the old fabric is in rags or the colour and design do not harmonize with the intended surroundings. It is as well to ask the upholsterer to strip the chair or settee right to the frame (if only for reasons of hygiene) and to make a careful examination of the piece in this stripped state. Note, first, if the beech or deal framing be old, and, if repaired, to what extent. This is highly important, as it is better to have a sound new frame than a rotten old one, especially if the covering fabric is to be expensive. At the same time, with a walnut easy chair, for instance, for which a high price is demanded (as it usually is), one must remember that the figure is being paid for four old legs, and more often for only two, as back legs are usually repaired, and do not amount to much anyhow. Personally, I cannot understand a large price being paid for such articles, other than for that class which must have everything old. There is a hatter's shop on the east side of St. James's Street, nearly down to Pall Mall, where the headgear of former generations is displayed in the window. Those old hats *ought* to be priceless, by the same reasoning. Perhaps they are—to the firm in question, as an advertisement!

If the front legs of our chair are of an unusually ornate description—if, in short, the price has been definitely paid for those legs—one should examine, with the greatest care, the joints where the side rails are tenoned into them. This is important, as I have often seen faked legs grafted on to an old chair, a little trick of which more will be said in a later chapter. Next, examine the legs themselves, at the cross-grain end (which the upholstery has hidden, hitherto) and on the feet where they rest on the floor. Are the latter surfaces worn, and, if so, in the right and natural way? Remember that any bruises or abrasions must be minute, as the tendency is always to polish them out by the friction of the legs on the carpet or floor.

With all walnut furniture of this period, the surfaces should be examined closely. There is a marked difference, to the expert, between original varnishing (no matter how much it may have been smoothed down by subsequent waxing and friction) and shellac-polishing. If the latter be well done (which it rarely is) the surface is too glassy, and there is no sign of that peculiar gummy appearance which is inseparable from varnishing. If the finish be the usual French polisher's "stiff shine," then the rubber streaks will be apparent. If the "dulling-brush" and pumice have been used (which leaves a multitude of minute scratches behind, the whole length or width of the surface) the piece should be viewed with great suspicion.

The fashion for marqueterie appears to have left behind it a taste for certain ornamental woods, in the walnut years. Thus, I have found thuja, amboyna, laburnum (used in the form of "oyster-pieces"), and both pollarded olive and elm, on pieces of this period. There existed a curious custom, at one time, of calling all spotted woods, especially "bird's eye" maple, by the name of "maza" or "mazer-wood," probably a corruption of the old German *masa*—a spot. The name is often used to describe pollarded olive, which has a greasy texture and rather a spotted surface, probably as a cloak to ignorance of the name of the wood itself.

Veneered walnut of the Queen Anne period is always banded with cross-cut wood, sometimes with a double "herring-bone" line between the banding and the veneer. The edge- or "cock-bead" is the usual finish to drawer fronts, and is an innovation of this date. It is curious that this striped English walnut, if veneered right over a table-top, for example, appears to be unfinished without a border of some sort, although one has not this feeling with any other wood.

Old varnished walnut has a rich brown or golden shade, in its original state, and this the faker vainly endeavours to imitate. Bleaching with acids always leaves the surface shaded (which old walnut never is), and renders the wood opaque and dirty. Also, with all carved furniture, whether of walnut or mahogany, there should be no "high lights," that is, the outstanding details should not have a scrubbed appearance. That is what the faker ironically calls an "antique" finish, possibly because no antique piece ever looks like this. Genuine old walnut may vary in shade from a brown to a pale gold, but it is *never grey*, and it is *always* transparent.

I recollect one instance which illustrates what Huxley called "the scientific use of the imagination." I had to give an opinion on a small walnut table, with cabriole legs and cut-out framing. This latter was of walnut, veneered on *pine*, and the shaping showed the edges of the white wood below. A moment's thought showed that no original maker who had the run "of the timber yard" would have framed up a walnut table in this way; whereas a faker, finding a piece of pine veneered with walnut, *and with the old surface intact*, would use it in just this manner; in short, he would be fettered by his material, whereas the original maker would be free. It is the same old question "Has the piece ever been anything else?" applied in a new manner. I have rarely found much difficulty in pointing out why a fake *is* a forgery (excepting in a court of law!), but I find it extremely difficult to get people to see for themselves, especially before they pay for one of their "bargains."

While the smooth cabriole belongs to the first years of the eighteenth century, it appears, in embryonic form, in the last decade of the seventeenth. Here are three chairs of 1695-1700, very similar in design, each with the square-sectioned cabriole as introduced from Holland in *circa* 1690.

Plate number One Hundred and Fifty-seven

The smooth cabriole marks the first years of the eighteenth century, but in these two Chairs the stretcher-
railing (here of H-form) is retained. The chair on the
left has the square-sectioned cabriole, finishing in the
"pied-de-biche," or goat's foot, of *circa* 1695; but in the
other the cabriole is rounded (a distinct advance in evolution), but both have the rounded "ear-pieces" and are
separately attached to the seat-framings.

Plate number One Hundred and Fifty-eight

The evolution of the cabriole is here illustrated in another way in these two walnut X-chairs. The X-type is copied from much earlier sources as at Knole Park, but the use of visible and finished walnut shows the eighteenth century. The chair on the *right* is interesting as it was once the property of Dr. Samuel Johnson the lexicographer, and was shown at the bi-centennial exhibition in his own house at Lichfield in 1907.

Plate number One Hundred and Fifty-nine

Left

A typical walnut hoop-back Chair with central splat and
heavy framing shaped to fit on the knee of the cabriole.
The legs have the usual escallop shell on the knees and
ball-and-claw feet.

Right

Walnut Chair of *circa* 1700. A perfect cultured example of
fine designing with very little ornamentation. The knee
of the cabriole here crests up over the seat-framing.

Plate number One Hundred and Sixty

Right

A walnut Chair of *circa* 1705, with the rounded "balloon" seat, central splat turning backwards in "paper-scrolls," and fine early cabriole legs of great vigour.

Left

The development of the broad splat, intended to show veneers of rich figure. Here the central splat is tied to the outer balusters. The finest quality of Queen Anne walnut.

Plate number One Hundred and Sixty-one

Left

The Chair on the left is of mahogany of the Lion years, *circa* 1735, but apart from elaboration, the older hoopback is retained. The later details are the eagles' heads, and especially the lion masks on the front legs.

Right

A walnut Chair of *circa* 1710 type, but having the later detail of the arms finishing in animals' heads. This chair is probably as late as the other.

Plate number One Hundred and Sixty-two

Left

A mahogany Chair of *circa* 1720 covered in red-ground floral needlework. The smooth cabriole and the plain arm is retained here.

Right

A walnut writing Chair of *circa* 1715, having the early arm finishing to the seat in an unbroken series of curves, but with the later type of front leg.

Plate number One Hundred and Sixty-three

Arm and Side Chair, mahogany, from a set of six single and two arm-chairs. While the date is as late as *circa* 1725 the earlier form is retained, but the significance of the use of the new wood, mahogany, is indicated by the absence of veneering and the use of carving on the seat rails. The arms are of the early form.

Plate number One Hundred and Sixty-four

Left

A walnut Arm-chair, parcel gilded, with tapestry seat.
The later evolution from the 1710 type into elaboration
which indicates the George I period.

Right

A fine walnut Arm-chair of *circa* 1710, but of Midland
origin. In Cheshire, Lancashire and Yorkshire, at this
date, the seat-framings of chairs were usually shaped out
and very heavily made.

Plate number One Hundred and Sixty-five

Right

A walnut Arm-chair of *circa* 1720, with the late detail of
the eagle's head used as an arm finish.

Left

A fine Arm-chair, probably made for gilding, as several
kinds of wood have been used. Here the eagle's head has
been used for the finish of the arms, and the legs are
typical eagles' claws, with the feathering carried up the
leg. *Circa* 1725.

Plate number One Hundred and Sixty-six

Right

Typical Queen Anne walnut Chair with scrolled-up cresting rail to the back, cabriole legs with knees carried up over the seat-framings, and broad central splat.

Left

A walnut Smoker's Chair with seat made for straddling instead of sitting. It has a reading desk at the back. Some of these straddling chairs were made with upholstered backs lunetted at the top for resting the chin when watching a "main" of cock-fighting.

Plate number One Hundred and Sixty-seven

A pair of walnut Hall Chairs from Lyme Park, Cheshire. Here is the smooth cabriole with plain club foot, turned cross-stretchering of legs (an early detail), and the knees are fixed under the cross-banded seat-framing instead of cresting over them. The device on the back of the one on the right is that of the Disley Ram, the device of the House of Lyme.

Plate number One Hundred and Sixty-eight

Plate number One Hundred and Sixty-nine

Side Chair and Settee (Love Seat) from an important set comprising fourteen chairs and two settees. Covered with modern fine ruby silk velvet, trimmed *galon* braid, but originally covered with home-made needlework. Satyr masks in centres of seat-framings; ball-and-claw feet.

Finest possible quality of *circa* 1730.

One of a pair of walnut Settees in the original Mortlake
tapestry. This example shows the vigorous early cabriole
of the 1705 period, finishing in the "club" or "spade"
foot. The legs are kept detached from the seat-framing,
and in the centre the knee is bifurcated.

Plate number One Hundred and Seventy-one

Plate number One Hundred and Seventy-two

Plate number One Hundred and Seventy-three

The cabriole is also to be found in the so-called "Burgomaster's" Chairs, similar to the above. Although usually regarded as of Dutch origin, it is doubtful whether they were not made in Wales and the Welsh bordering counties in the late seventeenth and early eighteenth centuries.

Plate number One Hundred and Seventy-four

Walnut Cupboard or Clothes Press, with the moulded and intricately
mitred cornice of the period.

Plate number One Hundred and Seventy-five

The type of the fall-front "Scrutoir" of the last years of the seventeenth century. Veneered with walnut of rich figure.

Plate number One Hundred and Seventy-six

Cabinet of 1700 elaborately veneered with "oyster-pieces" of walnut and laburnum.

Plate number One Hundred and Seventy-seven

Walnut Cupboard or Press of *circa* 1715-1720. The late date is indicated
by the detail of the cornice and bracket-plinth.

Walnut Bureau Bookcase of *circa* 1700. The "broken" pediment is usual at this date. Note the elaborate interior to the bureau.

Walnut Bureau Cabinet of *circa* 1700. Note the unusual ogee
cornice, the flat bevel of the silvered glass panel on the upper
door, and the inlaid lunette to the bottom drawer.

Plate number One Hundred and Eighty

Type of 1670 (very rare) on twisted-leg stand with pivot-hinged
"gate." Open and closed.

Plate number One Hundred and Eighty-one

Late seventeenth-century type, rather a secretary than a bureau. Lift-up top and fall-front. This example is veneered with pollarded elm with plinth of walnut. Concealed underneath are turned stump feet with leather bowl castors. This secretary type is also found in the cabinets and tallboy chests of drawers of the same period.

Plate number One Hundred and Eighty-two

The earliest Bureaux have the upper stage divided from
the lower either by a moulding (as in the example at the
top) or by a distinct overhang without moulding. (See
illustrations to chapter xi.) The later bureaux are always
flush sided.

Plate number One Hundred and Eighty-three

In the early years of the eighteenth century furniture was designed for utility, and many pieces serving a dual purpose were still made. The top of this Bureau is intended to support a dressing-glass as a fixture, and the central cupboard below is for shoes. The narrow drawers on either side are more useful for toilet implements than for documents or papers.

Plate number One Hundred and Eighty-four

One of the small walnut Dressing Tables with central shoe cupboard of the early eighteenth century. The central support to each pedestal is intended so that the piece will stand firmly on an uneven floor. These pieces are now rare, but are very difficult to forge for many reasons.

Plate number One Hundred and Eighty-five

Walnut Bureau on stand with cup-turned legs and wavy stretcher.
Late seventeenth-century type.

Plate number One Hundred and Eighty-six

Walnut Bureau on stand with cabriole legs. These bureaux on
separate stands mark the evolution of the bureau on plinth in the
direction of the pedestal writing table.

Plate number One Hundred and Eighty-seven

Various types of small Tables of the walnut period
from 1700 to 1725.

Various types of small Tables of the walnut period
from 1700 to 1725.

One of a pair of Card Tables (top shown at side) of walnut and laburnum inlaid with key-pattern of sycamore. Legs of this kind bridge the cabriole and the turned type. It is doubtful if these elaborate card tables were made for real play. They were probably intended as ornamental pieces of furniture serving no actual useful purpose.

Circa 1705.

Plate number One Hundred and Ninety

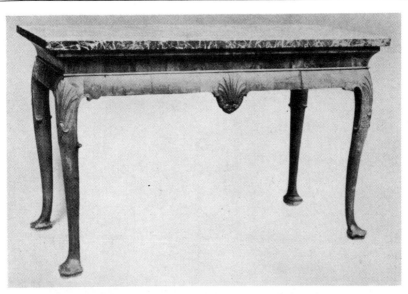

Above. Walnut Side Table with marble top.
Below. Red and gold lacquer Table.

Plate number One Hundred and Ninety-one

[Plate number One Hundred and Ninety-two was not used]

CHAPTER XV

MAHOGANY FURNITURE

IT appears to have been the custom, in all ages, for home-ward bound ships, which had failed to secure a return cargo, to ballast with timber, and, in this way, there is no doubt that mahogany from Central America had been introduced into England many years before its merits as a wood for furniture had become known.

Mahogany, *Swietenia mohagoni* of the family of *Cedrelaceæ*, appears to be native to the tropical belt, not only of America, but of Africa also. While the mahogany used throughout the eighteenth century appears to have been imported only from the West India Islands (Cuba and Hayti, the latter known also as San Domingo and Hispaniola), and, in the later years, from Honduras and Madeira (*Persea indica*), it is found also in Mauritius, Guatemala, Nicaragua and elsewhere. In the United States the Department of Forestry has collected valuable data regarding mahogany, with specimens, and there appear to be upwards of fifty definite sub-species known to the timber merchant at the present day.

Some knowledge of the different varieties of mahogany is necessary for the detection of forgeries, in fact it is one of the most powerful weapons in the armoury of the expert, as not only was the eighteenth-century timber of a very special kind, but it is one which is practically unprocurable at the present day.* The necessary study, therefore, can be undertaken in one of two ways: either to learn all the known varieties of mahogany, or to be able to recognize the wood from Hayti and Cuba beyond the possibility of error. The latter method is the easiest, but it is fraught with great dangers, as no two pieces of mahogany are ever exactly alike unless they are cut from the same log, perhaps, and even then they may vary. It requires a considerable amount of knowledge to be able to say, with precision, "That piece of furniture is later than the eighteenth century, because the wood is of a kind which was unknown at that date," yet the expert should have the necessary experience to be able to make such a statement, and with certainty.

* The reference here is rather to size and age than to any definite sub-species. The mahogany used in the eighteenth century is nearly always in very wide boards, obviously from very old trees, and jointing is rare in consequence.

The introduction of the new wood for furniture, in *circa* 1725, had the effect of greatly modifying the trades of the cabinet maker and the chair maker, both as regards designs and construction. The first mahogany to be imported was a dark heavy wood, without figure, and there was no reason for the doubtful economy of cutting it into veneers. The trade returned, therefore, to the former traditions of solid construction, and veneering presses, cauls, hammers, and sand-bags were laid aside for a while. This use of the solid wood lasted only until the finely figured mahoganies were discovered, and then veneering, or facing, was revived again.

Perhaps another reason for the return to veneering was the heavy tax which was levied on mahogany until 1747. The duty, either in the log or the plank, was £8 per ton of 2,240 lb., a formidable sum when the purchasing value of money, in those days, is remembered. It is equivalent to a present-day tax of about 10d. per square foot in the inch, or nearly the actual value of the wood as it is to-day. By an Act of George II the duty was reduced to £2 5s. 9d. per ton on mahogany imported in English ships, and £2 7s. 9d. in others where the master and more than one-fourth of the crew were foreigners. One tenth of the tax was allowed, by way of rebate, for cash payment, and a drawback of £2 2s. per ton was allowed if the timber, either in the log or made up into furniture, was re-exported within three years.

With these heavy duties it was obvious policy to import only the finest varieties of mahogany, as the tax made no distinction in this respect. The woods from the Bahamas ("Madeira wood") and Honduras were left alone as not worth the cost of transport and the duty. With a tax such as this, which must have involved Customs examination on the one hand and evasion of the duty on the other, there must have been many difficulties in the way of using the timber as ships' ballast.

This mahogany tax, in its action, arbitrarily selected the kinds of timber which were imported into England, and affords some assistance in segregating the work before and after 1750 (allowing three years for any stocks of timber, accumulated under the older conditions, to be dispersed), and a marked distinction does, in fact, exist. At the same time, there is a natural selective progression in decorative quality, due to greater knowledge and finer grading of the timber, and it is not until the era of Chippendale (1748-79) that we get the curl, the "plum-pudding," "fiddleback," "ocean-figure," and other elaborate varieties of mahogany used, as a general rule. With the earlier work, we find finely figured wood used here and there, but this must have been chosen, probably, from an entire shipment, and could not have been a staple article with the timber merchant.

Mahogany, in the natural wood, varies from a pinkish yellow to a deep brown; it is red only when it is stained with bichromate of potash. It is an ideal furniture wood, strong and durable, procurable in wide boards comparatively free from knots, shakes or sap, and, in the harder varieties, will take a good polish with waxing and friction, especially if the surface be oiled first. With the early Georgian mahogany, the usual finish appears to have been a thick coating of linseed oil, allowed to dry for several days and then rubbed with a flat cork and powdered brickdust. Later on, it appears to have been the custom to varnish the surface with copal or other varnish, but this could not have been the universal practice, as Thomas Sheraton, in his *Cabinet Dictionary* (1803), under the article "Polishing," still refers to the old oil-and-brickdust method, apparently the only one with which he was acquainted. The finish of the later mahogany furniture of the Chippendale period will be referred to again in the proper place.

The mahogany models of George I follow those of Anne, at first, the hoop-back in chairs and settees being retained. Later on, when the capabilities and limitations of the new wood came to be recognized, the flattened top rail came into vogue, but the hoop was again revived in the hands of Hepplewhite and his school. In the absence of veneers of striking figure, and the disuse of bandings (it is not until about 1780 that mahogany came to be banded again, and then only with strongly contrasting woods such as tulip, kingwood or satinwood), the former plain surfaces of the Queen Anne walnut were inadmissible, and doors were again panelled, with the styles and rails cut out in decorative shapes and moulded. Comparatively early we get two innovations: the breaking up of glass, as in bookcases or cabinet doors, by the use of latticework, and also the applied fret.

Frets are of two classes, the open and the closed. In the first the saw can enter and leave the wood without being detached from the sawframe; in the second it is necessary to pierce holes for the insertion of the saw, as each part of the pattern is complete and enclosed. The "wave-moulding" is an example of the first, the usual Chippendale fret of the second. Later on, when the possibilities of lamination had been discovered,* the fashion arose for the open-pierced frets, for pediments and the legs of small tables. These belong, however, rather to the Chippendale and the Hepplewhite periods than to the early Georgian mahogany.

As with marqueterie, frets must be cut in layers, usually four, with two waste layers to take the "rag" of the saw, and this promotes a tendency to duplicate furniture, as an alternative to throwing the over-

* A laminated fret, that one cuts from three or five layers of veneer, alternatley straight and cross-grained, is far stronger than one cut from the same thickness of solid wood.

113

plus frets away. In my early days, in workshops, it was not uncommon to see frets, in scores of bundles, hanging from the workshop walls, and for many years. This was before the era of mass-production had set in; the usual run of shops made only to order, and in small numbers, and the opportunities for using up spare frets were few. In the years from 1720 to 1750 it is doubtful if such conditions prevailed. True, there was no mass-production, but patterns were originated in the shops, and bought by their clients with little or no dictation; the same design might be made up again and again if it was popular. That some such custom did prevail we can imagine from what we know of the career of Thomas Chippendale. Commencing in London in *circa* 1748, he projected the *Gentleman and Cabinet Maker's Director* soon after, and actually published it in 1754. This was Chippendale's bid for success, to show the "Nobility and Gentry" what he could design and originate, and to popularize the "Chippendale Style," whatever the term may have implied. He did not see, at the time, that the day when the workshops originated patterns had gone by, and the proof that, in this sense, the *Director* was a failure is to be found in the fact that from his many subscribers to the book (and there are some notable names among them) there is no record of Chippendale ever making one of the patterns in the *Director* for a single one of them.* Instead, and almost to the day of his death, he worked to the designs and under the supervision of Robert Adam, or in manners utterly foreign to his own.

I have already attempted some classification of the various style phases in another book,† and cannot do better than repeat it here, thus:—

> From 1714 to 1725. Decorated Queen Anne.
>   „   1720 to 1735. The Lion period.
>   „   1730 to 1740. The Satyr-mask period.
>   „   1735 to 1750. The Cabochon-and-leaf period.

Some explanation of these sub-divisions may be necessary.

By the term "Decorated Queen Anne" I refer to the models of 1700-14, which were perpetuated, with greater elaboration, in the reign of George I. Thus the eagle's head on the arms of chairs and settees, the escallop shell on the knees of legs, and the club and the claw-and-ball foot belong to the earlier period, but, after about 1714, we get greater embellishment, the leaf-carvings of knees and feet, and the tendency to pierce the splats of chairs.

We find also the eagle's head used horizontally as a finish to arms,

---

* Chippendale claims to have made two, a chair and a dressing-table, but these are very different to the actual *Director* design.
  † *English Furniture of the Eighteenth Century*, Vol. II, chapter ii.

instead of vertically, as before, but, more often, these arms terminate in bold scrolls. There is also a marked tendency for the claw-and-ball to lose much of its earlier vigour. The earliest "Decorated Queen Anne" furniture is still in walnut, but when mahogany comes into general use certain notable modifications are observable. The most striking of these is the piercing of the splats of chairs, in patterns which simulate the interlacing of flat tapes, and these are generally more elaborate in the models where the older form of the hoop-back is retained. With the advent of the flattened top rail these piercings become more simple, the usual device being that of a vase, either in the solid or cut through.

Another modification, in chair design, is the provision of a carved rail, or "apron," between the front legs of chairs and tables, a fashion which develops until we get the preposterous "aprons" of the style incorrectly known as "Irish Chippendale," so called, perhaps, because the furniture is earlier than Chippendale and has nothing to do with Ireland, beyond being discovered, sometimes, in the huge houses of the older "absentee landlords," palaces which were used as lumber-rooms for unfashionable pieces discarded from the English mansions when they were refurnished.

It is a prevailing notion that the history of English furniture can be resolved into a number of periods and fashions, and that no single manner was ever revived at a later date. Unfortunately, I have proved this to be incorrect, over and over again. I have seen much of this "Decorated Queen Anne" furniture (apart from deliberate fakes, which are plentiful enough) which I was convinced was the reproduction of far later years, even of the nineteenth century. I based my conclusions on the timber, the design, the workmanship, and the evidences of the use of tools which were unknown in *circa* 1720. To write a book on English furniture and its development, one is compelled to systematize or classify (or one should be), but we can carry these classifications too far. Yet there is no other method available. It is as well to bear in mind, therefore, that when the possibility of the fake has been eliminated there still remains the question of the late copy or essay in the same manner, which has to be considered.

The "Lion period" is where the heads of lions are used as arm terminals or for the knees of cabriole legs, usually in conjunction with the lion's paw for the feet. Of late years this lion furniture (which belongs to the mahogany rather than to the walnut years, although I have found it in both woods) has become fairly plentiful, but thirty years ago it was exceedingly rare. There were several notable collectors of it between 1905 and 1914, and examples became very numerous and progressively impudent. I have seen original walnut or mahogany chairs where the simple front legs have been cut off just under the seat rails, and "lion" legs dowelled on, with little or no attempt at concealment. A practical chair maker would have laughed at them, but they sold— and became the "ornaments" of more noted collections than one. Another well-known device was to take a bold cabriole and to cut a lion-mask in the wood, but the projection was rarely sufficient, with the result that the lion looked as if it had been in a prize-fight—and had not emerged the victor! Beware of these flattened lion masks! Made in the original instance, there was no more need to have skimped the wood in this fashion than to have cut a cabriole leg from a square not thick enough to contain the shape. There was one of these defeated lions in the Shrager Collection, where a certain well-known expert (since deceased), who endorsed it, took refuge in the statement that it was Irish, as if everything bad must have come out of Ireland. Certainly, Irish humour is not bad, but with that the expert must have been unacquainted.

If the "lion" furniture be rare, that with the "satyr-mask" decoration is rarer still. The device appears to have been reserved for important pieces, such as large tables, and it is obviously inspired from the French or the German Renaissance, probably the latter, as a concession to the presumed taste of the first, or second, king of the House of Hanover. That neither cared for much beyond fat women is by the way.

The "cabochon-and-leaf" furniture carries us into the Chippendale period, if not beyond it. Here the device, used principally for the knees of cabriole legs, and, rarely, as the junction between arms and their balusters, is that of an uncut jewel surrounded with leaves and scrolls. The fashion begins about 1735, but I have found it in furniture as late as 1765, and it is usually regarded as typical of the Chippendale style. Unfortunately, the general idea of "Chippendale" has no connection either with the work or the published designs of Thomas Chippendale himself.

Dealers often use the expression "I do not like it," and, if the man have some knowledge and good experience, I always respect that as a genuine opinion. Beginning with some old basis (as all good fakes do), the material, or its absence, always fetters and circumscribes the faker. Many of these forgeries, or "beautified" originals, are photographically evident. I have attempted to demonstrate some of them here, in the accompanying pages to this chapter.

The study of timber varieties is not only desirable to the expert, it is indispensable. The first difficulty in making a collection of different species of mahogany, for example, is that the various pieces may include no examples of wood used in the eighteenth century at all; in fact, it is highly probable that they will not. One can hardly expect to buy authentic old pieces of furniture of this period to break up into pieces to add to this timber collection, but it is still possible to accumulate specimens from "wrecks" and by other means. Thus, the spare leaves of 1790-1800 dining-tables can still be bought cheaply, and if a section, say of 12 inches by 12 inches, be cut out, *and one half only scraped to the wood*, one will have an instructive example both of the actual timber and its contemporary finish. Similarly, the seat rebates of the "drop-in" chairs are not varnished or waxed, as a rule, on the inner faces, and one can examine the wood there in its natural state. The insides of wardrobe doors of 1760-90 are often left without surfacing, and there are the inside faces of solid, i.e. unveneered or unfaced, drawers which can all be studied. The scraping and re-surfacing of old mahogany pieces, which was the general custom less than forty years ago, was an act of utter vandalism, but it had its compensating value, so far as the older school of cabinet makers was concerned; these men had every facility for examining the bare wood, stripped of its overlying varnish, wax and dirt. Such opportunities, however, are gone, and, it is to be hoped, for ever. It is still possible, nevertheless, to learn the various kinds of mahogany used in the eighteenth century, if one embarks on such a study as a deliberate pursuit. When one has qualified sufficiently to be able to recognize these mahoganies from Hayti, Cuba and the Bahamas, then one has to begin with the same woods in the finished state, covered with oil, varnish, wax and accumulated dust and dirt. It may be a long study, but it is necessary. After all, it is not to be compared, in intricacy, with the account which Mark Twain gives of the necessary education of a Mississippi pilot, who was expected to know the configurations of both banks of that great river, the position of every sand-bank and "snag" (all of which were changing every week or so), and by night as well as by day. It is amazing what one can learn if one tries hard enough. It is only to the dilettante that every molehill of difficulty becomes a mountain.

Chairs from a set (for one of the settees see the illustrations to chapter XIII) in gesso and gilt, covered with ruby ground petit-point needlework in tapestry stitch. Typical example of George II period.

Plate number One Hundred and Ninety-three

The development away from the hoop-back in the early Georgian years.

The development away from the hoop-back. The identical splats in
the two chairs above show that the hoop-back and the flattened top
rail were used at the same period, *circa* 1730.

The strong similarity between these two chairs shows that design-influences were still localized in *circa* 1725. The chair on the left is in a small country church, where it has been for many years. Other genuine examples have been found which match this arm-chair exactly. The type is one which is often forged, but never with great success.

Plate number One Hundred and Ninety-six

Right

The development from the hoop-back. This type is known as a "bell- splatted" Chair, and must have been very fashionable.

Left

A "cock-fighting" Chair. The sitter straddled the seat and, embracing the back, rested his chin in the lunette while watching a "main" of cock-fighting. Mahogany, parcel gilt, and original needlework.

Plate number One Hundred and Ninety-seven

Left

A corner Chair in mahogany of the 1740 period. These corner chairs are almost unknown in walnut, and only began to be plentiful after 1730. They remained in vogue up to 1775 or later.

Right

An original Castor showing the leather "bowl" or wheel in four sections. The "brass-bowl" castor does not appear before about 1770.

Plate number One Hundred and Ninety-eight

Mahogany Chairs of the 1745 period. Needlework remained the fashionable covering for rich chairs until about 1780, and on large sets the designs differed with each chair. The knees of the cabriole legs here illustrate the device of the "cabochon-and-leaf," one borrowed from French sources, but extensively used in England from 1735 to 1770. It is incorrect to call this detail "Chippendale," as it is of earlier origin than the date when Thomas Chippendale commenced business in London.

Plate number One Hundred and Ninety-nine

Mahogany Chairs, Stools and Settees from a remarkable set formerly at Newhales, the property of the Marquis of Dalrymple. The tapestry coverings are in original unrestored state. It is impossible to attribute this set to any known maker. It is certainly prior to Chippendale, and

while of the finest quality, it may be of local make, possibly
the work of an Edinburgh craftsman. It has all the
appearance of Scotch work. The colourings of the tapestry
are brilliant, yet very refined. This is, perhaps, the finest
and largest complete set of furniture in existence.

Plate number Two Hundred and One

Two walnut Chairs of the mahogany years. On this, and the following pages, chairs have been illustrated in as orderly a progression of development as possible. The first change is the substitution of the flattened top rail for the older hoop-back. The second is the piercing of the central splats, at first in vertical lines, but gradually evolving towards an elaborate interlacing, something like a pattern made with a ribbon. With the advent of Thomas Chippendale in *circa* 1748, and the publication of the *Director* in 1754, this development stops. See next chapter for the succeeding progression.

Plate number Two Hundred and Two

Plate number Two Hundred and Three

Plate number Two Hundred and Four

The coupling of two or more chair-backs to form a settee begins in the early walnut period, probably as early as 1690. There is another development, illustrated on the next page, where, within the one top rail and pair of balusters, several splats are fixed. The Settee above is in mahogany and is a late use of the older hoop-back.

Plate number Two Hundred and Five

Two examples of the use of several splats in the one pair of outside balusters.

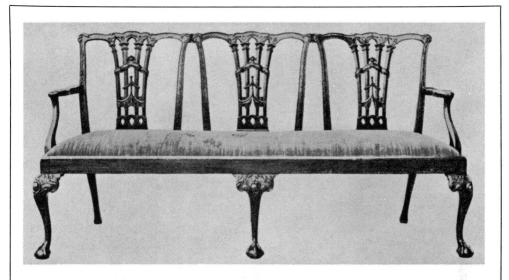

Two Settees in the so-called "Gothic" manner of the Chippendale school. The one below is exceptional, being in rosewood. It is curious to notice how the problem of the placing of the central legs, at the front and the back, has been differently solved in these two settees, and in neither with complete success.

Plate number Two Hundred and Eight

The introduction of the Lion mask as a decoration of furniture begins with George I, and may have been a tribute to the first of the House of Hanover, as the lion head was used, to a considerable extent, in German furniture. It begins with the walnut furniture, as in the settee above, where the Queen Anne hoop-backs and central veneered splats are retained, but the style really develops in the later mahogany years.

Plate number Two Hundred and Nine

The Lion decoration was also used in combination with gesso and gilding. The table and stool above were formerly a part of a large set, since dispersed. A settee from the set found its way to the Metropolitan Museum in New York, where the gesso and gilding promptly fell off, owing to American steam-heating conditions.

Plate number Two Hundred and Ten

A mahogany Chair showing the great projection of the lion heads.
This is always found in genuine examples.

Plate number Two Hundred and Eleven

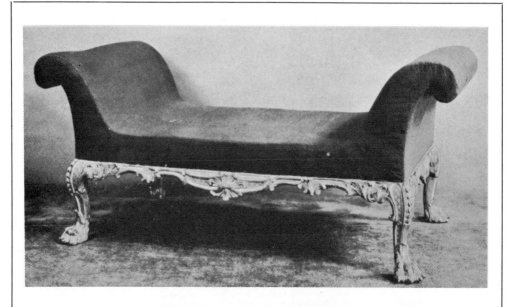

Plate number Two Hundred and Twelve

Mahogany Bergère Chair of the Lion period. The legs are bold in projection, with heavy carved "aprons" between.

Plate number Two Hundred and Thirteen

Plate number Two Hundred and Fourteen

Plate number Two Hundred and Fifteen

Plate number Two Hundred and Sixteen

The last phase of the Bureau on Stand in the mahogany years. These small bureaux (this one is only twenty-six inches wide) are very valuable and are, therefore, often made up from old parts. The stands should be examined first as they are the really valuable details in these pieces. The upper stage may have been cut down from an old bureau.

Plate number Two Hundred and Seventeen

Plate number Two Hundred and Eighteen

Plate number Two Hundred and Nineteen

Right

A very rare mahogany Powder Table. The type of the George II furniture which carries on the traditions of the later walnut years. The last development here is the scrolled foot.

Left

A mahogany Bottle Tray on cabriole stand. These occasional pieces are rare and valuable, and their forgery is seldom attempted, but all the same they should be carefully examined.

Plate number Two Hundred and Twenty

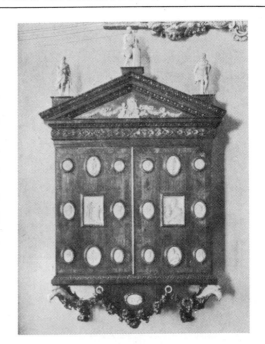

Right

An interesting mahogany hanging Cabinet with ivory figures and plaques. Said to have been made for Horace Walpole. It is in the architectural classical manner of the middle eighteenth century.

Left

A fine mahogany hanging Cabinet made to contain small articles. The details have been carefully studied everywhere, and the execution is of the finest quality.

Plate number Two Hundred and Twenty-one

Two examples of pre-Chippendale mahogany Bureau Cabinets with many details in common, some of which, such as the feet, have been borrowed from the chairmaker. The

carved akroter on the one on the left is of a type often found on Philadelphia furniture in the late eighteenth century, but it is rare on English pieces.

Plate number Two Hundred and Twenty-two

Two views (open and closed) of a mahogany secretaire tallboy Chest in the Philadelphia manner of the late eighteenth century, especially in the design of the pediment with its akroter.

These secretaire tallboys (they are never of the bureau or slant-front kind) show that the bedroom was still an important apartment at the date when they were made. Their elaborate character shows this.

Plate number Two Hundred and Twenty-three

Plate number Two Hundred and Twenty-four

CHAPTER XVI

THE WORK OF THE CHIPPENDALE SCHOOL

WITH the life and work of Thomas Chippendale this book has little concern. Those who are interested in the subject can be referred to other books;* it is proposed here to deal with the work of the Chippendale school.

I have coined the name, in default of a better, to describe those makers (many of whom are unknown) who flourished—or otherwise—in the years from 1745 to 1780. I am not referring to the authors or compilers of design books, as we have no evidence to show that men like Manwaring ever made furniture. He may have made a good deal, but we have no knowledge of any authenticated pieces. Similarly with Ince and Mayhew, who issued *A System of Household Furniture* in *circa* 1763; it was not until the year 1929 that I happened on a bookcase bearing their label. The piece and its label are illustrated here.

On the other hand, there are certain known makers, such as William France, whose furniture productions have been traced and identified, but who issued no design books or trade catalogues (which may be the better description of many of these "Directors," "Systems," "Companions" and "Darlings").

The study of English furniture has never been regarded seriously, in the scientific spirit, as it were, and the capacity for sifting and weighing evidences appears to have been totally lacking with many writers. The subject is really far more involved than one would imagine. The fact that a book was published, in which designs of furniture were illustrated, is no more proof that the author—or the one whose name figures on the title-page (which is not always the same thing)—was an actual maker than the present-day catalogue of a firm such as Maple can be regarded as evidence that the late Sir Blundell Maple was either a designer or a cabinet maker. In fact, he was neither. It is so easy, in compiling a list of the eighteenth-century makers, to take the names from these books, Chippendale, Copeland, Crunden, Darly, Hepplewhite, Ince and Mayhew, Johnson, Batty Langley, Adam, Lock, Manwaring, Milton, Overton, Paine, Pastorini, Pergolesi, Richardson,

---

* *Thomas Chippendale: His Life, Work and Influence.* Oliver Brackett. *English Furniture of the Eighteenth Century*, Vol. II. Herbert Cescinsky.

Shearer, Sheraton, Wallis and others, and to assume, without further evidence, that they were all cabinet makers. As a matter of fact, some were architects, others artists, and a third class only designers, with little or no practical experience of woodwork.

There is another pitfall, in this sifting of evidence, which should be mentioned here, the relation of documents to the pieces themselves. I recollect one notable example of this. There are records, in the Admiralty Office in London, of a clock presented to the Board by Queen Anne, made by the famous maker, Thomas Tompion. There is a long-case clock with the signature of Tompion on the dial, and a brass plate, affixed to the case, with the words engraved on it, "Presented by Queen Anne." Apart from the obvious fact that a royal gift to the Admiralty would hardly be acknowledged in this scanty fashion, the signature is a forgery, and the clock is by Eardley Norton, a maker separated from Tompion by nearly a century. Similarly, if one find a mention in an inventory of a certain piece of furniture, and one exists which corresponds, roughly, to the description, that, in itself, is no evidence that it is the actual piece. The original may have disappeared and its place been taken by another. I have found this quite frequently. Once any historical furniture has passed through an auction-room, the greatest care is necessary in its subsequent identification. I have known, on more than one occasion, of a genuine piece, bought at auction, which has been copied, and then sold as the original under the cloak of the catalogue description and provenance. Nor are all these substitutions the result of a deliberate deception. An idle tale of one generation may become the gospel of the next. I know one highly respectable family in the West Country, and in the house is a broken portion of what looks like an old soap-bowl of the kind used by barbers long ago. It is of maple wood, and as only a portion exists, the silver rim has disappeared. It may have been a "mazer-bowl," as the term is generally used in a very loose sense. I was assured by the family, however, that it was a portion of the original Holy Grail, and they told me they had the assurance of the great Richard Wagner himself on this point. They had absolutely no evidence as to whether Wagner had ever been in the house or had ever seen the fragment, and, in any case, to be the author and composer of *Parsifal* does not imply, necessarily, a profound archæological knowledge or a personal acquaintance with the Holy Grail; yet on no further evidence than this idle tale the fragment was accepted as genuine, and I was regarded a Philistine for daring to doubt it. It is still shown to visitors as the Holy Grail, so far as I can gather.

The next problem offered for solution is, what constitutes the Chippendale style? Is it the actual work of Chippendale himself, furniture made after his published designs, or the collective work of what is known here as the Chippendale school? Also, in any event, is the style simple or compound, and, if the latter, to what extent?

If the sum total of the designs in the *Director* be taken as the criterion of the Chippendale style, then we must also include many from Ince and Mayhew's *System*, and others. Of these designs very few indeed were ever actually executed in wood, and then only with serious modifications, which suggests that Chippendale himself was not the maker, as these modified pieces, if made by him, would be tantamount to a confession that his designs were impractical, in which event he would have been on the horns of a dilemma; on the one hand, he would have had to acknowledge that he, a practical cabinet maker, published impractical designs, or, on the other, that he was not the author of the designs at all.

If we take the known and authenticated work of Thomas Chippendale, as at Nostell Priory or Harewood House (the latter not as fully authenticated as one might have wished), none of this is in the *Director* manner. The bedroom furniture made for David Garrick, now in the Victoria and Albert Museum, is also not in the "Chippendale style." As a matter of fact, it is known that Chippendale worked largely to the designs, and under the supervision, of Robert Adam, therefore we must dismiss actual Chippendale work as being "Chippendale" in the style-sense used here. Those pieces which are usually regarded as "Chippendale" bear little or no relation to either the *Director* patterns or the work of the man himself. They are the collective productions of a certain school of cabinet makers, and they may date from as early as 1745 (three years, at least, before Chippendale came to London from Yorkshire) and as late as 1780 (one year after the great cabinet maker's death). They differ, widely, in many respects; that is only to be expected over such a period, and with little or no trade cohesion, but they have certain points in common, and keeping for the moment to the somewhat rough-and-ready title of "Chippendale," we can divide the style under several headings; these are:

(1) The cabriole style, which is a natural development from the earlier mahogany models, with many of their details still retained.

(2) The Gothic (often a bald travesty of the English national style of the fifteenth century, and earlier) and the Fretted.

(3) The Chinese manner, which is another variation of the Fretted.

(4) The plain square leg, on chairs, tables and the like, which is another development of the Fretted.

(5) The French, which is an Anglicized version of the Louis XV.

(6) The Tripod furniture, which is a definite innovation of the Chippendale school, both in design and in principle, as a three-legged table will stand firmly on an uneven floor.

Having thus classified the Chippendale style under these six headings, it must not be concluded that they are comprehensive; many examples can be found, such as the interlaced "Manwaring" backs in chairs, which conform to none. In a general sense, merely, can the furniture of this period be thus sectionalized, and then only as a working basis.

Those whose business it is to design furniture, in the manner of this period, will recognize the definite thread which runs through it all, especially in carving details. There must have existed some strong design-tradition, at the time, as it is not unusual to find, for example, identical backs on two chairs, one with carved cabriole, the other with plain square legs. As a matter of fact, the Chippendale manner (if one can call it by that name, as it has nothing to do with Chippendale himself) is much more widespread than this. We find it, as an ornamental design-style, not only in the furniture books of Ince, Darly, Copeland and others, but also in other fields widely separated from furniture. Staffordshire pottery—of the transfer kind—was frequently ornamented with "Chippendale" patterns, and tradesmen's cards of the time are often in the same style.* A manner borrowed from such artists abroad as Blondel and Meissonier, it became very general in England. It must not be imagined that it originated with Chippendale and spread to others; in reality, it is an engraving and not a furniture style at all, and it cannot be employed by the wood-carver without drastic modifications. At a somewhat later date Robert Adam used a similar unconstructional manner with his composition and carving ornaments, where he had to seek the aid of wire cores to give stability to his swags, festoons, and pendants.

The Chippendale school used the finer figured mahoganies, especially the curls, very extensively, and as veneers had still to be cut by hand, they are often found as thick as one-eighth of an inch; more in the nature of facings than true veneers.

As chair makers they were unrivalled. A chair designer knows that the problem of a successful pattern only really commences when his sketch and full-size drawing have been made. There is the problem of the double shaping, which distorts lines, to be considered, and this becomes even more serious with the work of the Hepplewhite school, where the shield and the oval are used for the backs of chairs. At the same time, there was a definite progression towards economy in manu-

* See Ambrose Heal, *London Tradesmen's Cards of the Eighteenth Century*, Plates XCI, XCII, XCIII, XCVII, XCIX, C, and CI.

facture. The layman cannot understand that there is more work in a simple hoop-back walnut chair of Queen Anne pattern, with veneered splat and "balloon" seat, than in a full-blown Chippendale "ribbon-back." Veneering, in itself, necessitates complicated construction, and the Chippendale workman used solid mahogany wherever possible.

In the estimation of the quality of this eighteenth-century furniture, both as regards design and workmanship, one must not forget that nearly all of it has undergone a double selective process. First, there is the ordinary wear in use, which would, after many years, tend to weed out the badly made pieces. Secondly, during the long period of neglect, practically throughout the whole of the Victorian era, when even the finest was regarded askance as something hopelessly out of fashion, only the really outstanding examples would be likely to be preserved. Any judgment of the furniture of a country, over a given period of time, must—or should—include both the good and the bad. That of the Chippendale period contains examples of both. One thing must be said in its favour. Labour was too poorly paid in the eighteenth century to make deliberate scamping of work a commercial economy. The bad pieces suffer rather from lack of tradition and design rather than from poor workmanship. So long as a country has an enforced system of apprenticeship, its artistic handicrafts do not readily fall below a certain level. It is only when apprenticeship (which implies, or should imply, a certain measure of training) falls into disuse, when a lad begins his trade in a more or less haphazard fashion, that there is real danger of decay.

This Chippendale furniture varies from the very simple to the extremely ornate, and one must remember that it is a paying commercial proposition to carve up pieces of the plainer kind. That such practices have been general, in the last twenty years, is suggested by the present-day scarcity of these simple models; they have been adorned with gorgeous plumage since. Take a plain chest-of-drawers, with serpentine front, top with a moulding of good section, a simple cut-out plinth, and with the drawers edged with cock beads. A serpentine-fronted chest must have splayed angles, as a necessary result of the shape. Such a piece, with drawer interiors of quarter-sawn oak, may be worth from £28 to £40, no more. Now carve the top moulding, apply frets to the rails, some carving to the splay sides, and yet more to the cut-out plinth, and it is promoted to the dignity of a commode, and may be enhanced in price (if not in value) ten times. If the handles are unduly elaborate, other than on a piece where the ornament is an integral part of the design and could not be added, suspicion should be aroused. I know that original brass handles were ruthlessly scrapped in the Victorian period and replaced with knobs, but if there are signs of old handles (holes where the bolts have gone through the drawer fronts, and the marks of the securing nuts) one should ask the question, why the present handles—which must be replacements—should be so ornate? If the piece has been "beautified" in this respect, there is every possibility that it has been also in others. Of course, if the plain chest-of-drawers price be asked, there is not much harm in any event, but if the figure demanded be of commode size, then it is as well not to be too trusting. It should be borne in mind that a really fine piece should have an equally fine pedigree; elaborate Chippendale furniture was never made for the cottage. If a source be stated, this should be investigated, and one should keep an eye, all the time, on the possibility of a copy of an original kept in the background.

I am especially sceptical of chairs with square legs and stretchers where the former are carved in the manner of frets and the latter pierced through in the same manner. I have rarely found one specimen in a hundred which would bear examination with a powerful glass. People have, and always have had, a habit of resting their feet on the under-rails of chairs. Why should these be weakened by open fret cutting, which, at the best, is ornament in the wrong place?

Tripod tables are especially selected by the faker for attention. Thirty years ago the plain varieties of these could be bought by the truck-load. They would hardly have been used for firewood, yet where are they to-day? During the same period the numbers of elaborately carved tripods have increased enormously. Where have these come from? To say that the simple tables have been thrown out, *and have disappeared*, and that the ornate ones have been carefully concealed, waiting for a boom, demands a credulity and a faith which I, for one, do not possess.

One should beware of the chair which has been "restored." What is implied by this term? If the additions (other than legitimate repairs) add materially to the appearance and value of the chair, then one must suspect that "improvement" is the word which should be employed. Stripping and re-surfacing may disguise many faults and additions; there is no reason why a Chippendale chair-frame should ever be thus stripped at all.

Unfortunately, any generalities on the subject of faking must be inaccurate just because they *are* general. To say that the faker *usually* does this or that must be incorrect. He does nothing in the way of "improvement" which is *usual* at all. He finds an old piece which permits of definite embellishment, but he may never find another which admits of "improvement" in just the same way. He is conditioned, all the time, by the old base on which he works. To write of faking in all its branches, therefore, would be to describe and illustrate every piece which has been "beautified" since faking began, and that is obviously impossible, in this or in any other book. Even if the necessary data were available, a whole library would not contain it.

Two views of a mahogany so-called "Architect's" Table. These pieces were made as reading and drawing tables, probably for wealthy amateurs. They are far too elaborate and costly for professional use.

A rare and interesting "four-way" pedestal Writing Table. Each pedestal contains, alternately, drawers or a cupboard.

Plate number Two Hundred and Twenty-five

A mahogany Table of exceptionally large size, with centre
made to lift on struts to support heavy volumes.

This Table is double-sided and the pedestals have wide
drawers back and front.

Two views of a Writing Table in the style of Adam or Hepplewhite, with curious hinged flaps made to cover in the whole table when not in use.

These two Cabinets (shown here with the secretaire
drawers open and closed), although not identical in

Plate number Two Hundred and Twenty-eight

design, are obviously from the same hand. The workmanship and details are excessively minute.

Plate number Two Hundred and Twenty-nine

Side view.

Above. View of upper stage with doors.
Below. Side view of open stage.

Plate number Two Hundred and Thirty

Detail of Stand. In the frieze of each stage is a shallow drawer.

Plate number *Two Hundred and Thirty-one*

These Tables, intended for trinkets, are usually known as "silver tables." Two examples show the detail of the triple-cluster column, where the joining together of the three spindles results in greater strength than the fragile appearance of the legs would suggest.

Plate number Two Hundred and Thirty-two

Right

The Wardrobe as realised by a practical craftsman from one half of the design in Chippendale's *Director* of 1763.

Below

Plate 104 from the 1763 edition of Chippendale's *Director*. A comparison between the left-hand half and the wardrobe above will show the modifications made by the craftsman.

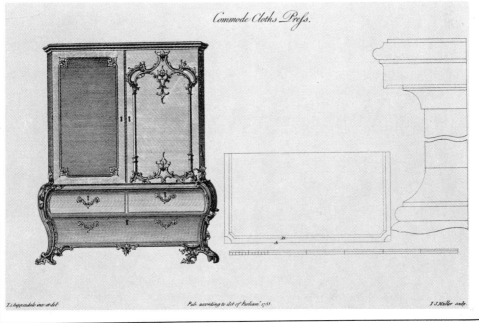

Commode Cloths Press.

Plate number Two Hundred and Thirty-three

A set of twelve Chairs (six with arms and open fretted backs, six
without arms and with solid upholstered backs) covered with

original petit-point needlework. Details shown to larger size to
show the carving details.

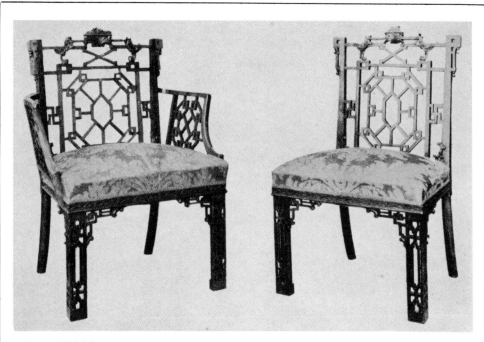

Above. Arm and single Chairs in the fretted Chinese manner of the
Chippendale school.
Below. Arm and single Chairs and Stool from an important set.

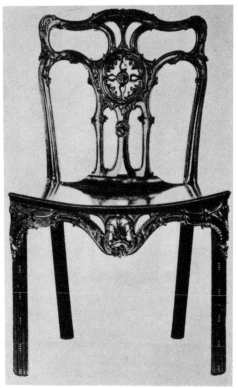

Above. Rare examples of Chippendale Side Chairs.
Below. Leather-covered Library Chairs trimmed with brass-headed nails.

Above. Examples of ladder backs.
Below. Square leg Arm-chairs of simple type.

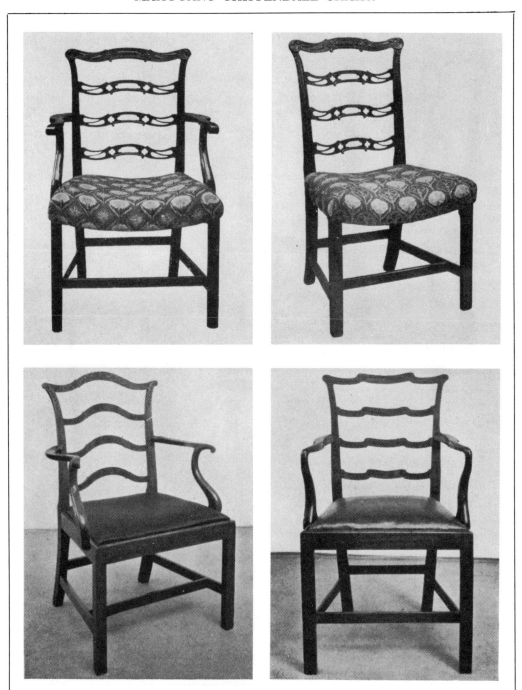

Examples of ladder-back Chairs with open and solid "rungs."

Plate number Two Hundred and Thirty-nine

The two examples on this page illustrate the so-called "Gothic" manner of the Chippendale school. While the designs have little or nothing in common with the true Gothic style, they are fine in proportion and detail, and the carving, in these "Gothic" chairs, is

nearly always of high quality, combined with the use of hard and heavy Cuba mahogany of the kind usually known as "Spanish." Chairs of this type are valuable and offer an inducement to the faker. They should be carefully examined, therefore.

Plate number Two Hundred and Forty

Chairs of this kind are generally fine in proportion and detail,
although the timber is often not of the best.

Plate number Two Hundred and Forty-two

Plate number Two Hundred and Forty-three

This Table was made by William France for Kenwood, the Hampstead mansion of the Earl of Mansfield, Lord Chief Justice of England and premier Earl of Scotland.

William France was a competitor of Thomas Chippendale, and on one occasion acted as the guarantor of the latter for an advance of money made by Lord Mansfield.

Plate number Two Hundred and Forty-five

Plate number Two Hundred and Forty-six

Plate number Two Hundred and Forty-seven

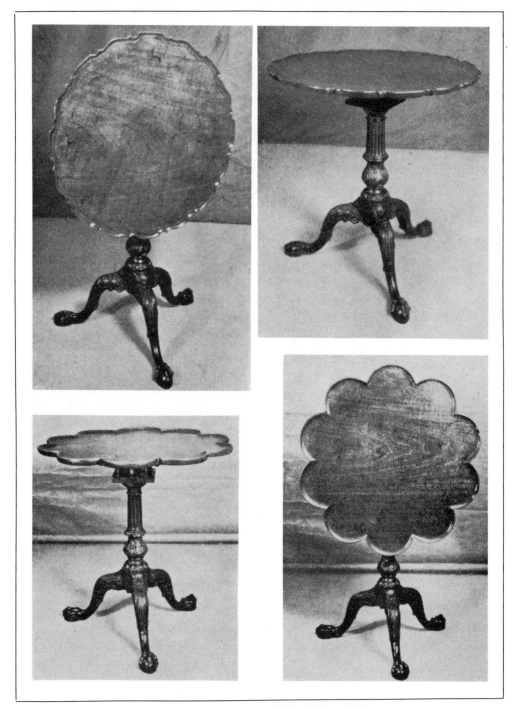

Plate number Two Hundred and Forty-eight

Plate number Two Hundred and Forty-nine

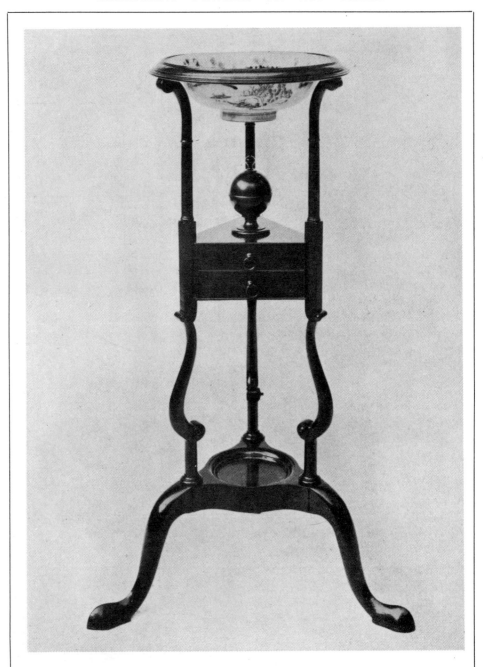

These Tripod Stands were made to support bowls to contain hair powder. They were usually kept in the small "powdering closets" which one finds in the older Georgian houses.

Plate number Two Hundred and Fifty

CHAPTER XVII

FURNITURE OF THE HEPPLEWHITE SCHOOL

F the history of George Hepplewhite of Cripplegate in the City of London we know very little. He died in 1786, and it was not until two years later that the *Cabinet Maker and Upholsterer's Guide* was published by "A. Hepplewhite & Co.," the initial being that of his widow, Alice. Whether the man or the firm originated the style which we know as "Hepplewhite" matters very little here. There is one notable distinction, however, between the *Guide* and the *Director* of Chippendale. The designs in the former are uniformly practical, which is much more than can be said for those in the latter. That the *Guide* patterns were not original to Hepplewhite, at the time when the book was first published in 1788, we know from the preface, where the fact is acknowledged. The references here, therefore, are to the work of a school rather than the creations of a man.

In *English Furniture from Gothic to Sheraton* (published in the United States) I have attempted a classification of the Hepplewhite styles, which it may be convenient to repeat here.

(1) The work showing the influence of Robert Adam, which may be conveniently designated as "Adam-Hepplewhite."
(2) Models borrowed from the Louis XV, which may be called "Curved or Cabriole Hepplewhite."
(3) Those taken from the Louis XVII, the "Turned-leg Hepplewhite."
(4) The "Taper-leg Hepplewhite," which is, perhaps, the most original and representative work of the school.

In the case of chairs, further classification is possible, thus:

(1) The bridge-pieces which overlap with the Chippendale, of which the ladder-back chairs are examples.
(2) The serpentine top-rail, sweeping down to the outer balusters of the back in unbroken lines, only one remove from the Chippendale.
(3) The hoop-back, almost a revival of the earlier Queen Anne or the early mahogany period.
(4) The shield-back in its various forms.

(5) The oval-back, sometimes found in conjunction with the French cabriole.

(6) The pear-shaped or cartouche-back, nearly always borrowed from the French, with little, if any, modification.

(7) The interlacing, heart-shaped back, usually in conjunction with the tapered leg with moulded toe.

(8) Variations on two or more of the above.

To avoid the confusion so usual in dealing with the chair designs of Hepplewhite and Sheraton, it may be as well to state here that none of the above forms are characteristic of Sheraton's style, which is quite distinct. An oval or a shield-back chair is never Sheraton.*

Hepplewhite's wall furniture, bookcases, cabinets and the like, is generally simple in outline, with ornamentation added, instead of being an integral part of the design.

In his plainer models he follows very closely in the wake of the Chippendale school. The Hepplewhite style or styles were adopted as standards by other firms, such as Seddon, Sons & Shackleton of Aldersgate Street, or Gillow of Lancaster, shops of importance, but as they published no *Directors* or *Guides* their names have fallen into obscurity. Gillows, at least, were making Hepplewhite pieces from 1790 onwards until the middle of the nineteenth century, and, after the long interval of time, it is only possible to segregate their work from that of the eighteenth-century London style by certain small mannerisms—one can hardly call them provincialisms, as Gillows were established in London in 1790. Throughout the entire history of English furniture it is possible to separate the work of the Midland Counties, especially Yorkshire and Lancashire, by reason of certain definite crudities of line or proportion. Scotch work is similarly unmistakable. With both it appears that "prettiness" was a deadly sin, to be avoided at all costs.

Hepplewhite wall furniture, possessing, as it does, merely extraneous ornament, as distinct from that of Chippendale, where the carving is often an integral part of the design, lends itself readily to "improvement." With Chippendale, the embellishment was always by carving or fretwork,† but with Hepplewhite we have, in addition, inlay, and, in other woods than mahogany (such as satinwood or sycamore), painting, and solid and parcel-gilding.

To veneer and inlay a representative piece of Chippendale would be a glaring imposture, but it is quite easy to take, say, a plain mahogany Pembroke table and to overlay it with marqueterie. Nor do the inlaid

*I am aware that Sheraton illustrated two shield-backs in his *Drawing Book*, but, as designs, they are failures.

† We know that Chippendale made inlaid pieces, but we are dealing here with the representative work of a school, not the individual work of a man.

designs of the period offer anything like the same difficulties as with the earlier scrolled marqueterie of William III and Anne. Hepplewhite marqueterie is always made up from detached units, medallions, pateræ, festoons, scrolls or swags of flowers, and engraving was also practised, to minimize the work of the cutter. There is one important guide in detecting original eighteenth-century work, that is, in the satinwood with which so many of the pieces were veneered. The East India *Chloroxylon Swietenia,* a native of India and Ceylon, was always used. It is a lemon-coloured wood, comparatively free from figure, other than a faint longitudinal striping. West India satinwood, *Ferolia Guianensis,* a native of Guiana, is more of a golden yellow, and with a close rich figure. It does not appear to have been imported until 1800, but it may have been known, in England, at an earlier date, as I have found it, *used in decorative panels only,* on true Hepplewhite pieces, of mahogany and East India satinwood. On the other hand, I have never known of a single piece completely veneered with the wood. If known at all, it could only have been used in small pieces.

The late Lord Leverhulme—who, considering the enormous amount of furniture which he bought (he had three or four great houses simply packed with pieces), seemed to have had a positive genius for buying fakes—had a pair of cabinets veneered with this West India satinwood. When they were on exhibition, at the sale in New York in 1926, a practical cabinet maker, and one whose opinion was of the highest value, condemned them as later work on this point alone, and when they were carefully examined we found a maker's name on the locks who was not in existence before 1835, and comparatively modern hinges and screws. With much of this so-called Hepplewhite furniture, it is the later copy of which one has to beware, rather than the modern fake.

When improvements, which materially affect the value of pieces, can be effected at no more cost than the sticking on of carved pateræ, the carving of a few flutes, or the adding of a "swan-necked" pediment, the temptation to thus improve must be very strong. In the parlance of the trade it is "easy money." Later veneering with satinwood is difficult, as the original plan, with a table top, for example, was to glue up pine in narrow strips to minimize shrinkage, and to face with moulded mahogany at the edges, before laying the veneer. The faker who takes a piece and veneers it has to lay his veneer on a bed of solid mahogany; he has no other alternative. To turn the table upside down and examine the under side of the top is always advisable, therefore, and satinwood laid on mahogany, without any facing or clamping, is always highly suspicious.

With painting, especially where decorated medallions, flowers, swags, etc., are added, it is possible to produce the most genuine crackled appearance in one of two ways. The surface will craze badly if it be shellac-polished before the paint has dried hard, but this will make gaping cracks which do not look genuine at all. The better method is to apply the last coat of paint with a quick-drying medium (turpentine with a little mixing varnish will do), and then to coat it over, before it has thoroughly dried, with a thick coating of starch. This, drying almost at once, imprisons the paint below and prevents it from shrinking as it sets, with the result that it crazes instead. It is possible, with practice, to produce quite decorative effects by this crackling process, which appear to be "utterly genuine" by the way. If a panel of, say, four feet by three feet be taken, and the last coat of paint be stippled from the edges towards the centre, and if a very quick-drying medium be used, the crackle will be pronounced in the centre (where the paint was applied last) and fade away to nothing at the edges. The nearer the paint is to absolute hardening before the starch is applied the smaller will be the crackle. The yellow lacquer cabinet from the Shrager Collection, which I have illustrated in the chapter on "Lacquer," was crazed in this manner. That is why it fogged at least one "expert" in that case completely; it looked so genuine.

The oval- and shield-back chairs of the Hepplewhite school are, perhaps, the most beautiful models which English furniture can show, *when they are fine*. It is very difficult to design either properly, as an oval or a shield, if correctly drawn, will distort badly if bent concave, as nearly all these chair-backs are. To obviate this, it is necessary to distort the design, so that when bent it will look right, and that is by no means so easy as it appears. The only satisfactory way is to make a concave model and then to draw the outline afterwards. Other proportions are just as important. Half an inch, more or less, in either the height or the width, in one of the Hepplewhite backs, will make all the difference in the world. If the man who makes a cabriole leg has to rely on his eye for the final shaping, still more has the chair maker to do so when he fashions a shield or an oval back. The easy way is, of course, to omit the concave shaping, but a flat shield or oval looks bad in itself. If a fine model be difficult to make, it is just as difficult to copy. The proof of this is in the fact that, even in the 1780-90 years, with all the trade traditions which the trade must have possessed at this period, really perfect Hepplewhite chairs are remarkably rare.

The old makers nearly always used beech for their seat-framings, and models intended for painting or solid gilding were often made of the same wood throughout. The modern chair maker nearly always uses birch instead. Seat-frame braces of the eighteenth century are generally of the open kind, the solid ogee-brace being a later innovation. It is rare, however, to find these original open braces intact, other than on important chairs of a kind which would have been well preserved at all times. The open brace is not as strong as the closed one, the latter permitting of being well screwed, in both directions, to the framings.

Hepplewhite furniture is more varied than that of Chippendale. Thus both the sideboard and the dining-table are familiar pieces with the former, but practically unknown with the latter. In addition, we find many varieties of the writing-table, such as the kidney-shaped and the shutter- or tambour-fronted, and such articles as "harlequin" tables, where a concealed nest of drawers rises when a spring-catch is released. Both four-post bedsteads and tray-wardrobes begin to multiply, although they are not unknown to the Chippendale school. It may have been possible that Hepplewhite, or the firm that bore his name, or the trade which adopted his manner, were lucky enough to strike a period of refurnishing among the "Nobility and Gentry"; certainly the Hepplewhite manner became very popular, judging only from the examples which have persisted to our day, and that is more than can be said for the *Director* manner of Thomas Chippendale.

The shield-back Chairs of the Hepplewhite school vary enormously in proportion and quality of detail, and, consequently, in value. Anything short of the finest should be rejected by the discriminating collector. Above is an enlarged detail of a shield-back where the execution of the carving is of high quality.

Plate number Two Hundred and Fifty-one

Plate number Two Hundred and Fifty-two

Plate number Two Hundred and Fifty-three

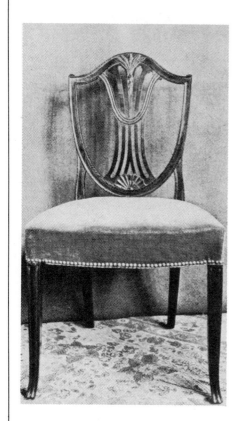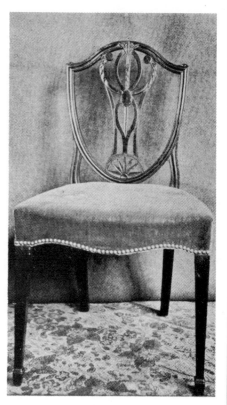

These Hepplewhite Chairs appear to have been made both for dining- and sitting-room use. When in mahogany they are generally carved, sometimes inlaid, and occasionally both. Those intended for the dining-room were made in sets, often of large size, as upwards of twenty-four have been found of the one pattern and consecutively numbered under the seat-rails.

Plate number Two Hundred and Fifty-four

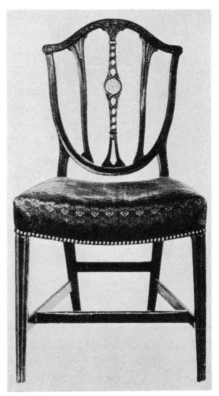

The shield-back Chairs on this page appear to have been made for drawing-room use, and when made in sets a settee and a pair of window-seats were generally included. While usually in mahogany, they were sometimes made in beech intended for painting in colours and parcel gilding. Occasionally the seats were caned, with loose squab cushions.

Chairs of the types shown above were often made in satinwood as well as mahogany.

Dining-room Chairs were often dipped in the seat. In the two examples below will be noted the overlapping between the manners of Hepplewhite and Chippendale.

[Plate number Two Hundred and Fifty-eight was not used]

CHAPTER XVIII

FURNITURE OF THE SHERATON SCHOOL

THOMAS SHERATON, native of Stockton-on-Tees in County Durham, is the last of these eighteenth-century designers who published books. He was already somewhat advanced in years when he made his pilgrimage to London in 1790, the fatal year of the French Revolution. He could hardly have chosen a worse time in which to make his great adventure. How much Chippendale, Hepplewhite and their schools had owed to the patronage of the brothers Adam it is difficult to estimate, but it must have been considerable, yet in two years Robert Adam was to die, and within four the great practice of the "Adelphi" was to be wound up and to cease. With the guillotine busy, commencing with the heads of a king and a queen, and from thence to those of the aristocracy, old and young, male and female, with the streets of London thronged with refugees bringing tales of horror from Paris, with the sound of the tumbrils almost in the ears of the English populace, especially those of wealth and station (in this respect the aristocracy have notoriously sharper ears than the democracy), it was hardly the time to preach the gospel of a new style, as Sheraton found to his cost. Nor had he much in his favour, personally. In his fortieth year, a man with only his trade behind him (and he *was* a practical cabinet maker), burdened with a wife and a small daughter (blessings become burdens under the stress of poverty), with the rancorous and narrow disposition of a Narrow Baptist, with no capital and no experiences of London and its ways (especially of the "Nobility and Gentry," who, in any event, had their minds occupied with far more urgent matters than the furnishing of their homes, and who were in considerable doubt as to whether they would have any homes at all, for long), it would have been a miracle had Sheraton succeeded, and miracles did not happen in the eighteenth century, or at any other time.

Sheraton's book, *The Cabinet Maker and Upholsterer's Drawing Book*, is significant in its title. Here we have no *Director* or *Guide*, simply a *Drawing Book*, and Sheraton imagined that he could vault into the position of a renowned teacher of drawing to the furniture trade of his time. If the trade wanted anything at all, other than patronage (which must have been lacking somewhat in 1790), they required new designs.

131

Sheraton, in his book (which was issued in parts in 1791), gave them treatises on perspective, the Five Orders, and drawing in general, but of new designs very few. The *Drawing Book* must have been more or less complete before he left Stockton-on-Tees, advanced enough to procure five hundred and twenty-two subscribers, many of which must have been gathered on the road south, and we can guess that the journey must have been made largely on foot, with many stoppages. Certainly post-chaises, or even stage-coaches, must have been utterly beyond Sheraton's means.

Sheraton soon found, in London, that the book as projected was a bad selling proposition. The original parts of the first edition ranged over the years from 1791 to 1794, and contained one hundred and eleven plates and text. A second followed in 1793 (thereby overlapping the first) with one hundred and nineteen plates, and a third in 1802 with one hundred and twenty-two. The additions were by way of an "Appendix" and an "Accompaniment," and were larger than the number of plates indicated, as some of the original matter of the first edition was curtailed.

Sheraton was principally a designer in London (if we except the writing of scriptural tracts and some occasional street-corner preaching); he certainly made no furniture, as we have no record of his possessing even the most modest workshop at his London addresses, at 41 Davies Street, Grosvenor Square, in 1793; at 106 Wardour Street, Soho, in 1795; and, lastly, at 8 Broad Street, Golden Square. Those collectors, therefore, who seek for actual Sheraton furniture will search in vain. There is one record of Sheraton's activities as a designer, which I only discovered four years ago. When the Leverhulme Collection was sold in New York, in 1926, it contained a piano, made by Broadwood for Don Manuel de Godoy, Prince of the Peace, and presented by him to the Queen of Spain. The case was of satinwood, banded with mahogany and inset with Wedgwood medallions. Accompanying it was a coloured drawing, the right-hand corner partly torn away but the name ". . . eraton, Inv: et del:" could be seen. The sketch was dated 1796. I had no doubt, at the time when I had the opportunity of examining the drawing, that it was from Sheraton's own hand. It may have represented an important commission at the time, to one in Sheraton's circumstances.

Hepplewhite's *Guide* had also passed through three editions, in 1788, 1789 and 1794, so the last must have overlapped with the *Drawing Book*. There is every evidence to show that Sheraton must have been well acquainted with the earlier editions, as he not only helped himself very freely, but also made some sarcastic remarks about Hepplewhite in his Preface. That is only natural, perhaps, at least I have found it so. In many respects, however, and especially with chairs, Sheraton did break new ground, and, within the limits of the rectangular back, he showed an amazing fertility in invention. He illustrated two designs only of shield-backs, neither of which compare with those of Hepplewhite, and, in any case, are in a totally different manner.

Sheraton's chairs have had a great popularity with the trade, judging by the number which one finds at the present day. They are both refined and decorative, and have the advantage of being much cheaper to make than most of the Hepplewhite patterns. Sheraton is also the only one of his date to revert to the old Stuart principle of constructing a chair with the top rail of the back tenoned *between* the outer balusters, in the early Restoration manner. There is no single pattern, from Queen Anne to Hepplewhite, which I have seen, where this principle of construction is observed; to Sheraton alone belongs the credit for its revival.

There is very little, if any, distinction between the wall furniture of Sheraton or Hepplewhite. Both probably took the current patterns of the trade and embellished them in various ways. It is impossible, for example, to state whether a wardrobe or a bookcase is from the one school or the other. Both are alike in one respect. It is possible to find pieces of furniture which have actually been copied from the respective books, and with practically no modification, and the same cannot be said of Chippendale and his *Director*.

Forgeries of Sheraton pieces are rare, for the simple reason that it rarely pays to make them; the price which the originals fetch is not high enough. At the same time, later copies of the nineteenth century are plentiful. Gillow of Lancaster, the Seddons, Edwards & Roberts, Wright & Mansfield, Jackson & Graham, Johnson & Jeans, and Cooper & Holt, of Bunhill Row, all specialized in "Sheraton" until about 1880, when the trade again became depraved by the "Domestic Gothic" of Eastlake and the "Early English" of Talbert, with a few other style-atrocities thrown in. These were still the days of the "hand shop," where the "Cabinet Makers' London Book of Prices" governed and piece-work was the rule, so the distinctions between the original Sheraton of 1790-1800 and the copies of 1840-1880 are often very fine indeed, and cannot be explained in a book. I have often been told that one cannot succeed in the antique trade if one knows too much, or is too particular. Perhaps this is true, with Sheraton furniture at least. After all, many of these 1880 copies are very antique by now.

133

The manner of Thomas Sheraton has been usually regarded as peculiarly his own, yet above is a silver Candelabra by Septimus Cresswell, which is typically Sheraton, yet is dated 1771, twenty years before Sheraton came to London.

Plate number Two Hundred and Fifty-nine

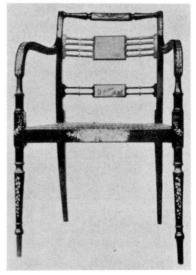

With the chair designs of the Sheraton school we have a reversion to original type of plain solid construction, without torturing of timber.

These Chairs are graceful and charming and far less expensive than those of Hepplewhite.

Plate number Two Hundred and Sixty

It is characteristic of Sheraton's Chairs that the workmanship is all on the surface without any costly single or double shaping of the wood.

Plate number Two Hundred and Sixty-one

Settees, such as the three above, were usually made to match arm
and single chairs to form a suite.

Plate number Two Hundred and Sixty-two

CHAPTER XIX

ENGLISH WALL MIRRORS

THERE are no articles, in the whole category of antique English furniture, which are forged so frequently as wall mirrors. For the expert, therefore, the subject is one of considerable importance, and must be considered in detail.

It may be as well to begin with some attempt at classification, as the remarks which follow do not apply to all alike. Before proceeding to do so, however, a few words as to the mirrors themselves, that is, as distinct from their frames, may be advisable.

Mirrors of polished metal or silvered glass have always been highly esteemed from very early times. They were regarded as prized possessions for three reasons. In the first place there is no substitute for a reflecting mirror; secondly, a silvered glass (which is the most efficient form) was very costly in the seventeenth and eighteenth centuries (and that which is very expensive is always highly prized, in fact, the thing may cost a good deal of money just because it *is* esteemed); and, thirdly, the possession of a costly thing implies wealth in the owner, and the next best thing to being actually wealthy is to have that appearance.

Small mirrors, chiefly from Venice, seem to have been imported into England early in the seventeenth century, but the manufacture of silvered glass had become an industry in this country in the reign of William III, as heavy duties were imposed in 1695, repealed in 1698 at the instigation of the Duke of Buckingham (who was largely interested in the Foxhall or Vauxhall factory), reimposed in 1745, and, finally, abolished by Sir Robert Peel a century later.

Apart from these duties, plates of any size were very expensive to make, and were generally imperfect. The old silvering was by the mercury process, where quicksilver was "floated" on the back of the glass, adhering only by its cohesion with a perfect surface. Quicksilver, being very heavy, would be liable to fall off if the glass had any irregularities (and old glass is rarely perfect), and this would leave the mirror either fogged or spotted after a while. Added to this, the mercury being on the back, any discoloration of the glass would be noticeable on the front, and eighteenth-century glass nearly always has an unmistakable bluish tinge. At the present day the silvering of mirrors is done by the "patent" process, where silver-foil is used in place of mercury. A good test for an old mirror, even if it has been re-silvered, and by the "patent" method, is to hold a sheet of white paper up to it and observe the reflection. The blue tint of the old glass will be noticeable at once. The mercury process is still done at the present day, principally for the faker, as patent silvered glass would deceive no one with the slightest knowledge.

Some idea of the cost of glass, in large sheets, may be gathered from the bills of Chippendale. Thus, in 1769, he supplies to the Earl of Mansfield, Lord Chief Justice of England and premier Earl of Scotland, two large mirrors for Kenwood at Hampstead, with "French Plates," 74 inches by 44 inches, at £69 10s. each, but the two carved frames are only priced at £16. Money at that date had a far greater purchasing power than at the present day (probably more than four times), but apart from this the disparity between the cost of the glass and the frames is remarkable enough.

Mirror frames of the seventeenth century are usually small in size, and correspond, in style, with the plain walnut, marqueterie, and lacquer furniture of the same dates. In addition, there are two other classes, those where the frame itself is of glass, etched and coloured from behind, and others where needlework, "petit-point," stump-work or bead-work is used, framed either with wood or tortoise- or turtle-shell. The usual section of the mouldings which enclose the glass is a bold, but flattened, quarter-round.

From 1700 to 1715 we get a particular type, in walnut, but afterwards perpetuated in the mahogany period, where the moulding of the frame is of small section, with a carved and gilt ogee on the inner edges, the whole moulding being planted on a flat board, cut out, on the edges, in various patterns, and enriched with carved and gilded ornaments. The usual cresting at the top was a gilt eagle with outspread wings.

The early Georgian mirror is sometimes of walnut or mahogany, parcel gilt, but, more often, gilded entirely, with the flat surfaces sanded. Usually of architectural type, with "key corners," the pediments are generally of scrolled form with central akroter, or of the closed "portico" kind. At the present day the former are more in demand, and, in consequence, have the greater value.

At a slightly later date, and from thence throughout the whole of the eighteenth century, we find the convex mirrors, with enrichments sometimes of carving, more often of wired composition and always gilt; occasionally, but rarely, with a black circular band next to the glass. The distorting effect of these glasses is peculiar, but decorative.

From 1750 to 1775 the rococo "Chippendale" mirror becomes paramount, either made to hang on a wall and ornamented at top and bottom or of the pier-glass kind, with a flat bottom-rail made to stand on a mantelshelf or the top of a pier-table. Then Robert Adam sets the fashion for his Romanesque designs, from 1760 onwards, and his classical patterns finally submerge those of the Chippendale school, and persist almost to the end of the century. The last phase of all includes the rectangular frames, with cluster-columns at the sides, small ball-cornices, and often with painted scenes in the friezes or in separate panels above the mirror itself. These are, properly speaking, over-mantels rather than mirror frames, and they originate in the Sheraton period, *circa* 1790, and persist well into the nineteenth century.

As so many of these old frames are gilt, a few words as to gilding processes may be necessary. Two methods are employed: oil- and water-gilding. The former is used for outdoor work or when the gilding is exposed to damp and weather, as moisture will perish or remove water-gilding. This should be remembered, as to clean old water-gilding with soap and water is *not* the correct method.

With oil-gilding the gold is put on a coating of gold size (which is a quick-drying varnish); with the water process it is placed direct on the preparation, brushed over first with water. With both, however, there is the same underlying preparation, and this varies considerably according to the nature of the article itself.

Preparations are coatings of whiting and size, in the later applications with an admixture of coloured lead. Details intended to be burnished, with the agate burnisher, are finished, under the gilt, with a lead coating known as "blue burnish," but this is never found in old work, where the underlying coat is either red or yellow.

Gilders' size is usually prepared by boiling parchment shavings, straining the liquid afterwards to get rid of impurities and solids. Much of the success of the work depends on the purity of the size. This parchment size, mixed with powdered London whiting (which is finely triturated chalk purified by elutriation), forms a paste which is brushed directly on the carving or the composition, and soon dries. The surface produced is soft, and admits of cutting up, into finer detail, with pointed sticks dipped into water. With modern gilding the carving is generally finished, and the preparation applied thinly, but in the old work much of the fine detail was actually put in by the gilder, in a thick coating of the preparation. It follows, therefore, that to strip many of these old carved frames to the wood for re-gilding is to remove this finish of detail, and the result is disastrous. With composition (*carton-pierre*) this does not apply, as the ornament (of whiting, resin and glue) has a casting face when it comes out of the boxwood mould, and this cannot be improved by "re-carving" in the whiting preparation.

The old carving was generally prepared in three operations, of white, yellow and red respectively. With modern work a fourth coating, of the blue burnish, is added on the parts which are to be burnished with agate tools.

Taking our subdivisions in their order, it should not be difficult to detect a modern, or faked, plain walnut quarter-round-section frame, purporting to be of the Queen Anne period. The wood is always cross-banded, and on this cross-cut walnut it is practically impossible to produce anything which resembles an old surface. An example which shows signs of scrubbing, or "high-lighting," should be suspected at once. The wood back to the glass should also offer some indication, *not on its surface, but in the way it is cut at the edges*. Old glass is difficult to detect, as the mercury process is still used for fakes, applied on glass with an uneven back, which fogs and spots very soon. The old bevels are also closely imitated. They differ from the modern in being very flat (almost as if they had been moulded with the glass instead of being ground with the sand-wheel), with an almost imperceptible line of demarcation between the bevel and the face of the glass itself. On the other hand, very few old glasses have survived, and new plates (provided they are made in the old manner) do not seriously detract from the value of an old frame.

Marqueterie mirrors, especially where the inlay has been applied on an old frame, offer many difficulties to the expert, as the surface available for examination is usually very small. *It is the marqueterie which has to be inspected*, as if this be genuine the rest of the frame matters very little. On the other hand, if the frame itself be old, beyond question, that is no guarantee that the marqueterie itself is not later, as a genuine old marqueterie mirror is far more valuable than a corresponding one of plain walnut. Much the same applies in the case of lacquer, with one distinction; it is almost impossible to imitate the old surface of *fine* lacquer, and inferior work should have very little value to the collector, in any event. Rubbish, in any art-craft, can be faked quite easily, as there is no possible standard for judgment.

With the frames of glass, coloured and etched from behind, the colours themselves, the design and its execution, are the only criteria, and to judge by these alone demands a degree of taste as well as of knowledge. These original "Muranese" mirrors (as they are called) are exceedingly rare, and always of the highest quality. The glass itself was of such value, at the time when they were made, that it was only commercial common sense to employ the finest artists. To have done otherwise would have been akin to making a rough casting in solid gold, and then leaving it without chasing.

The mirror frames of the Chippendale school are remarkable more for the vigour of the cutting than for the logical character of their designs. It is so easy to forget that wood has its limitations as well as its possibilities, and this the Chippendale carvers appear to have utterly ignored. Working in a style which is essentially that of an ornamental designer, rather than of a woodworker, it is amazing to note how they circumvented the inherent drawbacks of the material in which they worked. Unfortunately for our present purpose, not only is the present-day carver just as clever, but the style also, as far as mirrors and frames are concerned, has never lost its popularity, even in the days when other Chippendale furniture was regarded as second-hand rubbish. Once the design principles of the style are properly appreciated, and granted a state when the same motives are used continuously from 1750 right down to the present day, any attempt at dating examples of the various periods must be one of enormous difficulty, largely a matter of intelligent guesswork. To explain the subtle differences between a Chippendale frame of 1760 and of 1860, where both have been gilded, and where the time has been sufficient for the gold to tone properly, is impossible in a book such as this—or in any other.

Modern water-gilding is toned in various ways, the more usual, and the best, being to brush over the gold with Vandyke brown and umber in turpentine, wiping off the colour afterwards on the exposed places. This gives the gold the metallic appearance of the old work. In the eighteenth century, instead of using the gold-leaf thicker (which would have been impossible in practice), it was not uncommon, with the best work, to doubly and even trebly gild it. The final finish, after the burnishing of the high-lights was completed, was to brush over the gold with a transparent parchment size, to act as a preservative coating. The ageing of sized gold has a very different appearance to that of the metal when it is left bare.

Needlework and stump-work mirrors have been left to the last, as there is very little to be said about them. Costs of labour preclude the faking of stump-work, and modern "petit-point," with aniline-dyed wools, cannot be mistaken for the old vegetable dyes, by anyone with an eye for colour, even apart from the mellowing action of time. There is one caution, however, which may be necessary. It was a usual practice, at one time, to "restore" these stump-work mirror-frames by sticking down the satin to the wood beneath. A frame treated in this way is ruined, as it can never be properly restored again. It is the essence of the art of the stump-worker that his work requires periodical attention with the needle, and this is impossible where the satin back is glued down. There are fakes, and ruined antiques, and the second is worth rather less than the first as a rule.

Mirror Frame of walnut
inlaid with floral marqueterie.

Mirror Frame of walnut
with elaborate pierced pediment.

These late seventeenth-century Mirrors are nearly always
of small size, as glass was not only very costly at this date,
but the greatest difficulty seems to have been experienced
in the making of large sheets. Where the glass has a
shaped top, it is usually made in two sections, butted
together with a bevel, to minimise any loss in breakage.

Plate number Two Hundred and Sixty-three

Late seventeenth-century glass-framed bevelled Mirrors. The fashion for a central plate of silvered glass inner-framed with glass sections pieced together appears to have originated from Murano, but was copied in the Duke of Buckingham's Vauxhall or "Foxhall" factory at Lambeth. In the illustration on the right the glass frame is etched and gilt from the back. The outside framings and the pediments in both are of carved gilt wood.

Plate number Two Hundred and Sixty-four

I

2

(1) A large Mirror Frame in the walnut manner of 1705, but here decorated with black and gold lacquer. The pediment is flat, pierced and decorated in the same style.

(2) A type of Mirror which remained in fashion for many years, where the pediment is a flat veneered board cut out in various shapes. The glass is in two sections, the upper one brilliant-cut on the sand wheel.

Plate number Two Hundred and Sixty-five

1　　　　　　　　　　　　　2

(1) A type of Frame, usually veneered with English walnut with gilded enrichments, which was also very popular and the vogue for which extended to the mahogany years. Frames of this pattern were generally made in pairs, and are very valuable.

(2) A fine type of Frame of the George I period in walnut and gold. This is a furniture-maker's frame as distinct from others which appear to have been the product of a distinct trade.

Plate number Two Hundred and Sixty-six

I   2

Two designs of Frames, one fully gilt, the other in walnut
and gold. Both were made in pairs. The constructional
method is the same in both, the glass inset in a solid
board with the mouldings and enrichment applied. No. 2
is of a type found also in mahogany, and became very
fashionable in Philadelphia in *circa* 1750.

Plate number Two Hundred and Sixty-seven

It is generally supposed that the surmounting eagle, as in both examples on this page, was a device which originated in America on the eastern seaboard, but the eagle's head and claw (the claw-and-

ball) was a defined motif in English furniture in the reign of Anne, that is, earlier in date than any known American furniture in mahogany.

Plate number Two Hundred and Sixty-eight

Plate number Two Hundred and Sixty-nine

Plate number Two Hundred and Seventy

Plate number *Two Hundred and Seventy-one*

Plate number Two Hundred and Seventy-two

Plate number Two Hundred and Seventy-three

Two designs for Mirror Frames reproduced from the
original drawings, now in the Metropolitan Museum,
New York, made for the *Director*. As designs for execution
in wood, both are impossible.

Plate number Two Hundred and Seventy-four

A comparison between these flamboyant Mirror Frames, as actually made, with the designs in Chippendale's *Director* (see opposite page) and other books such as those of Ince and Mayhew, Lock Copeland and others, is interesting in showing how the published designs had to be modified for execution in wood. This inevitably suggests

that the designers (as distinct from the makers) were not practical craftsmen, and we know, from the original *Director* drawings now in the Metropolitan Museum, that Chippendale was not the actual designer of many of the plates in his book.

Plate number Two Hundred and Seventy-five

Above is a typical example of a Mirror Frame designed by Robert Adam, where the use of composition, reinforced on wire cores, is a logical necessity. It is an instance of a designer working with no knowledge of the possibilities and the limitations of his material.

Plate number Two Hundred and Seventy-six

CHAPTER XX

LONG-CASE AND BRACKET CLOCKS

S this book has been written with the idea of supplementing and reinforcing, rather than duplicating, others already published, it is not proposed to enter into a technical description of long-case and bracket clocks, highly desirable as such information may be. Those who are interested can be referred to another book,* where the whole subject is dealt with *in extenso*. There is no space here for recapitulation.

The intention in the following pages is to show how these old clocks can be forged, altered or vandalized, or, in any other manner, rendered undesirable for the collector. The fine period—that is, where specimens may be said to possess more than a mere furnishing value—extends from 1675 to 1800, but with certain large reservations. The following is a list of the points which make a clock worthy of the attention of a discriminating collector.

(1) The dial should be signed by a good and recorded maker.
(2) Both movement and case should be original, plus reasonable restoration or replacements; it should neither be vandalized nor "improved."
(3) The clock itself should be a good specimen of its period.
(4) It should possess some unusual features.

Clocks of all periods can be roughly divided into two classes, good and bad. At all times depraved examples appear to have been made which, while they belong to their date (in other words, are not imitations or fakes), yet possess no more than a mere furnishing value, or as timekeepers.

I have not included timekeeping qualities in this list (although these have a definite application, as we shall see later), because when we say that a long-case clock keeps good time all that we really mean is that the pendulum is adjusted to the correct length, and the movement is clean and properly lubricated, nothing more. When we come to clocks of precision, those with dead-beat escapements or mercury pendulums, for example, they come under the heading of possessing unusual features.

* *English Domestic Clocks*, by Herbert Cescinsky and Malcolm R. Webster.

A word or two as to timekeeping, although this does not concern us here very greatly. When we are told that a clock "keeps beautiful time" what is really meant, as a rule, is that it keeps good *average* time. A clock may be exactly right at, say, nine o'clock in the morning and the same time at night, yet may have varied considerably in the hours between. Variation is a question of temperature, which affects the actual length of the pendulum and thus causes the clock to lose or gain as the case may be. This inaccuracy may counterbalance itself, in twelve or twenty-four hours, but a precision clock is one which varies only fractionally in the same period. No clock ever made keeps *exact* time; it either gains or loses, but this is immaterial so long as it does the one or the other, and not *both*. A clockmaker of the old school will have a fine regulator clock in his shop, and he will tell you he knows its "rate." If you ask him the time, he will look at the dial and tell you to a second, but the time he will give you will *not be the one which the hands indicate*. He knows his clock's rate. It may give or lose, but it does the one only, say, two minutes in a day (which is bad timekeeping with a really fine clock), and he makes a mental calculation from the last adjustment of the hands before he answers your question.

It is practically impossible, in these days, to forge a fine clock, such as those made by the leading makers, Tompion, East, Clement, Knibb, Quare, Gretton, Graham, Dutton, Mudge and others, but deceptions are practised in many other ways. So many fail to realize what a fine clock really is, and form their opinion on the case only, which is a very unsafe criterion. While it is impossible—or uncommercial would be the better word—to fake a fine movement, with its dial-plate punched or "matted" by hand, corner-pieces beautifully chased and water-gilt, intricately pierced and carved steel hands, and engraved hour and seconds ring (in the high-grade clocks these are often of solid silver), the cases, which are of oak, as a rule, either veneered with walnut or ebony inlaid with marqueterie or decorated with lacquer, can be faked or "improved" in exactly the same way as other furniture. In any event, the attention should be first concentrated on the dial and movement; the case is only of secondary importance, especially with renowned makers such as Tompion, Knibb, Clement, or Quare, whose clocks were practically all in plain cases. Another point to be remembered is that with two twelve-inch square-dial clocks, for example, they can be transposed from the one case to the other quite easily, and to one unacquainted with the case-styles of the two makers the transposition would never be noticed.

Perhaps the best way to impart information about the early and valuable clocks will be to take the four points, as stated before, and to deal with each separately.

(1) *Signatures on dials.*

Dials of long-case clocks are nearly always signed in one of three positions: (a) across the bottom of the brass dial plate; (b) at the lower edge of the hour ring, between the V and VII; or (c) on a separate oval plaque fixed to the dial just under the hand collet. The first is the most usual with early clocks. *An unsigned clock should be viewed with great suspicion.* If the value can be increased by the stoning out of a more or less unknown maker's name and the insertion of another, such as Tompion, for example, there is a material inducement to do so. The methods of detecting such an imposture are: (1) by an examination of the signature itself, and a comparison with another on an authentic dial; (2) by noticing, in the case of a gilded dial (and Tompion's dials were always water-gilt), whether the gold runs into the engraving itself, *or whether, in other words, the engraving has been done before or after the dial-plate has been gilt* (the latter would be an obvious absurdity with an original clock), and, last, by a study of Tompion's movements, which have many peculiarities found only in the work of high-grade makers.

To avoid confusion in terms, it must be pointed out that a "signature," in the way in which the word is used here, is not a copy of a maker's handwriting, but an engraving of his name, either in script or in separate lettering. Tompion often signs his dials "Tho: Tompion; Londini; Fecit"; and Edward East, Court Horologist to Charles II, in much the same manner, thus: "Eduardus East; Londini; Fecit:". One would have imagined that such explanation would have been quite unnecessary, but, in the oft-quoted Shrager case, there was a "Tompion" clock with a forged dial, and I pointed out my reasons for stating that the signature had been put in later. One of the defendant's "experts" (who began his evidence, by the way, by saying, outright, that he knew nothing about the "works" of clocks) made the amazing statement that the name was not Tompion's signature at all, it was his engraver's work. After such a gem his preamble must have been quite unnecessary.

That these old makers' signatures varied on different clocks is as much as to say that they did not always employ the same engraver. The marvel is not that they vary, but that they do not differ far more than they actually do. Yet there is always something definitely recognizable about them. Their names were sometimes imitated by rival makers, contemporaneously. I have a bracket clock signed "THO: TOMKIN, LONDINI. FECIT", which has all the appearance of Tompion's work, and is certainly of Tompion's date. Here a deliberate attempt has been made to obtain a notoriety by a *similarity* only of signature. It is not a true forgery at all, which is, in itself, a proof of contemporary date, as in *circa* 1700 the Clockmakers' Company was powerful enough to suppress actual forgeries and to punish the perpetrators.

(2) *Originality of movement and case.*

It is far more usual to find ignorant additions, or restorations, than actual improvements intended to enhance values. Thus, one meets with dials where the original corner-pieces or spandrels have disappeared, and have been replaced with others, roughly cast, without chasing, and coarsely lacquered instead of gilded. Clock hands are rarely found in original state, especially the minute hands, which, while more delicate than hour hands, as a rule, yet, being used to alter the time, are liable to get broken. There must have been a definite practice, at one period, of replacing old hands with others of a later fashion but of far inferior workmanship, as one meets with so many dials which have suffered in this way. Again, in modern times, I have known of so many water-gilt dial-plates which have been renovated by the electro-gilder, and, needless to say, spoiled in the process. This, however, is all utter vandalism; it is practically impossible for a faker to meddle with an old clock in a way which will improve its value. If he attempt to cut down a 12-inch movement to miniature size (these small 7-inch "grandmother" clocks are rare and valuable) he will find he has left no room for the going and striking trains. He can add no extra engraving, as the finest clocks of all have practically none. Take a fine Tompion dial, such as the one illustrated at the end of this chapter, and, after studying it carefully, and learning to appreciate its delicacy and refinement, its beautiful hands and corner-pieces, and narrow hour-ring, note how there is literally nothing left on which the faker can exercise his "improving" hand.

With the cases, also, his sphere is very circumscribed. He can take a small bracket-clock case, of the "basket top" kind, and veneer it all over with fine scrolled marqueterie (which may increase its market value quite considerably), but, with a "grandfather," this is a doubtful commercial proposition. A really fine case is very good indeed, in proportion and detail, but a second-rate one is correspondingly as bad, and it is only these which are available for this "improving," and here everything is wrong from the start. To inlay a genuine plain Tompion case with marqueterie, so far from enhancing its value, would be to detract from it very much. Marqueterie cases are not in great demand, and their market price is certainly not the value of plain walnut plus the cost of the inlay.

One usually finds these old cases either in a badly dilapidated state or in an altered condition, which is even worse. The English long-case clocks must have passed through a long period of neglect to have got into the condition in which so many were found up to twenty years ago, that is, when the attention of collectors was first directed to them. We do know, as a matter of fact, that the long-case clock fell into disrepute in the years from about 1740 to 1760, for the simple reason that no examples are found between those dates, and it is reasonable to suppose that none were ever made, and that this type of clock went out of fashion. Actually, the long-case clock never really accorded with the decorative styles of 1740-60, where bold surbases and skirtings were the rule; their place was in panelled rooms of the oak period with no projecting mouldings. In any event, there is every reason for believing that these tall clocks, from the finest to the most mediocre, found their way, not into lumber-rooms or attics (where they would have been untouched other than by dust and decay), but into low-ceilinged cottages, and it may be instructive to point out why we *do* know this, as it affords a good object lesson in the art of deduction.

A long-case clock must stand firmly on the floor, or the pendulum will get "out of beat," and the clock will either not keep time or will stop. This implies an even floor, such as few cottages possessed at this period; rough tiles, which were washed with water and a mop, were the general rule. One measure of adjustment would be to wedge up the base, and then to screw or nail the back of the case to the wall. To do this, in the ordinary way, one hole only would be necessary, yet if we examine many of these old cases, it will be found that the backs are riddled with holes. Why is this? There are two reasons. First, a frequent change of position, if not of habitat, is implied, yet this alone will not account for many holes in the back. Let us remember now that the cottages of the period (that is, of much older date than 1740, as labourers' dwellings were not built, to any extent, in the eighteenth century, as we know from those which remain, in country districts, to this day) were generally of wood and plaster, coated with whitewash, or sometimes of irregular brickwork. A position being found for the clock, the problem was then to get a fixing, either between the joints of the brickwork or into a wooden stud. The result would be many abortive attempts, each of which would have to be made through the back of the case, and would result in a separate hole.

Again, with these early clocks, while the cases were not unusually tall (ninety inches is about the maximum), there were usually no doors to the hood, and the dial had to be exposed, for winding, by sliding up the hood on grooves and runners at the back, which involved the raising of the hood itself nearly twelve inches, and thus increasing the room-height demanded by the clock, when it had to be wound, to nearly nine feet. In the majority of these cottages such a height was not available, so several things may have happened; either the base was sawn away or the hood-slides removed and the front cut and hinged to form a door, but with no inner wood facing being provided for the dial. If the hood had a carved cresting (which was the usual finish to early clocks), this

145

would be removed first, and, in the usual way, lost. The fact that these old clocks came into cottages at all shows that they must have cost the new owners little or nothing, and, therefore, could have been esteemed only as timekeepers, if that.

The proofs that these happenings did occur are evident. It is rare to find a sliding-hood case with its original runners. I have never seen one in nearly forty years. On the other hand, I have found dozens where the front of the hood has been roughly cut and hinged to form a door, without any attempt being made to provide a wood bezel for the dial, which would be the workmanlike way of making such an alteration. Again, it is exceedingly rare to find one of these old clocks with its original base, in fact, it is doubtful whether any of the step-moulded plinths which one so often finds on these 1680-1710 clocks ever belonged to the cases at all. Certainly, in the very few examples which have been found with the original bases, these moulded plinths are absent, turned stump-feet being provided instead.

The lower doors, that is, of the trunks of these long-cases are always of oak, clamped at the top and bottom, and provided with half-round "shutting-beads." Being veneered on the front over the clamps, any breaking away of these must crack the wood on the face, and to restore such a door will involve the re-laying and re-surfacing of the veneer. Such a catastrophe must have been of frequent occurrence, judging by the present state of the majority of these cases.

(3) *The clock should be a good specimen of its period.*

If there were good and bad furniture makers in the eighteenth century, there were certainly fine and poor clock makers. The clocks of Lancashire and Yorkshire are huge and bad, and the more elaborate they are the less I like them. A rhinoceros does not become a pretty animal by being overdressed. If one require a clock to keep time only, and have a really big space of wall to fill up, then the Yorkshire clock may be ideal, but it will not compare, for a moment, as a piece of furniture, with a fine Tompion or a Knibb. Their cases are quiet, refined, of good proportion, and not assertive in any room or with any scheme of decoration. The dials are nearly of eye-height, as a dial should be. Big Ben may be an excellent timekeeper, but it is not exactly an ornament to a room. The hour-circles of these early dials are narrow and beautifully engraved; the hour and minute hands are not only works of art, but they differ as widely as possible, so one is never in doubt as to whether the time is 9.30 or 6.45. The workmanship is superb, as all mechanism which has a duty to perform should be. A German "regulator" may keep as good time, but it will be always in the clock-jobber's hands.

Apart from the refinement, I find a great deal of pleasure in studying the devices which these old makers contrived so that their clocks should be treated with respect. Take the "bolt-and-shutter" maintaining power, which one never finds on inferior clocks. The power which drives the mechanism is the fall of a weight, which, in the act of winding, is suspended by the lifting of the weight on the winding key, and a good clock will "trip," i.e. go backwards. To obviate this, the winding holes are closed by shutters, which have to be opened by pulling a string or depressing a lever, and this puts a spring in action which drives the clock for the few moments it takes to wind it. Then, again, think of the idea behind that apparently clumsily contrived sliding hood in place of an opening door. This was devised to foil the careless person who usually winds a clock *without opening the trunk door*, and who stops only when the rising weight crashes against the seat-board of the movement, and causes the gut line to break, incidentally. Behind the trunk door is a rocking catch, something like a pivoted slender spoon, which the shutting of the lower door forces back, and engages the other end forward into the hood. *It is impossible, therefore, to raise the hood without first opening the trunk door.* Then there is the 61-inch pendulum, which swings once in a second and a quarter, found only on clocks of the highest class. I suppose it is common knowledge, in these days, that a pendulum of one metre in length, about (to be exact, 39·1393 inches from the point of swing *to the centre of gravity of the entire pendulum*), will take one second of time to make one swing, *in the latitude of London*, no matter if the arc be one yard or one inch. (After my experiences of "clock experts" in the Shrager case in 1923, I began to doubt if they knew *anything* about clocks, but, perhaps, "the man in the street" may be more knowledgable.) The margin of error, therefore, in the twelve-hour going of a clock is an inaccuracy, in pendulum-length multiplied by 43·200 (60 x 60 x 12), so the initial error, per swing, must be inconceivably minute. At the same time, with the second-and-a-quarter pendulum (again, to be accurate, of 61·155 inches effective length) the degree of error will be reduced in the proportion of 48 to 60, as the long pendulum swings only forty-eight times in a minute.

Again, there is the problem of duration between windings, *in a striking clock*. With a case of a given height, which means a certain distance for the fall of the weights and no more, it is possible to gear for the fall of the "going" weight by leaves and pinions and a shallow "release" to the escape-wheel. With the striking train the problem is quite different. Here the weight falls only when the clock strikes, and, during the time that the pin-wheel revolves, one pin-space for each stroke on the bell.* Now, the two weights must fall together, more or less, as a clock where

* For further explanation, see *English Domestic Clocks*.

the going train had to be wound once a month and the striking train once a week would be absurd. Joseph Knibb solved the difficulty in a very ingenious manner. He provided two bells, of high and low tone respectively, a double locking-plate, and a pin-wheel with pins on both sides, and the striking was arranged on the Roman numeral system, one blow on the deep bell for the V and two for the X. The other numbers were struck on the high bell, and the order was like this:

```
                                 o
           o            .   o   o   o   o
  .  .  .     .   .   .   o      o   o   o
 .  .  .  .  o  o  o  o  .  o   o   o
 I  II III IV V  VI VII VIII IX X  XI XII
```

It will be noticed that the 4 has here been written IV instead of the IIII usual on nearly every clock.

On the Roman numeral clocks only the number is engraved IV, and if one meets with a dial numbered in this way, it may be as well to examine it further, as this Roman-numeral striking increases the value of the clock materially.

The distance through which the striking weight falls in the twelve hours being a matter of bell strokes rather than time (as the weight does not fall at all until the clock strikes), by Knibb's method there is an economy of thirty blows in the round of hours, as compared with seventy-eight in the usual way.*

The advantages are, the possibility of getting the necessary falling space in a small clock with a duration of thirty, instead of eight days between windings, and the ease with which twelve o'clock can be counted, four blows instead of twelve, that is, for those who prefer to tell the time by ear rather than by eye.

Another ingenious device, more usual with bracket than with long-case clocks, was the provision of a repeating mechanism, generally with a pulling string, where the clock could be made to strike the last hour, sometimes with its halves and quarters. With watches, this repeating mechanism often extends to the minutes, and, in enabling the wearer to tell the time in the dark, it is the eighteenth-century equivalent of the modern luminous timekeeper.

(4) A clock should have some unusual feature.

Some of these have been already indicated, such as the "bolt-and-shutter" maintaining power, the "second-and-a-quarter" long pendulum, repeating work, finely pierced hands, narrow hour circle (preferably of solid silver), well-chased spandrels, and water-gilding of dials.

* It is usual to regard this Roman-numeral striking as peculiar to Joseph Knibb's clocks, but I have found one, on the same system, by Dan Quare.

To these may be added "skeleton-dials," where the spaces between the Roman numerals are cut away to show the matting of the dial-plate beneath, the numbering of each minute, from 1 to 60, in the outer ring of the hour-circle, and extra duration between windings in excess of the usual eight-day. Thirty-hour clocks, or those where the winding is effected by pulling up the weights on cords or chains, especially of the long-case kind, are nearly always depraved and worthless examples.

While with "grandfathers" a fine plain walnut case is just as valuable as one inlaid with elaborate marqueterie (none but the highest class movements are ever found in *good* walnut cases), the same is not true of bracket clocks, where marqueterie cases are exceedingly rare. (There are plenty of forgeries if one is satisfied with these.) If I had to place early bracket clocks, prior to about 1740, in their orders of case value, other things being equal, I should make the progression in something like this order, on an upward scale, the cases and movements being otherwise equal.

(1) Plain black cases.
(2) Ditto, ornamented with chased brass.
(3) Lacquer cases, tortoise-shell and cream being the rarest colours.
(4) Marqueterie cases.
(5) Cases overlaid with real tortoise-shell.
(6) Cases overlaid with mother-of-pearl.

Of the last I have only seen one genuine example in forty years.

I should place the values of long-case clocks, of exceptional duration between windings, in an arithmetical progression of value something like the following, taking the usual eight-day as the unit, and assuming movements and cases to be otherwise equal.

(1) Eight-day non-striking.
(1½) Eight-day striking.
(2) Month non-striking.
(2½) Month striking.
(3½) Three-month non-striking.
(4) Three-month striking.
(5) Six-month (clocks of this duration do not strike, as a rule, for obvious reasons).
(7) Year clocks.

Rarity increases value, naturally, and certain makers' clocks are more exceptional than others. George Graham, pupil and favourite apprentice of Tompion,* made many bracket clocks, but very few "grandfathers" indeed. A long-case clock, from the hands of this maker,

* They are buried, in the same grave, in Westminster Abbey.

therefore, is valuable, but it is to be hoped that this will not be taken as an incentive to engrave Graham's name on a few by other makers such as Dutton, Mudge, or Harrison.

Clocks of precision are usually of the regulator type, with dead-beat escapements, and pendulums of the Ellicott, Graham mercury or Harrison "grid-iron" type,* and are rarely strikers. Plain cases are the rule, either of walnut or, at a later date, of mahogany, but I have found one, in a lacquer case, by a small maker in the obscure village of Cuckfield on the road to Brighton (or Brightelhemstone as it was then), of the finest quality, with a dead-beat escapement and a seconds dial *below the hand collet*, which has necessitated an inverted anchor-escapement. I have examined this clock at my leisure, as I have possessed it for years, and have it still.

English clocks are still to be found in the most out-of-the-way places. I have unearthed specimens in tiny villages, not only in England, but in Spain and in Austria. How they migrated to these remote places is a mystery which I do not even endeavour to probe. I found a superb month-clock in a barn, with a fine marqueterie case which had been "restored" out of all knowledge, but where nothing had been added or lost; the case had been taken apart and simply jumbled together, something like a man with his boots on his head and his hat on his feet.

This reminds me, being a month-clock, how to tell one in a rough-and-ready manner. The eight-day clock has a train of four wheels from main wheel to escape, and winds from left to right. Duration, being a matter of gearing (it is also a great deal more, but that does not concern us here at present), a month, *with a seconds dial*, has *five wheels*, and, in consequence, must wind from *right to left*. If the clock to be examined is not in its case, and has its weights detached (one usually finds them in this condition), the thing to do is to get a key and insert it. If it turn from *right to left* it is a month-clock, but if it turn from *left to right* it may be either an eight-day or a *three-month*. With the latter, however, the weights would be about fifty-six pounds in weight, and, in consequence, of arresting size.

There are not many clock collectors.† There should be a great number, as English domestic clocks offer a fascinating field, and one where exact knowledge (as distinct from mere opinion, however cultured) must tell heavily in favour of its possessor. The absence of really fierce competition has its advantages, therefore; it offers a comparatively unexplored field for the one who collects with an eye to the future, and, incidentally, loves fine things for their own sake.

*See *English Domestic Clocks*.

† One of the most erudite, D. A. F. Wetherfield, died less than three years ago, and his remarkable collection was dispersed.

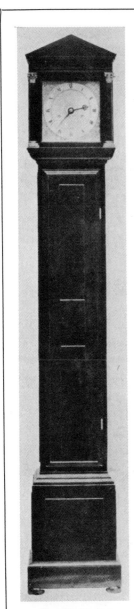
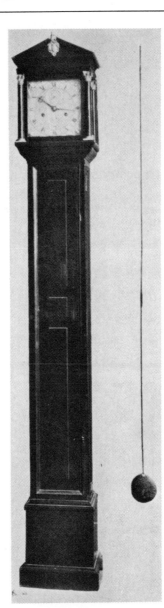

Joseph Knibb
Ebony-veneered case.

William Clement
61 inch (1¼ seconds)
pendulum, shown at side
to same scale.

Samuel Knibb
Three-train strike
and chime movement.

Plate number Two Hundred and Seventy-seven

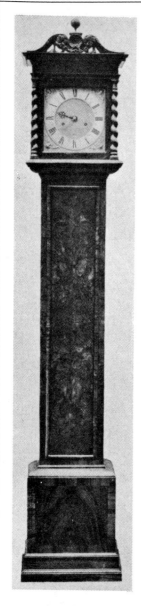

Joseph Knibb,
London.

Eight-day striking Clock in oak case veneered with walnut. Carved pediment with central ball spire; rising hood supported on spiral click spring on backboard. The small trigger just below the dial (in the right-hand view), with its spoon end just below the base of the hood, locks the hood itself when the trunk door is shut. The object of this was to prevent anyone from winding the clock without first opening the trunk door and thus marking the rise of the weights when the clock was wound.

Plate number Two Hundred and Seventy-eight

1 2 3

1 and 2 are early examples of marqueterie Cases without plinths. It is possible that these cases were made to stand in separate box plinths which could be adjusted to the floor by screw feet. None of these separate bases appear to have survived.

Plate number Two Hundred and Seventy-nine

1   2   3

1. "All-over" Arabesque marqueterie.   2. Jointed and figured walnut.
3. Floral marqueterie in panels.

Plate number Two Hundred and Eighty

Thomas Tompion, London.

Three-month Striking Clock; ebony-veneered case; bolt-and-shutter maintaining power; arched dial. The arch is a late detail, and only three with this feature are known of Tompion's make. The one in the Pump Room at Bath was made in 1709. Tompion died in 1713.

Plate number Two Hundred and Eighty-one

Edward East
Chased spandrels; early hands,
1670-5.

Edward East
Hour ring in two sections; the outer one
revolves once in a year, 1680-5.

Joseph Knibb
Roman numeral striking, 1690-5.

William Clement
Non-striking clock, 1690.

Plate number Two Hundred and Eighty-two

Low arch, with hour ring divided
into quarters on inside, 1735.

High arch; hour ring not divided
on inside, 1760.

High arch, with mechanical figures,
1780.

Arch with moving figures. Dial
completely silvered, 1790-1800.

Plate number Two Hundred and Eighty-three

Three-train Chiming Clock. Portico top, 1680.

Striking Clock. Portico top, 1680-5.

Basket top, 1690-5, with skeleton dial.

Skeleton dial with each minute separately numbered.

Plate number Two Hundred and Eighty-four

Basket top.

Back plate.

Basket top veneered with tortoise-shell.

Basket top inlaid with floral marqueterie.

Plate number Two Hundred and Eighty-five

Basket top
Pierced and chased brass basket and enrichments;
fine handle and spires, 1700.

Plate number Two Hundred and Eighty-six

Basket Top
Chased and pierced brass basket with fine handle,
1700-5.

Plate number Two Hundred and Eighty-seven

Bell Top, 1730-45.

Inverted Bell Top,
1745-1800.

There are many other types of cases which cannot be illustrated here owing to want of space. The full progression is illustrated in *English Domestic Clocks*. Many of the later patterns such as the balloon and the lancet cases, with their variants, are not strictly indicative of a defined fusion, but persist from the late eighteenth, right through the nineteenth century.

Plate number Two Hundred and Eighty-eight

CHAPTER XXI

DISCURSIVE AND CONCLUSIVE

HAT fashions should exist, in antiques as in everything else, and that these fashions should regulate current values and prices is only natural, perhaps, but as they come and go—and come again, very often—it is difficult to refer to them without the danger of becoming obsolete almost at once.

In this present year of 1930, and for some years prior to this, satin-wood had been out of fashion. Thirty years ago it was in demand, and realized high prices. Its time may come again, and it is as well to bear in mind that, providing the thing be beautiful in itself, and worth collecting, the absence of a vogue—which artificially inflates prices—may be to the advantage of the far-seeing collector. There are other pieces which have lost favour for quite different reasons. Thus, four-post bedsteads are not desirable articles at any time. The side-rails, secured by coachscrews or bolts, especially when the wood is old and rotten (as it frequently is), may be hiving places for vermin. Also, these "four-posters" are incomplete without draperies of testers, upper and lower valances, back-cloths and curtains, all of which modern hygienic considerations condemn, and rightly too. Again, there is the tallboy double-chest, where a step-ladder is necessary to examine the contents of the upper drawers. Similarly, the tray-wardrobe, which was admirably suited to the costumes of the eighteenth century, is of very little practicable value with modern garments, and as America has largely influenced prices by its demands, and as the wardrobe itself is a piece of furniture which the American refuses to recognize (he uses the fitted clothes-cupboard instead), these eighteenth-century pieces fetch little more than second-hand prices. On the other hand, any of these pieces, "four-posters," "tallboy" chests, or wardrobes, of outstanding character, are still expensive. The remarks made here only apply to those of the plainer kind. It may be taken as some consolation to the budding expert that the antique which commands no more than second-hand price is not likely to be forged, for obvious reasons.

A word or two as to pedigrees and provenance may be of value. Pedigrees, as a rule, where furnished at all, are usually of the most sketchy description. "A large house in the country" may mean anything from a

Stately Home to Maidstone Jail. Generally there is not the slightest attempt made to verify such sources. This leads, naturally, to another point, the selling by "planting." I know of several private country houses where the furniture is always in a state of transit, coming and going. To call the owners dealers would be taken as an insult, but the fact remains that furniture is always being sold out of these houses, and replaced with other pieces, presumably bought. There is another possibility, that the additions are from the stocks of dealers, "planted" in those houses to satisfy those collectors who prefer to "buy direct." They are usually "blood brothers" to those who look for worm holes as evidences of authenticity.

As with stocks and shares, buying tends to inflate prices, and in this respect it is surprising how small the antique world really is. Years ago I knew of two collectors only of Cousins' prints, and prices soared amazingly while they were buying, and dropped flat when they were filled up. With the general buyer there is no such danger, as the dealers never know where to catch him, but the collector of, say, Queen Anne walnut, once he becomes known to the trade, will find prices creep up alarmingly; hence the remarkable price-fluctuations which occur from time to time. There is the other type of collector, he (or she) who seeks for the impossible, the pieces which never did and never could have existed. This class asks not only for the massive price, but for the fake into the bargain. Many years ago there were two famous gamblers in the early railroad days in the States, who each piled up fortunes at their game, whether honestly or otherwise matters very little here. The point is that both must have been of the class which the American styles "hard-boiled," to have succeeded at cards. Both these gamblers came from the same home town, and they returned, in their later days, and retired, each devoting his leisure to making a collection of English furniture. There was the keenest rivalry between the two, and, in a very short time, they passed the bounds of the possible and began to look for the miraculous. Both got it! A tripod table, for example, had to be carved over every inch of its surface before it was regarded as worthy of their "collections," and if a well-known unique chair existed, they were in the market for a set of the same pattern, with a settee and a couple of arm-chairs thrown in. That dealers, or fakers, played up the one against the other was only infantile commercial instinct. I saw the selected remains of both collections in America only three years ago. Both had been "weeded out," remember, yet I found no single piece which had not been "improved." I have illustrated several at the end of this chapter to show what was collected in America some forty years ago. There was hardly a single outright fake among the lot; the genuine article itself could be bought for very little in those days. Nearly every piece began on an old basis, but had been "improved" out of all knowledge. There were one or two copies of unique originals, such as the well-known arm-chair in Sir John Soane's Museum in Lincoln's Inn Fields, which had grown to a really remarkable set in this collection, and I saw one Chippendale chair, at least, which had been carved up *on the outside of the back.* The lucky purchaser (I do not know which of the two it was, as when I saw the "collection" it was a jumble of both) must have rejoiced when he secured that "find." History repeats itself, however, as I saw fakes just as barefaced, but not nearly so fine in quality, in the famous Shrager case of some years ago.

From this "collection" to the law, and the protection it affords, is an easy and natural stage. My advice to those who seek the aid of the law in their "bargains" is the same as that given by *Punch* to those about to marry. The law demands proof, and even the placing of the actual maker in the box is not "proof" to many judges, as they may hold that the faker has been bribed to make false statements. I have always that famous "Royston Hall Room" in mind, where not only the maker, but the drawings also, were produced in court, yet where the plaintiff failed on this point and on every other. To be able to produce the actual maker of a fake is almost impossible, especially in a case against the antique trade, as fakers live by the trade and not by the private collector, and bread and butter is thicker than sentiment. Another snag, in the proving of a fake in a court of law, is that the dealer who sells rarely buys from the faker who makes. There is always an intermediary. Consequently, if one gets discovery of documents, all that this will show is that dealer Brown bought the article from Smith, and one has no right to ask for the production of *Smith's* books, and if he be challenged as to where the piece came from, he can easily decline to give any information, and in this he will have the support of the Bench in nine cases out of ten. It is far better to buy wisely and leave the law alone. After all, one can pay an expert a really fat fee, and then be considerably in pocket as compared with a law-costs bill. Many of the strictures above apply to the enforcement of any guarantee given by a dealer. Who is to be the judge? Without a well-drawn form of contract, dealers' guarantees are, as a rule, worth little more than wastepaper price.

A few words may also be said here about experts in general. I know one American collector who told me the rarest thing he had was his expert. It took more trouble to "collect" him than all the works of art he ever possessed. I have seen expert evidence given, over and over again, which was too inaccurate to be attributable to gross ignorance only. Beware of the expert who professes a knowledge in too many branches; as a rule he is ignorant of them all. It takes a lifetime to know enough of English furniture to become an expert, and I have not the slightest doubt that with pictures, china, silver, jewellery, manuscripts and other works of art, it takes as long. The leading picture experts specialize, as a rule, in the work of one artist, certainly the work of one school, and they would hardly do this if they could obtain as good a knowledge of pictures in general in the same way. They prefer to acquire a thorough knowledge of the one thing to picking up a smattering of many.

My own ignorance of Continental furniture is abysmal. I can pick out a piece of Dutch, German, French or even Spanish furniture, or at least I think I can, but, beyond this, very little. Why? Because to obtain a knowledge of French furniture, for example, one must live in the country for many years, know French methods, timbers, and details, be well acquainted with the work of the leading *ébénistes*, both by study and comparison, and know the art of the brass founder and the chaser thoroughly. The price which I should pay for such experience—that is, if I could ever acquire it—would be to ruin my eye and spoil my judgment so far as English furniture is concerned. This is only a kindred art, the French *ébéniste* versus the English cabinet-maker; what can one say of the furniture expert who claims to have a profound knowledge of English, Continental and Oriental porcelains and enamels, with some such trifles as needlework, tapestry, ironwork, silver, and a few others thrown in?

Collecting offers many possibilities to those of knowledge, taste, and pertinacity. There is the pleasure of living with one's collection (and this should be both a joy and an education), the fact that a really fine thing cannot diminish much in value so long as civilization lasts, and, to crown all, that fine and rare things must become more and more scarce as the years go on, and thus rise in value. A dealer in stocks and shares, without experience, would fall a victim to "bucket shops" in a very little while, yet he can learn his lesson quite easily. Why should the collector of works of art of bygone generations be exempted from apprenticeship?

Now a few words on the subject of auctions. There are public sale rooms of very high and very low repute, but one and all they put a clause in their conditions of sale by which they exempt themselves from any liability, due to mis-description or other cause. Why do they do this? Why, when they catalogue a piece as "Chippendale," do they not guarantee it and stand by their description? Because, first, to do so is not business, and, secondly, they are not infallible, and they know it. Therefore, the buyer at an auction purchases with all faults and errors of description and must stand by his bargain. There is no such thing as the "guarantee of an auction room," the auctioneer offers no guarantee of any kind, and, what is more, he says so in his conditions quite clearly.

There is another little current fiction in the minds of many who frequent auctions. They have the idea that if they bid, say, fifty-five guineas for an article, and the underbidder, at fifty guineas, is a well-known and experienced dealer, they have bought the lot dearly to the extent of the five guineas, at the most, as the dealer would have given fifty. Would he? There is such a procedure as "trotting," that is, encouraging a bidder to go on, and many have an uncanny skill in knowing exactly when to stop, when to "drop it" on the bidder. It is akin to "forcing a card," which is the basis of nearly every card trick. Offer the "bargain" to the underbidder at his figure, and see what happens. Take off another ten per cent, and try again. One will find, as a rule, a curious disinclination to "come up to the scratch," and it may enter the mind that, perhaps, the lot belonged to the underbidding dealer, and that he was merely boosting his own property. One has to reckon with this always, especially when the catalogue is marked "Property of a Lady, and *Sundry Properties*." Has anyone, outside the closed ring of dealers and auctioneers, any idea of the appetite of a modern auction-room? The contents of the Hotel Cecil were dispersed in *four days*. In a good season the turnover of Christie's may run into millions. Think of the insatiable maw which can swallow and regurgitate goods to this amount in a single year. Think, also, what it would mean if they guaranteed each lot and stood behind their guarantee, prepared to refund if necessary.

Speaking of furniture (the subject of this book), and leaving out forgeries of china, enamels, tapestries, needlework and a hundred other examples of works of art, each factory has its own hall-mark, as it were, if one can only train one's eye to recognize it. A maker of bogus "Chippendale," for example, will employ the same carver, whose "handwriting" should be recognizable after a while. With such things as frets, inlays and the like (which must be produced in quantities), the temptation to duplicate must be strong, as the faker is a commercial man who cannot afford to throw things away. The same is true of his patterns. To evolve an original creation implies drawings, templets, "jigs," and possibly models, and to pile the cost of those on to the one piece is not good business. The dealer, at least—he who reaps what rewards are going—will not stand for it. The fake may be exposed, in which case it will not fetch even second-hand price (very few will buy a fake with open eyes), and that is the risk he takes, and for which he expects a large reward when he does "plant" something.

With a really good furniture fake the incompetent or ill-equipped expert has no chance whatsoever; he is beaten before he starts. But really good fakes are costly to make, and therefore rare. This is his salvation. Yet expertize is not, or should not be, a game of guessing.

One should either know or not, and, if the latter, confess his ignorance. Yet *that* is not good business—for the expert. That reminds me of another caution, to expert and collector alike: a really fierce price is no guarantee of authenticity, and, at the other end, only a dealer in stolen goods can afford to sell much under market value.

What of the future of the antique trade? Allowing for circulation, antiques being bought and thrown again on the market, the time must come when the source will dry up. This day is not far distant. What then? Is it possible that fine forgeries, recognized as such, may become valuable in their turn? Remember it is only while the prices of antiques are high that it pays to make these fine fakes. To "antique" a good reproduction may double its cost. Here is a possibility of the future: the collecting of fine fakes. It opens up a vivid prospect! Fancy a piece of the future being catalogued or described as a "genuine fake; guaranteed"! Fancy the new school of experts which may arise to meet the new demand! One can visualize some of those white and blue circular plaques being affixed to houses and the ruins of factories. "Here lived (or died) ——, the noted faker." W. S. Gilbert died many years too soon.

CONCLUDING REMARKS

ANTIQUES have their fashions, or periods of demand. Thirty years ago satinwood in the Hepplewhite and Sheraton styles realized big prices, then it fell under a cloud, and has remained so ever since.

What is more remarkable is that fakes have also their fashions, and if one examines the "collections" made half a century ago it will be found that many of the pieces bear little or no resemblance to anything to be found in a dealer's stock at the present day. There have been "collectors" who have demanded the unknown and the impossible at all times, but seldom or never have they particularized what they DID want; they were merely on the look-out for the unusual—and the very expensive. Fashions in fakes, therefore, only show the difference between what satisfied these seekers after the miraculous fifty years ago and what is offered to whet their appetites for the wonderful at the present day. In the following three pages are given examples of the "improved" pieces which were much sought after some fifty years ago.

[*Plate number Two Hundred and Eighty-nine was not used*]

A Bureau Bookcase which started life as a simple piece, but has been
"improved" since. Note the elaborate pediment and feet, and the
carved mouldings.

Plate number Two Hundred and Ninety

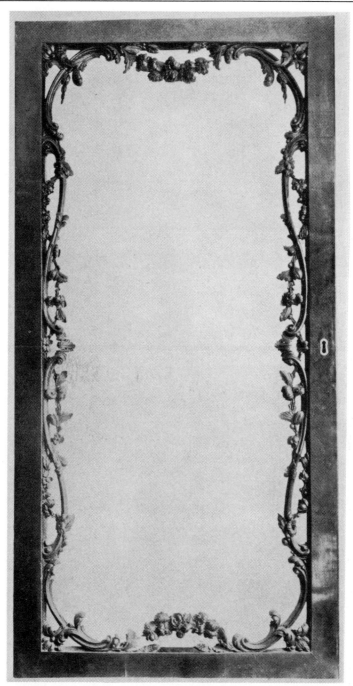

The doors of the Bureau Bookcase on the opposite page. The original simple lattice-work has been removed and the elaborate carved inner framing substituted. At no time in the eighteenth century would panels of glass as large as this have been used in a bookcase door.

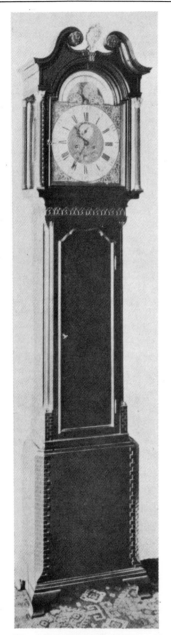 

Two depraved examples of Long-case Clocks which have been embellished
to the last degree. To the clock collector both *look* wrong, even in the
illustrations. The one on the right may be of Philadelphia make, but the
original case was plain without the carving in the base panel.

Plate number Two Hundred and Ninety-two

INDEX

*A*CER *pseudoplatanus*, 78
Adam Brothers, 105, 106, 131
Adam, Robert, 114, 119, 121, 131, 137
Additions to genuine pieces, 16, 17, 33, 35, 37
"Adelphi," 131
Admiralty, clock at, 120
Almond wood, 29
Altars, edicts against use of, 43
Altered pieces of furniture, 35, 37, 42
 and woodwork, 42
Amboyna wood, 109
America, collecting in, 152, 153
 collectors in, 152, 153
Anachronisms; weapons for the expert, 57, 58
"Antique finishes," 7, 109, 110
Antique, the; its merits, 13, 14, 15, 16, 17, 18
Antiques; demand enhances value, 152
 fashions in, 151
 obsolete; what becomes of them? 86
 prices and values of, 151
 types which have little sale, 157
 which do not pay to fake, 7, 8
Antiquity without quality, little merit in, 80
Appliqué work, 100, 101
Apprenticeship; its value, 123
Architects, effects of on woodworker, 69
"Ark"; old name for a chest, 19
Arkwrights, 19, 21, 24, 44, 48
 and carpenters compared, 45, 46, 48
Articles which do not pay to fake, 7, 8
Arts in Middle Ages emanated from the Church, 22
Aubusson tapestries, 100
Auction rooms, 120
 bidding at, 155
 danger of bidding in, 154, 155
Average time, with clocks, 142

*B*ABLAKE SCHOOLS, Coventry, tables in, 49
Bahamas, 112, 117
Barnstaple, 58
Beadwork, 136
Beauvais, tapestries of, 100
Beds of Restoration period, needlework on, 100
Beech; used for chair framings, 128
Beetle in wood, 107
Belton House, 69
Berlin wool, 97
Biblical scenes often illustrated in needlework, 99
Bichromate of potash, 113
Biddenden Church, 26
Bidding at auctions, 155
Bideford, 58
Bitumen varnishes, 62
Blistering of veneers, 89
Board, shooting. *See* Shooting board
Boards, jointing of, 70
Bolt-and-shutter maintaining power, 147
Books on fakes, difficulties in writing of, 3, 4, 5, 53
Bracket clock types, 144
Brackett, Oliver, 119
Brettingham, architect, 69
Broadwood piano; designed by Sheraton, 132
Bromley-by-Bow, panelled room from, 41
Brussels carpets, 101
Buckingham, Duke of, 135
Bullion, 100, 101
"Burl" veneers, 29
Burr veneers, 29

*C*ABINET DICTIONARY, THE, 113
 Cabinet Maker and Upholsterer's Drawing Book, The, 131, 132
Cabinet Maker's London Book of Prices, The, 133

Cabinet maker *v.* chair maker, 104
Cabinets, square, lacquered, 94
Cabochon-and-leaf furniture, 114, 116
Cabriole leg; marks an era, 103
  "collaring" of, 104
  method of making, 103
  skill required in making, 103, 104
Caning, original, rarity of, 79
Canvas used for needlework, 99
Cards used as patterns for needlework, 98, 99
Carnation, the favourite flower used in early marqueterie, 87, 88
Carpenter, early, follows traditions of the stone mason, 22
  and arkwright compared, 45, 46, 48
  principal woodworker in Middle Ages, 19
  the, 65, 66, 69, 70
  v. cabinet maker, 38
Carpenters' Company, 21
Carvers, work of, in early pieces, 36
Carving, growing elaboration in seventeenth century, 43, 44, 61
  machines, 103, 104
  of mirrors; usually finished by the gilder, 137, 138
Catherine, St., Patron of Coventry Guild, 47
Caustics, salting of, 44
  their use, 41, 44, 62
Cefyn Mably, table at, 50
Cellini, Benvenuto, 46
Chair-back settees, 106
Chair designing, 122, 123
Chair maker; the advanced trade in seventeenth century, 65, 66
  did not always use walnut in Restoration period, 78
  v. cabinet maker, 104
Chairs, debased principles in, 80, 81
  Cheshire, 64
  development of high back in, 67
  difficulties in exact copying of, 68
  dignity of in early times, 49, 50
  Elizabethan, form of, 49
  Elizabethan, value of, 50
  hoop-back in, 113
  Lancashire, 64
  multiplicity in causes of evolution in, 66

Chairs (*continued*)—
  Restoration, 80, 81
  sets or pairs, 68
  Shropshire, 64
  Somerset, 64
  splats of, 115
  varieties in, 125, 126
  Warwickshire, 64
  Yorkshire, 64
Chamfer, 56, 57
Chancel screens at Bovey Tracey, 42
  at Bramfield, 42
  at Eye, 42
  at Ludham, 42
  at Ranworth, 42
  at Southwold, 42
  defacement of in Puritan times, 43
Changed character of pieces, 34
Channel Island furniture, 34
Chapman & Hall, 5
"Cheese glue," 70
Chemical analysis, value of, 102
Cheshire chairs, 64
China and Japan; furniture compared, 94
Chip carving, 23, 48
Chippendale, 36, 114, 116, 119, 121, 122, 131, 133, 136
  comes to London, 121
  furniture, variety of, 123
  mirrors, 136, 137, 138, 139
  period, 93, 113
  school, 119, 120, 121, 122, 123, 124
  style, 114, 116, 120, 121
  style, divisions of, 121, 122
Chloroxylon Swietenia, 127
Christies, 155
Chronological order of English Furniture, 25
Church woodwork, importance of, 31, 32
Claw-and-ball foot, 104
Clement, William, 17, 81, 143
Clifford's Inn Room, 41, 70, 72
Clock cases made in Holland, 81
  cases; usually plain with good makers, 142
  collecting still a profitable field, 150
  collectors, rarity of, 150
  dials, signing of, 17

Clockmakers' Company, 143
Clockmakers; import cases from Holland, 66
Clocks, characteristics of good, 141, 142, 146, 147, 148, 149
   classes of, 141, 142
   dead-beat escapement in, 150
   difficulties in forging, 142
   duration between windings of, 147, 148
   forgeries of, 143, 144
   good and bad in early times, 146
   good; rare, but still to be found, 150
   hands of, 144
   long case and bracket, 141, 142, 143, 144, 145, 146, 147, 148, 149, 150
   long case, period of neglect of, 144, 145
   long case, reasons for decline in fashion of, 145
   long case, sliding hoods of, 146
   maintaining power in, 147
   precision, 150
   regulator, 150
   Roman numeral, striking in, 148
   signatures on dials of, 17, 143
   unusual features in, 148, 149
Clubfoot, 104
Coil springs in upholstery, 105
Coincidences in the finding of pieces, 32
Colchester, old Siege House at, 58
"Collaring" of cabriole legs, 104
Collecting in America, 152, 153
   possibilities of future of, 154, 156
Collectors, 1, 3, 13
   types of, 152
Colours in lacquer, 94
   in needlework, 97
Commonwealth furniture, 61, 79
Composition ornament, 136
Construction in timber, 22
   of Post-Dissolution Gothic, 45
   of various periods, 38
   progression of, 49
   sacrificed to design, 79, 80, 81
Constructive principles, 80, 81, 82
Cooper & Holt, 133
Copeland, 119

Copy, the late, danger of, 17, 18
Costumes, a guide in estimating age of needlework, 99
Counterfeits, improvements in when exposed, 4
Counterpart in marqueterie, 87
Counties of England with distinct styles, 31, 65
Coventry, 23
   Drapers' Chapel in cathedral, 49
   Guild of Clothworkers, 47
   Guild throne at, 23, 42, 43, 46, 47
   St. Mary's Hall, 23, 42, 43, 46, 47
   St. Michael's Parish Church, 23
Cowdray Priory, table from, 49
Crafts, progress in always pendulum fashion, 67
Crazing of painting, 128
Credence, 47
Cromwell, edicts under, 43
Cross-stitch in needlework, 97
Crunden, 119
Cuba, mahogany from, 111, 117
Cupboard, evolution of the, 47
Curat's house, Norwich, 74, 75
Curl mahogany, 112
Cutting of boards, loss in cutting of, 37, 38
Curved rib panels, 56

"DARK AGES" of English Furniture, 15
Darly, Matthias, 119
Dating of pieces, 30
Deal, Memel, 70
   replaces oak; reasons for, 72
   stripped, fashion for, 75
Dealers, 1
   methods of, 153
   wide knowledge expected from, 2, 154
"Decorated Queen Anne," 114, 115
Decorators, 8, 9
Department of Forestry in U.S.A., 111
Depraved principles in furniture circa 1685, 79, 80, 81
Dersingham Church, chest at, 23
Development of furniture, from simple to complex, 19

Dials of clocks, fakes of, 143
  signing of, 17, 143
  types of, 143
Dining tables, rarity of in early eighteenth century, 107
Director, the; of Chippendale, 36, 114, 121, 129, 133
Dissolution of Monasteries, 19. *See also* Post-Dissolution
Districts of origin of furniture, 31
Documents relating to furniture, 120
"Dolly" or pounce; in marqueterie, 68, 87
"Domestic Gothic" of Eastlake, 15
"Donkey" of the marqueterie cutter, 89
"Double-bine" twist, 79
Dovetailing, 38
Drapers' Chapel, Coventry, table in, 49
Drawer construction at various periods, 38
Drayton Manor, panelling at, 69
Drop-in seats, 105
Durham Cathedral, stole and maniple at, 100
Dutch workmen migrate to England, 66
Dutton, clock maker, 142
Dyes, permanence of, 102
Dyrham Park, panelling at, 69

Eagle's head on walnut furniture, 104, 105, 114, 115
Eagle's head, detail borrowed from Chinese, 105
Ear-pieces to cabriole legs, 103
"Early English," 15
Early English Furniture and Woodwork, 31
East Anglia, original oak in, 42
East, Edward, 17, 81, 143
Edward VI, edicts under, 43
Eighteenth-century furniture, finish of, 6, 7
Elaborate pieces should be suspected, 16
Elizabethan chairs, types of, 50
  value of, 49, 50
Elm wood, 109

Embroidery frame, 101
End wood, 30
England in Plantagenet times largely French, 26, 27
English and French construction compared, 27, 28
English Domestic Clocks, 141, 150
English Furniture from Gothic to Sheraton, 125
English Furniture of the Eighteenth Century, 114, 119
English Furniture; period of neglect and its effects, 15
Engraving of marqueterie, 88
  not found in early work, 88
Examination of pieces, methods of, 32, 33
Exeter Cathedral, Vicars' Hall, 49
Expert examination, formulæ for, 25, 26, 27, 28, 29, 30, 31, 32, 33, 34, 35, 36, 37, 38, 39
  in furniture, must be technical, 3, 14, 70
  problems with old panellings, 74
Experts, 33, 34, 45, 53, 63, 68, 101, 111, 116, 135, 143, 153, 154, 155, 156
  and pseudo-experts, 33
  rarity of, 8, 153
  training of, 18
Eye-levels, Japanese and Chinese, 94

Fake, as a term, 6, 7
  definitions of the word, 6, 7, 35, 74, 85
  not a reproduction, 6
  rarely a literal copy, 15, 16
Faked rooms, definition of, 74
Fakers are the real experts, 4
Fakers' methods, 10, 11, 13, 41, 44, 45, 62, 63, 75, 76, 80, 82, 96, 105, 107, 108, 123, 124, 126, 127, 128, 138, 139, 155, 156
Fakes cannot be illustrated in photographs, 10, 11, 12, 53
  classes of, 7, 8, 9, 10, 11
  detection of, 9, 10, 11, 67, 68
  difficulties in describing, 124
  difficulties in the detection of, 1
  in chairs, 108, 109
  in clocks, detection of, 143

Fakes *(continued)*—
  in marqueterie, 89
  in needlework, 97, 98
  infinite variety of, reasons for, 17
  often illustrated as genuine examples,
    53, 54
  rarely made outright, 9
Faking, commercial considerations in, 4
  ethics of, 73
Fashions, fluid state of in early eigh-
    teenth century, 105
  in antiques; effects on values, 151
  in English furniture, importance of,
    15, 16, 30, 67
"Feathers" Hotel at Ludlow, 26, 42, 75
Ferolia Guianensis, 127
Fiddleback mahogany, 112
Finishes, original, 82, 113
Fire, Great, of 1666; its effects, 58
"Flair," useless in detection of fakes, 1,
    33, 35, 44, 68
Flamboyant Gothic, 48
Forgeries in Chinese work, 94
Formulæ for expert examination, 25,
    26, 27, 28, 29, 30, 31, 32, 33, 34,
    35, 36, 37, 38, 39
Four-post beds, decline in demand for,
    129
"Foxhall" factory, 135
France, William, 119
François Première style, 56
French and English construction com-
    pared, 27, 28
French Gothic, 27
French polishing, 62, 82, 109, 113
French Revolution, 131
Frets and fretwork, 113
  cut in layers, 113, 114
  lamination of, 113
Fruit woods, 20
Fulford, Great. *See* Great Fulford
Furniture bought by millionaires often
    not genuine, 12
  and woodwork in churches, 26
  antique; export to America, 2
  antique, fashions in, importance of,
    15, 16
  antique, made primarily for use,
    16
  antique, scarcity of at present day, 2
  early, original scarcity of, 1

Furniture *(continued)*—
  "improved" pieces, 34, 35, 63, 105,
    124
  "marriages" of pieces, 33, 68
  perfect, definition of, 66
  "planting" of, 39
  styles, divisions in, 44
  trade, divisions in after 1530, 19
  traditions in, 38
  types, 106, 107
  types, evolution of, 106, 107
  unfakeable, 32
  unusual, duplication of, 32
  valuable details in, 33
  values, 32
  worm in. *See under* Worm

GARRICK, DAVID; his furniture, 121
  Gauntlets, stump-work used for,
    100
Geffrye Museum, 22
Gentleman and Cabinet Makers' Director, 36,
    114, 121, 129, 133. *See also "Direc-
    tor"*
Genuine antiques often condemned as
    spurious, 65
Gesso, 44
Gilders' size, 137
Gilding processes, 137, 139
  preparations for, 137, 138
Gillows of Lancaster, 126, 133
Glass, silvered, cost of in eighteenth
    century, 135, 136
Glue, fallacies regarding, 30, 70, 71,
    72
  "cheese," 70
  how prepared in early times, 71, 72
  its uses, 66
  perfect, not invented, 71
Gluing, theory of, 71
  of veneers, 88
Gobelins, tapestries of, 100
Godoy, Don Manuel de, piano made
    for, designed by Sheraton, 132
Gothic design, basis of, 48
  Flamboyant, 48
  French, 27
  Post-Dissolution, 21
  tables at Fulford, 49

Gothic (*continued*)—
    tables at Penshurst, 49, 50
    tables very rare, 49
    wainscotings, 55
Graham, George, clock maker, 142, 149
Grail, the Holy, 120
Great Bealings in Suffolk, 31
Great Britain, population of in 1750, 2
population of in 1800, 1
Great Fire of 1666, 58
Great Fulford, table at, 49
Gretton, Charles, clock maker, 142
Gros-point in needlework, 97, 101
Guide of Hepplewhite, 132
Guild throne at Coventry, 23, 42, 43, 46, 47
Guilds, early, powers of, 21

HALF-TIMBER imitated with black paint, 42
Hardware on lacquer pieces, 94, 95
Harewood House, 121
Hayte, 111, 117
Heal, Ambrose, 122
Hepplewhite, 119, 125, 131
    chairs, fine character of, 128
    furniture more varied than Chippendale, 129
    inlay divided under, 126
    period, 113
    school, 122, 125, 126, 127, 128, 129
    style, divisions of, 125, 126
    wall furniture, 126
Hepplewhite's *Guide*, 132
Hispaniola, 111
Historical aspect of English furniture, importance of, 15
History of a nation's handicrafts the history of a people, 13
Hobbies; their vocabularies, 6
Holland, importation of furniture from, 27
    tapestries from, 100
Holy Grail, the, 120
Honduras mahogany, 28, 112
Hoop-back on chairs, 106, 113
Huchiers; mediæval name for arkwright, 19, 24
Huxley, T. H., Professor, 110

ILMINSTER, table from, 49
"Improved" furniture, 34, 35, 63, 105, 124
Ince & Mayhew, 119, 121
Inlay, definition of, 86
    revived under Hepplewhite, 126
Ipswich, Sparrowe's house at, 75
"Irish Chippendale," 115

JACKSON AND GRAHAM, 133
Johnson, Thomas, designer, 119
Johnstone & Jeans, 133
Joiner, 19, 65, 66, 69
Joints in wood, rubbing together, 70, 71
    in wood, difficulties in making, 71
Jones, Inigo, 69
"Joyner" or joiner, 19
Juglans regia, 77
Juglans nigra, 77

KENT, WILLIAM, 69
Kenwood, Hampstead, 136
K'hang H'si, 94
Kingwood, 29
Knee of cabriole leg, 103
Knibb, Joseph, clock maker, 17, 81, 142, 146
    Roman numeral, striking of clocks by, 148
Knife-and-hammer method of inlaying marqueterie, 86
Knife-cut veneer, 29
Knowledge, general, often inadequate, 2

LABOUR, laws regulating, in early times, 31
Labour, poorly paid in eighteenth century, 123
Laburnum wood, 29, 109
Lacquer, Chinese, 93, 94
    colours of, 94
    difficulties in obtaining knowledge of, 96
    elasticity of the term, 95, 96
    English, definition of, 95
    Japanese, 93, 94

Lacquer (*continued*)—
　Oriental, is insoluble, 93
　pieces, hardware on, 94, 95
　qualities of, 95, 96
　restoration of, 95
　the native gum, *Tsi*, 93
　work, 93, 94, 95, 96
　work, divisions of, 93
　work, localities of, 93, 94
　work, Oriental, 93, 94
Laminations, 113
Lancashire chairs, 64, 65
Langley, Batty, 119
Large panel in woodwork, the, 56
Late copies of furniture, danger of, 17, 18, 30, 44
Lavenham, Guildhall at, 57
Law cases dealing with fakes. *See* Shrager
　regarding antiques. *See* Shrager
Laying of veneers, 29, 30, 88
Legends regarding antiques, 75
Legh, Sir Piers; builds Lyme Park, 1603, 75
Leoni rebuilds Lyme Park, 1725, 75
Leverhulme, Lord; sale in New York, 127
　piano in sale at New York, designed by Thomas Sheraton, 132
Linenfold panelling, 56, 59
Lion mask on furniture, 105, 114, 115, 116
Localities of furniture, 31, 64
Lock, designer, 119
London-made furniture, 18
London Tradesmen's Cards, 122
Lopers; of draw-tables, 49
Low Countries, traditions imported from, 81
Ludlow, "Feathers" Hotel at, 26, 42, 75
　development of, 56, 57
Luminer, the trade of the, 43
Lyme Park, Cheshire, 55, 75

Macquoid, Percy, 51
　Madeira wood, 112
Mahogany, kinds used in old furniture, 3, 14, 28, 111
　duties on and effects of, 112, 117

Mahogany (*continued*)—
　early, description of, 111, 112, 113
　figure in, 112
　first used for furniture, 112
　furniture, 111, 112, 113, 114, 115, 116, 117
　origins of, 111
　staining of, 113
Maintaining-power in clocks, 147
Maniple and stole in Durham Cathedral, 100
Mansfield, Earl of, 136
Manwaring, Robert, 119, 122
Maple & Co., 119
Marqueterie, 78, 85, 86, 87, 88, 89, 90, 91
　carnation the favourite flower in early, 87, 88
　chopped-in kind, 86
　counterparts in, 87, 90
　cutter's "donkey," 89
　cutting described, 86, 87, 88, 89
　definition of, 86
　dying art in England, 85, 86
　engraving of, 88
　evolution of, 89, 90, 91
　fakes in, 89
　faking of, 85, 86
　intricate character of early, 87, 88
　kinds of, 89, 90, 91
　laying of, 88
　master-pattern in, 86, 87
　new methods in cutting of, 90
　old and modern, 85, 86
　original, rarity of, 85
　place of in English furniture, 91
　prickings, 88
　revived by the Sheraton school, 88, 113, 126
　saw, 87, 89
　secrets of, 88
　shading of, 87
　the taste for ornamental woods, 109
　undercuts in, 87
　use of the pounce, 86, 87
　vogue for, 89, 90
"Marriages" with furniture, 33, 68
Master-pattern in marqueterie, 86, 87, 97
Maza-wood, 29, 109
Mazer bowls, 120

Medullary ray of oak, 20, 41, 62, 75
ray of oak darkened by the faker, 41
Memel red deal; its early use, 20
Mercury silvering, 136, 138
Metropolitan Museum, New York, 45, 46
Milton, designer, 119
Ming, 94
Mirrors, English wall, 135, 136, 137, 138, 139
classification of, 135
duties on, 135
early, 135
early, costly, 135
from Venice, 135
large, costs of, 135
marqueterie, 138
methods of silvering, 135, 136
Muranese, 138
types of, 136, 137
Vauxhall factory for making of, 135
Modern indications in fakes, 3
additions to old furniture, 3
Monypenny pew in Rolvenden Church, 26, 32
Mortise-and-tenon, 23, 38
Mudge, Thomas, clock maker, 142
Muranese mirrors, 138
Museum pieces, 16

Nationality of pieces, importance of, 26, 27, 28, 45
Nationality of pieces affects values, 27
Needlework, 97, 98, 99, 100, 101, 102
faking of, 97, 99
importance of, 97
indications of faking, 99
mirrors, 139
old, on card tables, 98, 99
old, purpose of, 98
old, qualities of, 97, 98
old, silk used in, 98
old, stitches used in, 98
variety of, 98, 100
Nettlefold screws, 36

Newton, Lady, 75
Norton, Eardley, clock maker, 120
Norwich, Curat's House at, 74, 75
Nostell Priory, furniture at, 121

Oak, case-hardening of, 42, 75
furniture, elaborate, to be suspected, 63
furniture, list of types, 64
furniture, little variety in, 64
furniture, localities of, 64
furniture rarely found in original condition, 41
furniture, types unknown at the period, 64
not necessarily superseded by walnut, 61
old, will warp if sawn, 42
original finish of, 41, 42
probably painted in early times, 41, 42, 43, 44
quartering of, 20, 70, 72
rooms, hypothetical origins of, 54, 55
rooms, original, cohesion in design of, 73
splitting or riving of, 20, 69
the constructional wood for walnut and mahogany pieces, 61, 78, 81
the general wood for furniture in Tudor period, 20
varieties of, 14
"Ocean figure" in mahogany, 112
Ockwells Manor, Berks, credence at, 51
Old furniture and woodwork part of the history of a country, 44
Old wives' tales regarding antiques, 75
Olive wood, 109
Original condition, 41, 42
condition of upholstered furniture, 37
surfaces, 9, 10, 26, 82, 110
work, spontaneity of, 44
"Original state," 26, 62, 63, 67, 73
Output; its effect on evolution, 66
Overton, designer, 119
"Oyster pieces," 29, 78, 109

PAIN, W. AND J., 119
"Painted cloaths," 55
Painting of Hepplewhite furniture, 127, 128
  of oak darkens medullary ray, 41
  of oak furniture, 61
  of oak general on Continent, 43
  of oak in early times, 41, 42, 43
  of oak panellings, reasons for, 72
Paintings on walls, 55
Palladian manner, 69
Panel, large, sudden appearance of, 69
  large, in English woodwork, 69, 76
  large; new methods adopted, 70
Panelled rooms, high prices paid for, 59
Panelling; art known in very early times, 55
Panellings, 54, 55, 56, 57, 58, 59
  county styles in, 57, 58
  old and new methods of construction, 58, 59
Panels, pilaster type, 69
"Parchemin" panels, 57
Parqueterie, 78, 86
Parsifal, 120
Pastorino, designer, 119
Paw foot, 105
Pedigrees, 38, 39, 50, 59, 75, 76, 120, 151, 152
Peel, Sir Robert, 135
Pendulum, clock; its laws, 142, 147
Pendulum-knife-cut veneers, 29
Pergolesi, artist, 119
Persea Indica, 111
Pershore Abbey, chest at, 23
Petit-point, 97, 101
Pile carpets, 101
  of velvets, 101, 102
Pit-sawyer, 19
"Planting" of pieces, 39, 152
Plate tracery, 23
Polishes, shellac, 62
Pollarded woods, 29, 109
Pollock, Sir Edward; his judgment, 74
Population in Great Britain in 1750, 2
  in 1800, 1

Post-Dissolution Gothic, 21, 23, 44, 47
Pounce, use of in marqueterie, 86, 87
Pre-Dissolution period, 23
Price considerations in faking, 7, 8
Prices, inflation of, 152
  of antiques no proof of authenticity, 156
Primitive character not necessarily an indication of early date, 21
Problems of localities of furniture, 31
Progress in crafts always in pendulum fashion, 67
Provenance of furniture, 120
Provincial-made furniture, 18
Puritan fashions, 61

QUARE, DAN, clock maker, 17, 81, 142
  Quartering of oak, 20, 70, 72
Queen Anne, 107, 120

RAMSBURY MANOR, panelling at, 69
  Rasp, the, 104
"Rag" of saw in cutting, 87
Renaissance in England, 21, 22, 24, 55, 56
Renovations, 36, 37
Reproduction not a fake, 6, 7
Restoration chairs, spontaneity in design of, 80
"Restorations," 41, 62, 68, 124
Richardson, designer, 119
Riving iron or "thrower," 20
  of timber, importance of, 20, 65
Rolvenden Church, furniture in, 26, 32
Roman numeral striking of clocks, 148
Rood screens, 46
  lofts, 46
Rooms, oak, from Bromley-by-Bow, 41
  oak, from Clifford's Inn, 41
  oak, made up, 73, 74
Rotary-cut veneers, 29
Rotherwas, Hereford, room at, 78
"Royston Hall," room from, 54, 73, 153
Rye, Sussex, 58

S AFFRON WALDEN Museum, 55
St. Catherine, patron saint of Coventry Guild, 47
St. John of Bletsoe, Lord, 101
St. Mary's Hall, Coventry, 23, 42, 43, 46, 47
St. Michael's Parish Church, Coventry, 23, 46
"Salting" of caustics, 44
Samplers, 99
San Domingo mahogany, 28, 111
Sand-burning in marqueterie, 87
Saplings cut for veneers, 29. *See* "Oyster pieces"
Satin the usual base for stump-work, 99, 100
Satinwood, 127
Satyr-mask furniture, 114, 116
Saw-cut veneers, 29
"Scratcher," the old tool for making mouldings, 59
Seasoning of timber, 9
Seddon Sons & Shackleton, 126, 133
Settees, chair-back, 106
Shearer, cabinet maker, 120
Shellac polishing, 62, 82, 109
Sheraton, Thomas, comes to London from Stockton-on-Tees 1790, 131
Sheraton, 113, 120
    chairs, 133
    chairs, construction of, 133
    chairs, rarity of the shield-back form in, 126
    furniture; none exists, 132
    furniture; rarity of forgeries, 133
    his addresses in London, 132
    his design for a piano, 132
    only a designer in London, 132
    school, 88
    wall furniture, 133
Sheraton's book, subscribers to, 132
Shield-back on chairs peculiar to the school of Hepplewhite, 126
Shooting board, the, 71
Shrager, Adolph; case in Law Courts in 1923, 54, 73, 96, 116, 128, 143, 147, 153
Shrewsbury, old houses at, 42
Shropshire chairs, 62
Sideboard, evolution of the, 129
Signatures on clock dials, 143

Silk used in needlework, 98
Slang, value of, 6, 7
Slide-rest on lathe, 79, 80
Smooth cabriole leg, 103
    borrowed from Dutch sources, 103
Soane Museum, 153
Solomon and Queen of Sheba in needlework, 99
Somersetshire chairs, 62
Spade foot, 104
Sparrowe's House, Ipswich, 75
Spencer, Herbert, 19, 80
Spiral turning, 79, 80
    fashioned by hand before 1660, 79
"Splash-figure" in oak, 41
Splats of chairs, 115
Splitting of timber, importance of, 20, 65
Spokeshave, the, 104
Springs, coil; used for upholstery, 105
Staffordshire pottery in Chippendale style, 122
Stole and maniple in Durham Cathedral, 100
Stone and wood compared, 22
Strippers; their use, 41, 73
Stump-work, 97, 98, 99, 100, 101, 102, 136
    described, 99
    mirrors, 139
    satin usual base for, 99, 100
    used for gauntlets, 100
    usually in form of pictures, 100
Substitution, danger of, 39
Surfaces, original, 9, 10, 26, 82, 110
Swietenia Mohagoni, 111
Sycamore, 78
System of Household Furniture of Ince & Mayhew, 119, 121

T ABLES, DRAW-, 42, 49
    trestle form, 49
Tadema, Alma, 26
Talbert, Bruce J.; his "Early English," 133
Tambour frame in needlework, 101
Tapestries, 8, 99
Technical knowledge necessary for the expert, 3, 14
Templets, 103

Tent stitch, 97

Thuja wood, 109

Timber merchants, value of in study of timbers, 28
shrinkage in, 56, 72
used as ships' ballast, 111, 112

Timbers, knowledge of indispensable to the expert, 14
old, liability to warp if cut, 9
study of, 28, 116, 117
thicknesses of, 37, 38

Timekeeping, 141, 142

Tompion, Thomas, clock maker, 17, 81, 120, 142, 143, 146, 149

Tool chests, elaborate, 22

Tools, importance of, 36
in early times, 20
modern and old compared, 14, 15
provided by the shop, 22, 23
rarity of in early days, 23

Toothing plane, 30

"Top-sawyer," 19

Torregiano, Pietro, 22, 46

Trades of the woodworker, divisions of, 19, 21, 65, 66

Traditions, trade, importance of, 14, 15, 21, 22, 38, 70

Translation of pieces from one county to another, 31

Tripod tables; how "improved," 10, 124

"Trotting" at auctions, 155

Tsi, the native lacquer of China, 93

Turning of woods, difficulties in, 65, 66

Tusk-tenons on draw-tables, 42

Twain, Mark, 117

Twist-turning, 79, 80

Types in English furniture, origin of, 15
of furniture, 35
of furniture which never existed, 35, 36

UFFORD CHURCH, pew-ends in, 26, 42

Undercuts in marqueterie, 87

Unfakeable furniture, 32

Unusual, duplication of the, 32

Upholstery, early, 105, 106, 108

VALUABLE details in furniture, 33
Values of furniture, 32

Vanbrugh, Sir John, 69

Varnishes, 82, 109
original on oak, 62
removal of with alcohol, 62, 63

Vauxhall glass factory, 135

Veneer pins, 88

Veneers, blistering of, 89
knife-cut, 29
methods of cutting, 29
pendulum-knife-cut, 29
rotary-cut, 29
saw-cut, 29

Veneering, caul, 70
era of, 66, 70, 78, 112
hammer, 70
principles of, 81, 82, 88, 89
sand-bag, 70
sham of, 80, 81, 82

Vicars' Hall, Exeter, 49, 57

Victoria and Albert Museum, 41, 44, 49, 50, 55, 72, 95, 101, 121

"Vine" panels, 57

WAGNER, RICHARD, 120
Wainscotings, 57, 58

Wainscotings begin as close-boardings, 55
do not appear before sixteenth century, 55
early, fixing of, 58

Wall paintings, 55

Wallis, N., designer, 120

Walnut, American, 77
burr, 77
chairs, fragile character of, 78, 79
chairs frequently restored, 78, 79
chairs, usually caned, 79
classes of, 77
English, 77
English and Low Country, 27
first planted at Wilton Park 1565, 77
French, 78
furniture, plain, 62
importance of nationality of in judging pieces, 77
imported in log and plank, 27
Italian, 78

INDEX

Walnut (*continued*)—
mild timber compared with oak, 78
native of Persia and Himalayas, 77
pieces, charming character of, 83
Spanish, 78
supersedes oak for furniture, 61
Warwickshire chairs, 64
"Wattle-and-daub," 55
Wave moulding, 113
Wear, an unsafe criterion in judging antiques, 14
Wedgwood medallions, 132
Westminster Hall, 108
West Stow Church, wainscoting from, 55
West Wycombe Church, pews in, 26
Wetherfield, D. A. F., 150
Whitehall, Banqueting Hall at, 69
Wire-brush; a tool of the faker, 41, 73
effects of, 62
Wood, shrinkage in, 56
and stone compared, 22, 23
thicknesses, 37, 38
Woodwork and furniture in churches, importance of, 26
large panel in, 69, 76
large panel in, first appearance, 69
rich, rare in Kent and Sussex, 58

Woodworker, early, follows the stone-mason, 48
Woodworking trades, divisions of, 19, 21, 65, 66
Woodworm or beetle, 107
Wools in needlework, 97
Workmen, skill of in olden days and present day, 14, 15
Workshop training indispensable to the furniture expert, 3
Workshops sources of inaccurate information regarding timbers, 28
Worm-hole makers, 80
Worm holes; when suspicious, 107
in wood, 80, 107
in wood, difficulties in removing, 108
killers, 108
Wren, Sir Christopher, 69

XESTOBIUM TESSELATUM, 107

YORKSHIRE chairs, 64, 65

Dover Books on Art

Dover Books on Art

MASTERPIECES OF FURNITURE, Verna Cook Salomonsky.
Photographs and measured drawings of some of the finest examples of Colonial American, 17th century English, Windsor,
Sheraton, Hepplewhite, Chippendale, Louis XIV, Queen Anne,
and various other furniture styles. The textual matter includes
information on traditions, characteristics, background, etc. of
various pieces. 101 plates. Bibliography. 224pp. 7⅞ x 10¾.
21381-1 Paperbound $3.00

PRIMITIVE ART, Franz Boas. In this exhaustive volume, a
great American anthropologist analyzes all the fundamental
traits of primitive art, covering the formal element in art, representative art, symbolism, style, literature, music, and the dance.
Illustrations of Indian embroidery, paleolithic paintings, woven
blankets, wing and tail designs, totem poles, cutlery, earthen-
ware, baskets and many other primitive objects and motifs. Over
900 illustrations. 376pp. 5⅜ x 8.   20025-6 Paperbound $3.00

*AN INTRODUCTION TO A HISTORY OF WOODCUT, A. M.
Hind.* Nearly all of this authoritative 2-volume set is devoted to
the 15th century—the period during which the woodcut came of
age as an important art form. It is the most complete compendium
of information on this period, the artists who contributed to it,
and their technical and artistic accomplishments. Profusely illustrated with cuts by 15th century masters, and later works
for comparative purposes. 484 illustrations. 5 indexes. Total of
xi + 838pp. 5⅜ x 8½. Two-vols. 20952-0, 20953-9 Paperbound $7.50

ART STUDENTS' ANATOMY, E. J. Farris. Teaching anatomy
by using chiefly living objects for illustration, this study has
enjoyed long popularity and success in art courses and home-
study programs. All the basic elements of the human anatomy
are illustrated in minute detail, diagrammed and pictured as they
pass through common movements and actions. 158 drawings,
photographs, and roentgenograms. Glossary of anatomical terms.
x + 159pp. 5⅝ x 8⅜.   20744-7 Paperbound $1.50

COLONIAL LIGHTING, A. H. Hayward. The only book to cover
the fascinating story of lamps and other lighting devices in
America. Beginning with rush light holders used by the early
settlers, it ranges through the elaborate chandeliers of the Fed-
eral period, illustrating 647 lamps. Of great value to antique
collectors, designers, and historians of arts and crafts. Revised
and enlarged by James R. Marsh. xxxi + 198pp. 5⅝ x 8¼.
20975-X Paperbound $2.50

Dover Books on Art

THE COMPLETE BOOK OF SILK SCREEN PRINTING PRO-DUCTION, J. I. Biegeleisen. Here is a clear and complete picture of every aspect of silk screen technique and press operation—from individually operated manual presses to modern automatic ones. Unsurpassed as a guidebook for setting up shop, making shop operation more efficient, finding out about latest methods and equipment; or as a textbook for use in teaching, studying, or learning all aspects of the profession. 124 figures. Index. Bibliography. List of Supply Sources. xi + 253pp. 5⅜ x 8½.

21100-2 Paperbound $2.75

A HISTORY OF COSTUME, Carl Köhler. The most reliable and authentic account of the development of dress from ancient times through the 19th century. Based on actual pieces of clothing that have survived, using paintings, statues and other reproductions only where originals no longer exist. Hundreds of illustrations, including detailed patterns for many articles. Highly useful for theatre and movie directors, fashion designers, illustrators, teachers. Edited and augmented by Emma von Sichart. Translated by Alexander K. Dallas. 594 illustrations. 464pp. 5⅛ x 7⅛.

21030-8 Paperbound $3.00

CHINESE HOUSEHOLD FURNITURE, G. N. Kates. A summary of virtually everything that is known about authentic Chinese furniture before it was contaminated by the influence of the West. The text covers history of styles, materials used, principles of design and craftsmanship, and furniture arrangement—all fully illustrated. xiii + 190pp. 5⅝ x 8½.

20958-X Paperbound $1.75

THE COMPLETE WOODCUTS OF ALBRECHT DURER, edited by Dr. Willi Kurth. Albrecht Dürer was a master in various media, but it was in woodcut design that his creative genius reached its highest expression. Here are all of his extant woodcuts, a collection of over 300 great works, many of which are not available elsewhere. An indispensable work for the art historian and critic and all art lovers. 346 plates. Index. 285pp. 8½ x 12¼.

21097-9 Paperbound $3.00

Dover publishes books on commercial art, art history, crafts, design, art classics; also books on music, literature, science, mathematics, puzzles and entertainments, chess, engineering, biology, philosophy, psychology, languages, history, and other fields. For free circulars write to Dept. DA, Dover Publications, Inc., 180 Varick St., New York, N.Y. 10014.